The Northwest Essentials cookbook

The Northwest Essentials cookbook

Cooking with
the Ingredients
That Define a
Regional Cuisine

Greg Atkinson

SASQUATCH BOOKS
SEATTLE

In memory of Flip

Printed in the United States of America
Distributed in Canada by Raincoast Books, Ltd.
03 02 01 00   5 4 3 2

Cover and interior design: Kate Basart
Cover and interior illustrations: Suzy Pilgrim Waters
Copy editor: Susan Derecskey

Library of Congress Cataloging in Publication Data
Atkinson, Greg, 1959–
    The Northwest essentials cookbook : cooking with the ingredients that define a regional cuisine / Greg Atkinson.
            p.   cm.
        Includes index.
        ISBN 1-57061-179-3
        1. Cookery, American—Pacific Northwest style. I. Title.
    TX715.2.P32A85 1999
    641.59795—dc21   99-15346

SASQUATCH BOOKS
615 Second Avenue
Seattle, Washington 98104
(206) 467-4300
www.SasquatchBooks.com
books@SasquatchBooks.com

Contents

Acknowledgments

I thank my wife, Betsy, for reading every word I write, for tasting every new dish I cook, and for encouraging me to make each word and each mouthful as good as it can be. I thank Chris and Alice Canlis for their boundless support. I thank Gary Luke for seeing this book in me and encouraging me to write it. Thanks too to Lila Gault for leading me to rich sources of information about apples and cherries. And I thank Susan Derecskey for the attention she paid to each recipe. What could have been a chaotic jumble became consistent and coherent under her care.

I thank my parents for providing me with a safe home where I learned to cook, where the kitchen was never off limits, and where there was always enough to eat. I thank them especially for giving me wings to fly from that home and make one of my own in the Pacific Northwest. I am thankful that such an awesome place exists and that I am allowed to live in it.

Portions of this book have appeared in slightly different form in *The Journal of the San Juan Islands, Pacific Northwest Magazine,* and *Seattle Homes and Lifestyles* magazine. The recipe for Mussel Soup with Saffron and Cream first appeared in *Northwest Best Places Cookbook.*

Essential Ingredients

Start with the best ingredients and you can't go wrong. But what are the best ingredients and why are they the best? More often than not, the best ingredients are the ones that are grown nearby, harvested at their peak, and eaten within a reasonable distance from their source. Certainly that's true here in the Northwest. We're very fortunate. Our region is home to some of the most compelling native ingredients found anywhere in the world, and the local climate supports a wide variety of things from far away. The harvest season is long, and the yields are abundant.

The best ingredients may also be defined by a kind of alchemy that comes with familiarity. As we eat and cook with the plants and animals that thrive all around us, our own experience with these ingredients adds to their inherent value. Stopping at the same farm stand for raspberries or fresh corn first as a young couple, then with kids in the car, lends a ritual significance to the ordinary rhythm of the seasons. Visiting the same mushroom patch year after year, or fishing from the same special spot on a mountain stream, gives each year's harvest a kind of poignancy, and each summer's catch a kind of relevance that would never come to the one-time forager or the casual diner. Ingredients become essential when they link us to the rest of our lives.

The first time I tasted a local oyster, it made me long for the oysters of my childhood, the Apalachicola oysters of the Gulf Coast where I came to know the taste of the sea. I could hardly appreciate the local oyster for what it was, because I was so keenly aware of what it wasn't. Now, after two decades of tasting Northwest oysters, I appreciate them more. Each one reminds me of a place, a time, a particular occasion. How much more local oysters mean to me now than they did when I brought that first quivering mollusk to my mouth!

Who could have known where it would lead? Dorée Webb, the woman who gave me one of my first Washington oysters, owned Westcott Bay Sea Farms with her husband then, and she wanted me to try her oysters so that I would serve them in the restaurant where I had just come to work. I presented those oysters to our patrons in myriad ways, simply chilled on the half shell, steamed open and drizzled with butter sauce, grilled open, baked with savory toppings, puréed into velvety bisques for a succession of Valentine's Days, and for one special New Year's Eve, stewed whole with saffron, cream, and flakes of 18 karat gold. Who could have guessed that Dorée would visit me again in the same kitchen seven years later when she knew, but I didn't, that she was dying and that in just a few days, she would give up food altogether to die in her home by the oyster beds?

How could I have known the first time I pondered a seed catalogue with a farmer one dark January afternoon to talk about what he might grow and what I might cook the following summer that we were developing a relationship that would help nurture us both for a decade or more? Who could guess that we would sing soulful songs together in his garden, toasting our new babies with red wine and sharing his wife's sourdough bread? Who could know how I would come to miss him when the season for seed catalogues came around and I had moved away?

Even the barely edible wild roses that captured my senses the first time I saw them growing beside the freeways are so thoroughly tied now to my understanding of the changing seasons that I can read the months of the year by the condition of the rose bushes along my favorite trails. They contribute next to nothing in the way of my actual food, those roses. But the rose-petal jellies and rose-scented teas I occasionally enjoy, and often think about, keep me grounded on the great wheel of time, even as the years spin uncontrollably by.

Berries, mushrooms, leafy greens, sacks of potatoes, and the bounty of the sea are more than just food, they are vital links to the elements that formed them and to the people who grew and gathered them. A cornmeal-crusted trout sizzling in bacon fat connects a happy camper to the lake and the water that tastes like the stones from which it sprang. A beet pulled shaking with dirt from the garden is a bridge to the very earth that bore it. The foods that thrive here in the Northwest are more than items on a list of ingredients, they are points of departure; they are almost, but not quite, the raison d'être for the recipes they inspire. But of course producing something good to eat is the real purpose of any recipe. And linking a collection of recipes to the people and the places that inspired them is reason enough, I hope, for a collection like this one.

I have never been able to accept that old analogy of man as machine and food as fuel. In the great scheme of things, I imagine that we are not machines at all, but we are something between animals and angels, and food is the golden chain that keeps us connected to both worlds. To the degree that we devour it unthinkingly, we are like the former, and to the degree that we celebrate it with understanding and gratitude, we are like the latter.

The Northwest Essentials Cookbook

Selecting the Essentials

In the chapters that follow, I hope to share some insights into the foods that have shaped my understanding of Northwest cooking. The selection of ingredients is not arbitrary, but it is subjective. When in the course of researching and writing this book I asked people what they considered the essential ingredients of Northwest cooking, they quickly volunteered apples and salmon. Then after a pause, a few added berries, oysters, or mushrooms. Some people seemed surprised that I found twelve ingredients that warranted inclusion.

I might have included more ingredients than I did. I thought of adding a chapter on wheat; Washington grows a huge proportion of the nation's winter wheat, but wheat is not unique to the Northwest, nor do we use it in ways that are peculiar to the region. Besides, wheat and its myriad uses constitute a book in their own right. I think Northwest vegetables are exceptional, but like wheat, the subject is too vast and too universal to be confined to one of these chapters

A couple of ingredients intrigued me, and I came close to including them. Rhubarb, for instance, is produced almost exclusively in the Northwest. We grow over 90 percent of the nation's commercial rhubarb crop, but even if we grew 100 percent, it would hardly provide enough material to warrant a chapter of its own. Pears, too, are closely associated with the Northwest; in fact, the vast majority of the nation's commercial pear crop is harvested here. But pears, at least to my mind, are best enjoyed more or less unadulterated. So I have afforded them a brief discussion and a few indispensable recipes in the chapter on apples, to which they are closely related.

In the end, twelve chapters seemed like the right number and so I stopped there, and around that set of twelve ingredients, I built my lists of recipes to bring out the best in each one of them.

Each recipe is a point of departure, for the formulation of any dish is an adventure, a little journey from a point where we have a disparate set of ingredients to the moment when they all come together to form a dish that is a thing in itself. Ultimately, I hope the essays and recipes gathered here will be stepping stones along the way for other cooks relishing their own gastronomical journeys through life.

Apples &
Pears

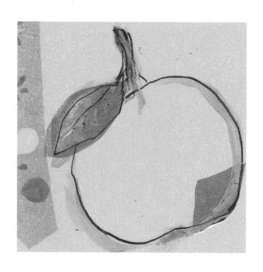

Many people have fond childhood memories of apple trees, apple pies, and apple blossoms. Not me. I was sixteen before I ever saw an apple tree. It was laden with fruit and I felt an urge to bow down before it. It was like seeing snow for the first time. Some things just aren't found in Florida, where I grew up. Now, though I have lived with apple trees for longer than I ever lived without them, they still seem otherworldly, and apples on a tree are magical. 🍃 In early evening, they are Chinese lanterns hung out to celebrate a holiday. At night they are planets, dangling from the limbs of

Apples

the tree that bore them. They rival the moon with their round yellow light. In the morning they are apples again, slowly ripening, sweetening in the late summer sun. 🍃 Some years they are less abundant than in other years, and in some hot sunny years, I am almost superstitiously afraid that they will ripen early, heralding summer's early end. Anything could happen. The weather here is fickle, and winter breathes down the neck of the snow-covered mountains all summer long. But if the apples ripen early or ripen late, or refuse to ripen at all, I would know, because whenever apples are ripening near my home I follow their development closely, almost involuntarily.

Once there was an ancient apple tree that grew behind a café where I cooked for several years, and in the fall I climbed it every day, gathering just enough apples to make the soup or the tarts I wanted to run as a special. The limbs of the tree were tangled with the limbs of a holly tree. I gathered apple blossoms to decorate the café in springtime, and at Christmastime, I gathered branches of the holly. So I was careful to avoid getting scratched by the holly when I picked the apples, and careful to avoid breaking the apple branches when I picked the holly.

Now the tree is gone, and I have probably inflated its worth and the quality of its apples. In the spring, it wore its blossoms in the same matter-of-fact, no-nonsense way that it bore its fruit in the fall. Without any tending or pruning, the tree presented its apples, and the tree bore them perfunctorily, without ceremony. The solid and well-balanced apples were possessed of a plain flavor, neither acid nor sweet, but steady and pleasing in a way that promised and provided good, plain nourishment. Oh, if only I had grafted its branches.

Happily, other old trees thrive in backyards and neglected corners of expanding towns all over the Northwest. When I lived on San Juan Island, I used to pass a circle of withered old trees that delivered a few fragrant apples every fall from an otherwise unoccupied lot near my home. They were like a gathering of old ladies allowed by grace to outlive their expected time, and they bore their few fruits in a giddy way. They seemed to delight in the fact that most of it was enjoyed by birds and deer who wandered out of the forest at night. Once, I rounded the corner and came upon the trees unexpectedly. Their branches were held in ridiculous angles, and they looked as if they had suddenly frozen in place. For a moment, I imagined that they saw me coming.

I have watched with keen interest the progress of a neighbor's young tree that looks entirely too small for the apples it produces. It strains under their weight in a valiant, awkward, pre-adolescent show of prowess. It is a dwarf, the product of some overly ambitious student of botany perhaps. And its fruit, though large and flavorful, falls mostly wasted on the grass, because the people who live in the house in its yard leave it ungathered.

More than once, I have boldly knocked on the doors of homes like that one to ask if I could gather the windfalls. "Help yourself," the people say. They hate to see their apples go to waste. Then, burdened with more apples than I can really use, I go home smiling with visions of pies and salads and jars of applesauce. Often I make applesauce and apple jelly from the same apples, using the pale tender pulp for sauce and the peels and cores for jelly. I peel and slice the apples at the kitchen table with my boys, who like to practice their cutting skills. With dazzling twists of the sharp little blade I reluctantly allow them to use, they scare the wits out of their mother and me. That is my favorite way to eat apples, crisp and unadorned at the table with my family. But I like apple jelly too. I like the look of it in jars. I'd like to have a pantry full of applesauce and apple jelly, but I never seem to manage more than a few sparkling jars to remind me in winter of the shining fruits as they hung during these last days of summer.

It seems appropriate to make jelly from apples and let it stand in jars on a shelf, because apples are timeless. If other summer fruits like cherries, plums, and peaches are fleeting, and remind us of the too short lease we have on life, apples are the reassurance of eternity. They may fall like rain in summer, and rot on the ground, but they do so slowly, and they come again every year. A few of them will last all winter.

Apples, the quintessential Northwest fruit, are one of the most versatile foods in the kitchen. They perform well in soups, salads, entrées, and of course in desserts. Sometimes, it's difficult to recommend specific varieties for a recipe because several varieties may be equally suitable. Still, certain varieties are better than others for cooking, and some apples are really not suited for cooking at all.
Some are all-purpose, good for cooking and eating out of hand, but their fragrance or texture might be either compromised or enhanced by cooking or baking.

Apple Varieties

I CAN'T SAY WITH ANY CERTAINTY JUST HOW MANY VARIETIES OF APPLES ARE grown in the Northwest. But I do know that over a thousand were under commercial cultivation in the United States in 1900, and the Washington Apple Growing Commission asserts that some 7,500 varieties exist worldwide. Only a few of these find their way to market. Growers and grocers are compelled to offer only those products that maximize profits and minimize risks, so they offer varieties that are most likely to sell and least likely to perish. Hence the preponderance of the ironically named Red Delicious.

One year when the busy season started winding down on the heavily touristed and well-appled island where we lived, my wife and I decided to take a couple of days and wind down ourselves. We packed our new baby into his car seat and gave our old dog the run of the back seat. Then, without any real plan, we crossed the mountains and drove down into the dry hills of central Washington. Leavenworth, Cashmere, Wenatchee, and Winthrop welcomed us in from the west as we made the Cascade loop.

My only other ventures into the eastern realms had been on the interstate, and I had never seen the heart of apple country. I had heard of course that Wenatchee was the apple-growing capital of the world and I had seen the colorful labels that used to be pasted on the sides of apple crates, but nothing prepared me for the contrast between the stark desert hills and the lush irrigated orchards. No matter how many times I see it, the image of that Eden in the desert still captures my imagination.

As we drove past the first orchards outside Cashmere, I was taken with the color of the apples. From the highway, they looked purple. Surely this was some new breed, some well-kept secret of the eastern kingdom that never leaked to the other side of the mountains. We stopped at the first likely looking place and my wife nursed the baby while I walked the dog beside an open orchard. I was a little younger then and considerably more innocent, and I didn't even think of trespassing. I approached the trees as if they were public property, or a national monument.

Up close, it became apparent that the mystery apples were only Red Delicious. Those incredibly dark fruits I had seen from the road were the same old apples I'd seen all my life. "Well," I thought, "I bet they'll taste better right off the tree. The freshness alone will make this apple a memorable one."

So I plucked a huge, perfect-looking fruit and tried it. The skin was thick and unyielding, the flesh firm and wet but basically tasteless. The apples bore no fragrance, no mystery, and no real flavor. I looked around me at the heavily laden trees that extended as far as I could see. "They are all the same," I thought, feeling a little panicky. The trees were motionless. No breeze stirred their leaves. "They are all exactly the same."

I called the dog and made my way back to the car. At the edge of the orchard was a lone, thin little tree with a few irregular fruits hanging precariously from its nearly leafless frame. I tried one of these. The flavor was explosive after the bland Delicious. Here was a real apple! This fruit had flavor and aroma and tartness. Why wasn't the whole valley filled with fruits like this one?

A terrible mistake had been made, I thought. And as we drove on, it dawned on me that all that time and money spent helping those trees to grow had been wasted. "No one really even wants those Red Delicious apples!" I said to my wife. "They're dull and stupid." From then on, I looked at the purple fruits with a jaded eye. My eyes combed the fields for signs of variety, but those signs were few and far between.

Golden Delicious was the most obvious exception to the rule of Red Delicious, but there were a few bright Jonathans, small dark Winesaps, and big Rome Beauties. None of them was half as captivating as a Gravenstein from my mother-in-law's backyard. None of the commercially grown apples we saw were as good as the apples whose names had been forgotten that grew on old trees all around the island where we lived. When we got home, I felt like Dorothy returning from Oz. "If I ever go looking for perfect apples," I said, "I won't look any farther than my own backyard."

Fortunately, many orchardists feel the same way I do and more and more interesting apple varieties are appearing on the market. Some, like Cox's Orange Pippin, are old heirloom varieties brought back into cultivation. Others like Jonagold and Elstar are newer hybrids, carefully derived from crossing existing varieties.

Still others are random mutations that sprouted from seeds and produced inter-esting fruit, like the little sapling I found on the corner of that orchard in Wenatchee. The Red Delicious started that way. It was a seedling that appeared by chance on an Iowa farm in the late 1800s and was mowed down several times before the farmer finally let it grow and sampled its history-making fruit.

My subjective notes on a few varieties of Northwest apples follow.

Braeburn Like Fuji, this is a sweet apple that is best eaten out of hand, but it is an all-purpose fruit and makes a decent pie. Its greatest attribute may be its tender fra-grant skin, which smells like just-pressed cider and vanishes like rice paper in the mouth. It came from a chance seedling in New Zealand and thrives in the volcanic soil of the Northwest.

Cameo A new apple, Cameo is a spontaneous variety, not an intentional hybrid. It sprang up in Eastern Washington, was allowed to grow, and proved itself a winner. It is a great dessert apple, perfect really, alone or with cheese. The Washington Apple Growing Commission rates it as excellent for pies, applesauce, and snacking—a rare honor. Apple growers love it because it keeps almost as well as Red Delicious. I predict that con-sumers will like Cameo because it looks like an older variety. It is unevenly colored: pale gold with random red stripes and appealing freckles. If it had a little more perfume, it might completely steal my heart. As it is, I already count it among my favorite apples.

Criterion The subtle complexity of this apple with its perfumey balance of sweet and tart flavors makes some first-time samplers swoon. A chance seedling from Washington, its progenitors probably include Red Delicious and Winter Banana. A word of warning: Long before its shiny skin begins to wrinkle, Criterion goes mealy inside, so be sure the apples you buy are very fresh, and keep them refrigerated. Criterion is often my first choice for picnics, salads, and other situations where I want uncooked apples, but it is an all-purpose apple. It bakes pretty well and makes a good applesauce.

Elstar A cross between Golden Delicious and Cox's Orange Pippin, or perhaps one of its descendants, this Dutch variety has recently surpassed Golden Delicious as Europe's most widely grown apple, and it's a popular choice for Washington orchardists expanding their varieties. This gold and red streaked apple tends to russet—that is, its skin shows some rough brown spots around the stem—so it doesn't match the glossy standard of perfection set by the more familiar standards. But what may have been the kiss of death to an apple at the height of the Red Delicious reign, may be a mark of character in this era of increasing diversity and longing for heirloom varieties. Certainly the sweet-tart flavor and cream-colored flesh make it a hit. It keeps its flavor and tex-ture when baked and makes good sauce.

Fuji The most sought-after apple in China and Japan, this big, red apple with golden highlights is bold and flavorful. But in spite of its Japanese name, its heritage is decidedly American. Fuji is a cross between Red Delicious and an obscure old variety known as Ralls Janet, which was grown by George Washington at Mount Vernon and by Thomas Jefferson at Monticello. It keeps better than any other sweet apple and stays crisp for weeks even at room temperature. It can spend a few weeks in a fruit bowl without turning mushy or mealy. You can get good results by cooking or baking with it, but this apple is best enjoyed raw.

Gala A really delicious apple for snacking, this early-ripening New Zealand import, now grown widely in the Northwest, is crisp and fragrant and juicy. But that famous crispness can become a little rubbery after any time in the oven, where this apple rapidly gives up its juice. And the ethereal fragrance that characterizes this apple when it's fresh all but vanishes when it's cooked. Don't try to bake with it; save it instead for salads, where its bright flavor is accentuated in the presence of vinaigrette, cheese, and nuts. Better still, since it's small and sweet, tuck it into a coat pocket or a kid's backpack for a snack.

Golden Delicious A soft and perfumey blonde, this American has been very well received in European orchards and markets. In Normandy, where I had gone in search of old French apple varieties, an apple farmer once confided to me that the Golden Delicious was his personal favorite. His bias is understandable. Golden Delicious may be common but, at its best, it is uncommonly versatile and flavorful. It makes sauce almost as good as the hard-to-find summer apples that are available only from small farms in the fall. This apple bakes well too, though it does become soft very quickly. It's popular with kids for snacking. Again, avoid apples that have been shelved too long. Look for the new crop of Golden Delicious from late September to the end of October. Out-of-season Golden Delicious is fine when it first comes out of storage, but if kept for more than a few days outside the refrigerator, it rapidly becomes bland and mealy.

Granny Smith This firm green variety is imported from Australia, where it sprang up as a chance seedling on the farm of a certain Ms. Smith. It has become almost as ubiquitous as Red Delicious. It's a good baking apple, and while it lacks some of the intensity of flavor found in more obscure varieties like Newton Pippin, it has a refreshing tartness. That tartness makes it especially useful in savory dishes where its characteristic firm texture allows it to stand up to rough treatment like grilling and pan-searing. Granny Smith is often a first choice for baking, but it is slow to soften.

Gravenstein A summer apple with a distinctive perfume and flavor, Gravenstein ripens in August and is typically gone with the first winds of October. For many native

Northwesterners, it is the first choice for applesauce and apple pie. Unfortunately, it doesn't keep well and therefore fails to meet the prime criterion for commercial growers. California orchardists do grow Gravenstein commercially, and many backyard orchardists and truck farmers produce enough of these apples to stock farmers' markets and roadside stands in the Northwest. They are worth seeking out. But eat them at once or make them into applesauce and can it.

Jonagold The number one choice for growers west of the Cascades in maritime Washington, this is a great apple. Intensely flavored and colorful, it's my first choice for an all-purpose apple. Different strains of the same apple range from dark red all over to almost pure yellow with just a blush of red on one side. Occasionally touched by a condition known as sugaring, in which portions of the apple near the core take on a translucent pineapple color, this apple has almost more flavor than it can hold. My only complaint about Jonagold is the brevity of its season. One can never find this apple before the first of October, and by Thanksgiving it's likely to have vanished. Any Jonagolds left on supermarket shelves by January have probably lost the characteristics that make them desirable in the fall.

Jonathan Of the three most commonly grown apples in Washington, this one has the most character. It doesn't hold its shape well inside a pie, but it makes good applesauce, and for flavor and texture it ranks several points higher in my book than either of the Delicious varieties. Jonathans are harvested late in the season.

McIntosh Usually thought of as a New England apple, the McIntosh is a Canadian apple that is the number one apple on the East Coast. It is also widely grown in British Columbia. Once in Florida, when my wife and I saw B.C. Macs in a supermarket, they seemed to radiate vitality, and they did not disappoint. The thick skin makes it less than ideal for snacking, but its smooth spicy flesh makes it worth the effort of peeling it. The apple also makes good sauce and pies.

Melrose A cross between Jonathan and Red Delicious, with a rustic, heirloom look that's not apparent in either of its parents, this all-purpose apple is the favorite of many amateur growers. The dull red skin is tart and perfumey, and the flesh is very sweet. It is late-ripening, and gains flavor and character for several months after it's picked. Some aficionados say you shouldn't even eat a Melrose until Christmastime. It's an excellent keeper; refrigerated, it stays firm and flavorful until Easter.

Newton Pippin This apple is as American as the proverbial apple pie, which, by the way, is never better than when it's made with this apple. It is the ultimate pie apple, fragrant, firm and slightly tart. It grew at Mount Vernon and at Monticello, and if it hadn't been for the invasion of Granny Smith, it would probably be the most important green apple on the market. As it is, it is a favorite for everyone who's in the know.

Red Delicious I know, I know, it's grown primarily to look good; it's the iceberg lettuce of apples. It will not stand up to cooking, and its somewhat insipid character makes it dubious even as a snacking apple. But like iceberg lettuce, a fresh Red Delicious apple is crisp, free from any off-putting flavors, and generally inoffensive. What's more, even in this era of increasing diversity in apple varieties, Red Delicious still accounts for 80 percent of all the apples grown in Washington. The harvest season for Red Delicious apples is late fall and thanks to Controlled Atmosphere Storage (a system that replaces ordinary air with chilled nitrogen gas), the apples are available year round. If they have not been left standing on supermarket shelves for too long, they can carry the illusion of freshness many months after they have been harvested. The sturdy skin that helps this apple survive long periods of storage is tough as shoe leather, so peel it off. Slice the peeled apple and toss it with a little lemon and sugar, and it's perfect for salads. Look for the new crop in the fall and if possible, sample a slice of apple before buying any to avoid those that may have been out of controlled atmosphere storage for too long. At home, keep them in the refrigerator; even though they look nice in a bowl on the kitchen table or countertop, they rapidly lose their texture and flavor at room temperature.

Spartan A cross between McIntosh and Newton Pippin, this British Columbian hybrid looks like a McIntosh. It is full flavored, good for snacking or cooking, though its flavor does fade a bit in the oven. Amateur growers appreciate its disease-resistant character.

Winesap My mother's favorite apple, and by sentimental association, one of mine. This late-ripening apple keeps extraordinarily well, and its dark red, maraschino-scented skin sometimes bleeds red veins deep into its tart, butter-yellow flesh. Winesap is an all-purpose apple and works well in pies and sauce, but I save it for salads and eating fresh with a paring knife at the table.

Yellow Transparent The first apple of summer, Yellow Transparent typically ripens in July and disappears by the middle of August. Its rosy scent and creamy white flesh make it a favorite for summer apple crisps and applesauce. This apple deteriorates so quickly that it should really be eaten or transformed into applesauce the same day it's picked.

*B*efore he finished graduate school, started a family, and threw himself headlong into his work, my friend Jeff Showman was a neighborhood renaissance man who flitted endlessly from one project to another. I was fascinated with his culinary inventions and learned from him the basics of pickling, preserving, and wine-making. Crocks of fermenting fluids in his kitchen would gradually evolve into bottles of dandelion wine or homemade vinegar. In his backyard, pots of homemade kimchee ripened in ceramic jars buried underground. ✑ Once, while walking by his

Pears

house, I noticed a half dozen bottles hanging from his pear tree. These, he explained, would later be filled with pear brandy. Over the course of the summer, as the pears grew and filled the bottles, other projects waxed and waned. Then, in the fall, the bottles were plucked from the tree with the full-grown pears trapped inside and the bottles were filled with cheap brandy which, by Christmastime, had indeed become infused with their essence.

Since then, I have seen pear *eau de vie* made not with cheap brandy, but with carefully distilled pear alcohol, utilizing the same clever technique of trapping a pear in a bottle. The practice has earned rave reviews for Stephen McCarthy of Clear Creek Distillery near Portland, Oregon. His product is infinitely more sophisticated than Jeff Showman's ever was, but I will always remember where I saw it first.

The pears that grew in Jeff Showman's yard were probably Anjou, the variety most commonly grown in the Northwest. Other types of pear trees grew up from hedge rows and along the back alleys on the south side of Bellingham, including tiny, sweet Seckel pears and soft, yellow Bartletts. On my foraging romps through the neighborhood, I gathered some of the fruit that would have otherwise gone to waste and made chutney. My neighbors, faced with more fruit than they could use, cheered my efforts and encouraged me to gather more.

Unlike apple trees, which demand pruning, pear trees seem to produce prolifically even when neglected. The fruit, however, is only good if it's picked before it's ripe. Left on the tree, pears develop grainy stone cells that proliferate as the fruit ripens. Anyone who has encountered a few of these cells in an otherwise smooth pear can well imagine how detrimental a host of them would be to a pear. In order to mature into the smooth, palatable fruit we love, pears should be removed from their source a couple of weeks before they would otherwise fall. This is a great advantage to commercial growers, who must harvest fruit green and pack it while still firm for shipping.

Pear Varieties

Anjou and Red Anjou Accounting for more than 80 percent of the commercial pear crop, Anjou might be thought of as the Red Delicious of the pear world if it were not for the fact that Anjou pears are as delectable as they are common. Available from October through June, Anjou pears are great for cooking, but like all pears they are probably best enjoyed fresh, sliced and served with your favorite cheese for dessert. Anjou pears are best served slightly underripe while they still have an element of crispness. They will be sweet and juicy well before they are soft. Red Anjous have a beautiful crimson color, but unless the pears are sliced very thin for a salad, it is better to remove the skin, for it is somewhat thicker and tougher than the skin on green Anjous.

Bartlett Red and yellow Bartlett pears are highly aromatic and even when ripe they're firm enough to survive a trip in a picnic basket. Like Anjou, Bartlett is sweet even when it's still crisp. A perfectly ripe Bartlett is fantastic for eating raw or for serving in salads. For cooking, use underripe specimens. Available from July through December, Bartletts should be watched closely for ripeness. The yellow variety will shift from chartreuse to golden during the last twenty-four hours of its ripening process. As soon as it's fully yellow, it should be eaten at once, because within hours it will begin to turn brown, the perfume will become overwhelmingly strong, and the flesh will go from firm to flabby. Red Bartletts will brighten from dark maroon to bright red.

Bosc With its slender swan's neck and its brown, russeted skin, this pear is a real showstopper. Fully ripe, it has an almost irresistible affinity for cheese. In fact, a ripe Bosc pear and a chunk of Oregon blue cheese comprise a classic Northwest dessert. Bosc is also the very best pear for poaching. For the most beautiful poached pears, choose slightly underripe Boscs and make sure the stems are firmly attached. Left on, they will give your poached pears character. Boscs are available from August through April.

Comice Available August through February, but not as widely grown as other pear varieties, Comice is the softest, sweetest, and juiciest of all the commonly grown varieties. It is what the French call a butter pear. The best Comice pears are completely free of any grit or stone cells, and their texture is as smooth as custard. They should be allowed to ripen beyond the crisp stage until quite soft. A very soft Comice can be sliced in half and eaten with a spoon.

Seckel Seckel pears are much smaller than other pears, and this makes them perfect for snacking. Officially they're available from August through February, but they seem to peak around the winter holidays. They are supersweet and can be eaten firm or soft.

Their maroon and olive skin makes them beautiful for centerpieces. I like to poach them and serve them as a garnish with other desserts such as pound cake, warm gingerbread, or homemade ice cream.

Ripening Pears

LIKE APPLES, PEARS ARE KEPT IN CONTROLLED ATMOSPHERE STORAGE AND shipped basically ready-to-eat. But ripeness is a more fleeting thing in a pear than it is in an apple, and a savvy consumer will know how to tell a ripe pear or gauge the time needed for one to ripen. On a trip to Italy, I was eyeing some pears at an outdoor market. I must have looked like I needed some help, because a woman in a fur coat shopping beside me asked me in Italian, "When do you want to eat the pears?" "Tomorrow," I said. "What time?" she asked. I said, "For lunch." She stripped off a glove and gently pressed a few of the pears between her fingers. "These will be perfect." And indeed they were.

Some pears will change color as they ripen, but most must be judged ready or not by touch. An unripe pear, hard as a potato, will need a few days to ripen. Place unripe pears in a brown paper bag and let them stand at room temperature. Test them every twenty-four hours. A ready-to-eat pear will yield readily to the pressure of a fingernail but will not give in to the pressure applied by the pads of your fingers when you pick them up. A pear that's too ripe will feel soft as soon as you pick it up.

Once the pears are ripe, eat them at once, or store them for a day or two in the refrigerator.

The Northwest Essentials Cookbook

Romaine and Apple Salad

Nothing is more refreshing than a crisp apple salad. Fuji, Gala, and Criterion are the varieties I usually reach for, but in a pinch, ordinary Red Delicious will do. The combination of cider, vinegar, sugar, and salt, will compensate for a lack of flavor or accentuate any already very flavorful apples.

- 1 head romaine lettuce
- 3 to 4 apples (about 1½ pounds)
- 3 tablespoons fresh apple cider
- 3 tablespoons apple cider vinegar
- 1 tablespoon sugar
- 1 teaspoon salt
- ½ teaspoon freshly ground black pepper
- ⅓ cup light olive oil or corn oil

Trim the romaine and cut the head lengthwise into quarters. Cut across into 6 parts to produce rectangular pieces of lettuce about 1½ inches long. Wash the lettuce and spin dry. Put in a salad bowl and set aside. In a jar or a small bowl, combine the apple cider, vinegar, sugar, salt, pepper, and oil, then whisk or shake the dressing to create a fairly smooth emulsion. If using Red Delicious or other tough-skinned apples, peel them; if using a thinner skinned apple, don't bother. Cut the sides of each apple away from the core to leave a square core. Cut each piece of the apple into thin slices and toss with the prepared dressing. The salad may be assembled at once, or prepared ahead up to this point and refrigerated for several hours. Just before serving, toss the marinated apples with the romaine and serve.

Serves 4

Warm Duck and Apple Salad

On a day in autumn when the apples have all turned sweet and the air is spiked with the smoke of the first fires of the season, this salad makes a meal that commemorates the change of season in a most satisfying way. Choose a flavorful Winesap, Fuji, or Criterion, or any fragrant apple.

> 4 cups mixed salad greens, washed and spun dry
> 3 tablespoons rendered poultry fat or olive oil
> 1 medium onion, thinly sliced
> 2 large apples, cored and sliced
> Salt and freshly ground black pepper
> ¼ cup Calvados, applejack, or apple cider
> 1½ cups leftover roast duckling, turkey, or chicken meat, cut or torn into 2-inch pieces

Arrange the salad greens on individual salad plates and set aside. Melt the fat in a skillet over high heat. Sauté the onion about 2 minutes, or until it begins to brown. Add the apples and sauté for 1 minute. Sprinkle on salt and pepper, then pour on Calvados. Add the duckling and sauté for 2 minutes, or until heated through. Divide the apples and poultry among the salad greens and serve at once.

Serves 4

Pear and Hazelnut Salad with Oregon Blue Cheese

The combination of ripe pears and tangy blue cheese is one of the classic flavor combinations. Served unadorned on a bare wooden board, a chunk of blue cheese and a pear could delight any serious gourmand. The two come together almost as easily in this salad, but the interplay is enhanced by the addition of a third and very agreeable component, toasted hazelnuts. A vinaigrette made thick and creamy with a puréed pear and some hazelnut oil brings all three ingredients together. I like to use red Bartlett pears when I find them, because the red skins look so good against the backdrop of pale green butter lettuce leaves, but any ripe pears will do.

2 heads butter lettuce
Pear and Hazelnut Vinaigrette *(recipe follows)*
3 large ripe pears, preferably red Bartlett
3 ounces roasted and peeled hazelnuts
6 ounces Oregon blue cheese

Wash and spin dry the butter lettuce, breaking the larger leaves into 4-inch pieces. Toss lettuce with 6 ounces vinaigrette, or enough to evenly coat the leaves, and arrange the dressed lettuce on 4 chilled plates. Slice each pear in half and spoon out the core. Lay the halves on a cutting board, flat side down, and slice each half on a bias into 7 or 8 even slices. Press the sliced pear halves lightly to fan them out and carefully transfer the pear fans to the beds of lettuce. Scatter a generous tablespoon of hazelnuts over each salad and heap about an ounce of crumbled Oregon blue cheese at the base of each pear fan. Serve at once.

Serves 6

Pear and Hazelnut Vinaigrette

A ripe pear, puréed in the blender with the other ingredients, makes this vinaigrette thick and smooth. The pear actually lightens the dressing, though, because it replaces most of the oil. If you choose a dark hazelnut oil made from toasted hazelnuts instead of a very light one made from raw nuts, the nutty flavor will be enhanced. If no hazelnut oil is available, don't be afraid to forge ahead and make the dressing with light olive oil or any good vegetable oil.

1 large ripe pear
¼ cup rice vinegar
1 tablespoon sugar
1 teaspoon salt
½ teaspoon pepper
¼ cup hazelnut oil

Peel, core, and chop the pear, and drop it into a blender. Immediately pour in the rice vinegar to prevent the pear from browning. Add the sugar, salt, pepper, and hazelnut oil and purée until smooth. Keep chilled until ready for use. Dressing keeps, covered and refrigerated, for several days.

Makes about 1 cup

Warm Spinach Salad with Pear Fans

I have always enjoyed a wilted spinach salad. But somehow the traditional combination of bacon and hard-boiled eggs leaves me feeling more like I've had the plowman's breakfast at a local diner than a salad. This version is still substantial and satisfying, and the pears give it a light sweetness that I really like.

> 6 cups baby spinach leaves, washed and spun dry
> 2 large ripe pears, preferably Bosc, peeled, halved, and cored
> ¼ cup olive oil
> 1 teaspoon sugar
> ½ teaspoon salt
> ½ teaspoon pepper
> 3 tablespoons balsamic vinegar

Divide the spinach among 4 salad plates and set aside. To make pear fans, slice each pear half lengthwise into 6 or 7 slices without cutting all the way to the top of the pear. Heat the olive oil in a large sauté pan over medium heat and add the pear fans. Cook 2 minutes on each side, turning carefully, then transfer the warm pears to the salad plates. Whisk sugar, salt, pepper, and vinegar into the pan, and when the mixture is boiling hot, drizzle it over the salads and serve immediately.

Serves 4

Curried Apple Soup

This soup is based on a recipe that was given to me by a friend who enjoyed it as child. I started making the soup with apples from a tree that once grew where a small hotel now stands in Friday Harbor. I have happy memories of climbing the tree in my chef's jacket and gathering the apples in my apron. I was never able to identify that variety with any certainty. The closest commonly available variety is Newton Pippin. Certainly this classic pie apple has the right texture and flavor to make this soup as good as it can be.

> 1 medium onion, thinly sliced
> 3 tablespoons clarified butter
> 3 apples (about 1½ pounds), preferably Newton Pippin or Granny Smith
> 1 teaspoon curry powder
> 3 cups chicken broth, boiling

1 cup heavy whipping cream
Whipped Yogurt *(recipe follows)* **and toasted slivered almonds, for garnish**

In a large, heavy saucepan over medium-high heat, cook the onion in the clarified butter, stirring now and then to prevent sticking, for 10 minutes, or until the onions begin to brown. While the onions are cooking, peel, core, and slice the apples. Stir the curry powder in with the onions, add the apple slices, and pour on the broth. Bring the soup to a boil. Cover the pan, reduce the heat to low, and let simmer for 20 minutes. Transfer the soup in small batches to a blender. Drape a dishtowel over the blender and place a hot pad over the towel. To prevent the hot soup from escaping, hold the lid down with the hot pad while the motor is running. Bring the cream to a boil in the soup pot, pour in the puréed apple mixture, and stir to combine. Serve the soup hot with a dollop of Whipped Yogurt and a sprinkle of toasted almonds.

Serves 6

Whipped Yogurt

½ cup heavy whipping cream
½ cup plain yogurt

Whip the cream until it is stiff. Stir in the yogurt. Serve immediately. Will keep several days in the refrigerator.

Makes about 1 cup

Cabbage and Apple Soup

Cabbage and apples soften together in this rich and compelling elixir. Built around a base of slowly caramelized onions like a classic French onion soup, it is positively thick with tender cabbage and apples. I used to make it with the same apples as for Curried Apple Soup (see preceding page) and with the dark green tightly curled leaves of Savoy cabbage, which a farmer friend of mine delivered regularly to the back door of my kitchen in late summer and early fall when the apples were ripe. Choose full-flavored apples firm enough to keep some of their shape when they are cooked. Newton Pippin works well in this soup. Members of the McIntosh clan with their heady scent are tempting, but most are too soft to keep any texture in soup or pie. Spartan, a cross between Newton and McIntosh, is an exception and makes a beautifully flavored soup.

¼ cup clarified butter or vegetable oil
2 medium onions, thinly sliced
4 cups finely shredded Savoy or other green cabbage
3 apples, cored and thinly sliced (about 1½ pounds)
1 teaspoon crushed garlic
1 teaspoon kosher salt
4 cups chicken broth, simmering

In a large saucepan or soup kettle, melt the butter and add the onions. Sauté over medium heat for 15 to 20 minutes, stirring to prevent burning, or until the onions are completely softened and uniformly browned. Add the cabbage and cook, stirring, until the cabbage is wilted, then stir in the apples, garlic, and salt. Continue to cook and stir for 5 minutes, then stir in the chicken broth. Simmer for 20 to 30 minutes before serving.

Serves 6 to 8

Fillet of Salmon, Sautéed with Granny Smiths and Cider

These two archetypal Northwest ingredients were destined to come together in one way or another. The salmon gets a crisp brown surface on one side, then it steams briefly over a bed of apples. The tart-sweet flavor of the apples is a perfect foil for the rich flavor of Northwest salmon.

4 tablespoons (½ stick) butter
4 salmon fillets (6 to 8 ounces each)
1½ teaspoons kosher salt
2 large Granny Smith apples, sliced
½ cup apple cider
Freshly ground black pepper

In a large skillet over medium heat, melt 1 tablespoon of the butter. Sprinkle the salmon fillets with salt and lay them, skinned side up, in a single layer in the skillet. Let cook, undisturbed, for 5 minutes, or until a crisp, brown crust forms. Do not try to move the salmon too early, or the surface of the fish will tear. Remove the fillets from the pan and add the apples. Stir-fry the apple slices for a moment, arrange the salmon fillets, cooked side up, on top of the apple slices, and pour on the apple cider. Cover and cook for 5 minutes. Transfer the salmon to plates and with a slotted spoon, lift out the apple slices and place them around the salmon. Swirl the remaining 3 tablespoons of butter into the juices left in the pan, whisking to form a smooth sauce. Season to taste with freshly ground black pepper, and pour the sauce immediately over the salmon and apples. Serve at once.

Serves 4

Charcoal-Broiled Breast of Chicken with Apples

A grill brings out the best in mild-flavored foods, and apples are no exception. The apple cider, with its generous allowance of sweetness and its hint of acid, becomes a kind of barbecue sauce for the chicken and the apple. An initial parboiling of the apples prevents them from turning brown before they go on the grill and gives them a jump start on getting tender.

> 1 cup apple cider
> 2 green apples, such as Granny Smith or Newton Pippin, cored and cut into ½-inch rings
> 1 cup chicken broth
> ½ cup heavy whipping cream
> 6 juniper berries, crushed
> 3 large boneless chicken breasts, split
> 2 tablespoons oil

Using a flavorful wood such as madrona, apple, or alder, build a fire in your backyard barbecue. Allow the fire to blaze and then settle into a pile of coals. A bed of embers spotted with small, lively flames is your goal. Position the grill rack about 6 inches above the glowing coals and wipe it with an oily cloth. Meanwhile, prepare the apples and the sauce. In a deep saucepan, bring the apple cider to a boil. Add the apple rings and cook for 1 minute, then remove and set aside. Add broth to the cider and boil until the mixture is reduced to 1 cup. Add the cream and juniper berries. Continue to boil until the liquid has thickened slightly and become translucent. Keep the sauce warm while the chicken is grilled.

Brush the chicken breasts with oil and broil the chicken for 7 minutes. (If flames shoot up, put them out with a squirt from a squirt gun or a splash from a pitcher of water.) Turn the chicken and broil for 5 minutes more. After the breasts have been turned, brush the apple rings with oil and broil them about 3 minutes on each side. To serve, top each broiled chicken breast with 2 or 3 tablespoons of sauce and garnish with grilled apple rings.

Serves 6

Pork Tenderloin, Baked with Apples and Bay Leaves

The combination of pork and apples is a nearly universal favorite. This dish is singularly festive because each person gets a whole, small baked apple, heady with the scent of bay. Choose a small flavorful apple like Criterion or Gala. If you have one of those apple peeler-corer gadgets, this is a great opportunity to put it to use.

3 pork tenderloins (1 pound each)
2 teaspoons kosher salt
1 teaspoon freshly ground black pepper
6 cups apple cider
2 bay leaves
12 small baking apples, peeled and cored, but left whole
½ cup (1 stick) butter, cut into 1-inch pieces
Fresh bay leaves, for garnish (optional)

Preheat the oven to 425°F.

The pork tenderloin has a thick end and a thin end. Holding a knife at a severe angle to the line of the tenderloin, cut each tenderloin in half lengthwise on the diagonal to make six even 8-ounce portions that will cook at a fairly even rate. Sprinkle each portion with salt and freshly ground black pepper, and arrange the tenderloins in a glass or ceramic baking dish large enough to accommodate them in a single layer. Brown the pork in the oven for 10 minutes.

Meanwhile, in a saucepan over medium-high heat, bring the apple cider and bay leaves to a boil. Add the apples, reduce the heat to low, and simmer for 5 minutes, or until the apples are heated through but not mushy. Add the apples and cider to the pan with the pork. Bake for 20 minutes more, or until the pork is browned and cooked through (160°F on a meat thermometer). Transfer the pork and apples to a cutting board and set aside. Pour the pan juices into a saucepan over high heat, then swirl in the butter to create a smooth sauce. Slice the pork on the bias and serve each portion with a roasted apple and some of the sauce. Garnish each serving, if desired, with a fresh bay leaf in the top of the baked apple.

Serves 6

Open-Faced Apple Tart

The simplest and most elegant apple tart is a rectangular, vaguely French, and very satisfying pastry with a single crust. The secret to success is very straight rows of perfectly sliced apples. Even rows of thinly sliced apples are easy to achieve if you cut the flesh of the apple away from the core in flat sections, leaving a square core behind. You will be able to slice the segments with the precision of a master pastry chef. Save the peels and cores for jelly. Choose a good baking apple with a red blush on its skin so the tart will have a nice color. Jonagold, Elstar, or Cameo would work nicely.

SWEET TART PASTRY

> 1 cup flour
> 1 tablespoon sugar
> ½ teaspoon salt
> 6 tablespoons (¾ stick) butter, cold, cut into bits
> 1 large egg, lightly beaten

APPLE FILLING

> 3 large apples
> ½ cup sugar
> 2 tablespoons butter, cut into bits
> ¼ cup apple jelly

To make the pastry, combine the flour, sugar, and salt in a food processor. Add the butter and pulse on and off for 1 minute, or until the mixture has the texture of coarse bread crumbs. Add the egg and continue to pulse for 1 minute more, or just until the mixture comes together to form a ball. Do not process any longer than necessary. Dough may be rolled and baked immediately or wrapped in plastic and refrigerated for up to 1 day.

Preheat the oven to 350°F.

Roll pastry into a rough 14 x 8-inch rectangle, then fold the edges to create a sharp 12 x 6-inch rectangle with raised edges. To make the filling, peel the apples, saving the peelings for apple jelly. Cut the sides from each apple, leaving a square core. Save the cores for making jelly. Lay the cut sides from the apple flat on a cutting board and slice very thin. Arrange the slices in two even rows along the length of the pastry. Sprinkle with sugar and dot with butter. Bake for 25 to 30 minutes, or until the pastry is golden brown and apples are tender. Warm the jelly in a small saucepan. Cool the baked tart for 10 minutes, then brush with hot jelly. Serve hot or at room temperature.

Serves 6

Cinnamon Crumble Apple Tart

Cinnamon is one of the most familiar and yet one of the most exotic scents imaginable. Once worth its weight in gold to the ancient Romans, it is now affordable to anyone, but it is still priceless in other ways. The smell of this tart baking on a cold, rainy day makes it seem that all is well with the world. For this open-faced tart, it's better to avoid drier Granny Smiths or Pippins; moist and tender Golden Delicious apples make the perfect filling, and the thin skin need not be removed. Avoid the temptation to use brown sugar in the crumble topping; it would become too dark and hard.

Sweet Tart Pastry *(page 25)*

CINNAMON CRUMBLE TOPPING

⅓ cup flour

⅓ cup sugar

1 tablespoon ground cinnamon

4 tablespoons (½ stick) butter, cold, cut into bits

1 teaspoon vanilla extract

APPLE FILLING

4 Golden Delicious apples

2 tablespoons fresh lemon juice

⅓ cup sugar

Prepare the pastry and refrigerate it. To prepare the topping, combine the flour, sugar, and cinnamon in a small mixing bowl or food processor. Add the butter and vanilla and mix with a fork or process until the mixture is uniformly crumbly. Set aside.

Preheat the oven to 350°F.

Roll the pastry into a 12-inch circle and press it into a 10-inch pie pan. To make the filling, cut the apples into quarters, core them, and slice them very thin. Toss the slices with lemon juice and sugar, then arrange them in the pastry-lined shell. Crumble the cinnamon mixture over the top and bake for 45 minutes. Serve warm.

Makes one 9-inch tart

Excellent Apple Pie

For years, the Washington Apple Commission rated only two varieties as "excellent" for pies. These were Golden Delicious and Newton Pippin. Recently, the new but as yet not widely available Cameo has been added to the list. Several others earn a "very good" rating. If an apple pie is not irresistible, then there is no point in eating it. The ultimate apple pie has a tender flaky crust and just a hint of spice in the filling. It should be bursting with apple flavor and aroma. Even the most flavorful apples can benefit from a boost of lemon juice and sugar. Extra butter makes the crust collapse down onto the apples as they shrink; this will help you avoid a gap between the filling and the crust, so don't skimp on the butter. And don't use shortening. The downfall of many apple pies is a doughy crust and crunchy apples, so resist the urge to pull the pie from the oven as soon as it's brown; leave it in until it's really done.

BUTTER PASTRY

2 cups flour

1 teaspoon salt

1 cup (2 sticks) butter, cold, cut into bits

⅓ cup cold water

EXCELLENT FILLING

6 or 7 Newton Pippin, Golden Delicious, or Cameo apples

2 tablespoons fresh lemon juice

1 cup sugar

3 tablespoons cornstarch

1 teaspoon ground cinnamon

½ teaspoon freshly grated nutmeg

To prepare the pastry, combine the flour, salt, and butter in a food processor or bowl and process or work with a fork until the mixture is uniformly crumbly. Add the water all at once and pulse the food processor on and off or stir gently with a fork until the mixture just comes together to form a ball of dough. Do not overprocess or overmix. Without handling the dough any more than necessary, press each half into a disk, wrap in plastic wrap, and refrigerate while making the filling.

Preheat the oven to 350°F.

To prepare the filling, peel the apples, cut the sides away from the cores, and slice the fruit into very thin slices. Toss the apples with the lemon juice in a mixing bowl, then stir in the sugar, cornstarch, cinnamon, and nutmeg and set aside. On a well-floured surface, roll out one disk of the pastry into a 12-inch circle. Fold it into quarters so that it can be lifted without tearing and unfold it into a 10-inch pie pan. Press the pastry into place without stretching it. Place the filling in the pastry shell. Roll the second disk of dough into a 10-inch circle and with a sharp knife or a small cookie cutter, cut a decorative pattern into the pastry. Fold the pastry to move it then unfold it over the top of the apples. Bring the overhanging pastry from the bottom crust up and over the top crust and crimp the two layers together. Place a baking sheet on the rack below the pie to catch any overflowing juices. Bake for 1 hour, or until the crust is well browned and the juices are bubbling out.

Makes one 10-inch pie

Honey-Poached Pears

One nice thing about poached pears is that they allow you a grace period to enjoy your pears once they have ripened. While ripe pears must be eaten at once, poached pears will keep, refrigerated in their syrup, for up to a week. They may be served warm or cold, alone or as an accompaniment to other desserts. In winter, when summer fruits are unavailable, I like to use thin slices of poached pears instead of strawberries on Peak of the Season Strawberry Tart (page 171).

> 3 cups water
> 1 cup sugar
> ⅓ cup honey
> 1 lemon
> 6 Bosc pears or 12 Seckel pears

In a large saucepan, stir together water, sugar, and honey. While working over the pan, use a special zesting tool to remove the colorful outer rind or zest from the lemon and allow the curls of zest to land in the syrup. Juice the lemon and strain the juice into the syrup. Place the pan over medium-high heat and bring the syrup to a boil. Reduce heat to low. With a vegetable peeler, peel the pears and leave their stems intact. From the blossom end, cut out the cores and discard. Add the pears to the simmering syrup and cook 25 minutes, or until fork tender. Serve warm or cold.

Serves 6

Honey-Vanilla Bean Canned Pears

With the sinewy rope-shaped pods of dark brown vanilla beans reflecting the curled brown stems of the pears themselves, whole pears, canned in wide-mouth quart jars, are so beautiful you won't want to put them in the cupboard. The pears can be served right out of the jar or used like poached pears in recipes. Still firm, barely ripe Bartletts are best for canning.

¼ cup lemon juice
5 cups water
12 firm-ripe Bartlett pears
1½ cups sugar
½ cup honey
5 vanilla beans

In a preserving kettle, sterilize three wide-mouth quart jars in boiling water and keep the jars simmering while you prepare the pears and syrup. Put the lemon juice in a large mixing bowl and add about a gallon of water. With a vegetable knife, peel the pears, keeping their stems intact. With a corer, working from the blossom end, remove the cores from each pear. Drop the pears as they are prepared into a bowl of cold water. In a large pot over medium-high heat, stir together water, sugar, and honey. Cook the pears three at a time in the boiling syrup for 6 to 7 minutes, or until heated through. Transfer the pears to the sterilized jars and cover with boiling syrup, leaving ½-inch headspace. Seal the jars with new lids and process in a boiling water bath for 30 minutes. When jars are removed from the hot water bath, allow them to stand undisturbed for several hours. Any jars that do not seal can be stored in the refrigerator for several weeks. Sealed jars can be kept in a cool, dark pantry for at least 1 year.

Makes 3 quarts

Apple Jelly

Almost any apples will make good jelly. Peels and cores are especially good for jelly because they have a lot of pectin, the substance that gives fruit jellies their wonderful texture. With some fruits, the balance of water, pectin, acid, and sugar can be delicate, even elusive, but a jelly made from apples never seems to fail. Whenever you make an apple pie or an apple salad and have ample peels and cores left over, put them into a saucepan and simmer them in just enough water to barely cover. When the apples are completely tender and have begun to disintegrate, strain the liquid into a measuring cup. You will be ready to make a small batch of the best jelly you ever tasted.

Small batches of jelly are less intimidating than large batches. This formula can yield a jar or two of jelly from the peels and cores left after making just one apple pie or tart. If you start with red apple skins, your jelly will have a wonderful rose color. Jonagold apples make a particularly nice jelly.

> **Apple skins and cores from 1 pound of fruit**
> **Water to cover the skins and cores**
> **Lemon juice (1 tablespoon for every cup of juice)**
> **Sugar (¾ cup for every cup of juice)**

Fill a saucepan with apple skins and cores. Add just enough water to barely cover and bring the apples to a boil over high heat. Reduce the heat to medium-low and simmer for 20 minutes, or until the apples are very mushy. Strain the mixture into a measuring cup and discard the solids. For every cup of liquid, add 1 tablespoon of lemon juice. Bring the liquid to a boil in a saucepan over high heat. Measure ¾ cup sugar for every cup of apple liquid and when the liquid is boiling hard, stir in the sugar all at once. At this stage, the boiling liquid will run from the back of a clean metal spoon in two distinct streams; but when the jelly is cooked, the two streams will come together. This is called "sheeting," and it occurs at 220°F. Cook the jelly until a thermometer or the sheeting test indicates that it is ready.

Transfer to sterilized jars and seal with new lids. Process the jars in a boiling water bath for 5 minutes. Turn the jars upside down for 5 minutes, then turn right side up and allow them to stand, undisturbed, for at least 1 hour to seal. Any jars that do not seal can be stored in the refrigerator for several weeks. Sealed jars can be kept in a cool, dark pantry for at least 1 year.

Makes about 2 pint jars

Applesauce

Some people who were present when their mothers or grandmothers canned applesauce have memories of laborious hours spent over steaming kettles. These people were witness to an era when huge quantities of home-canned goods were put by for winter, and for them, canning sounds like a chore. These days, smaller batches are more appropriate for most of us. A few precious jars of homemade applesauce can be put up in about an hour, making home-canning an enjoyable pastime. Even if this recipe did not produce the wonderful sauce that it does, the smell of apples boiling on your stove would be worth the effort. Summer apples, like Yellow Transparent and Gravensteins, which don't keep or transport well and therefore seem to be grown only in backyards, make the best applesauce. If you are using store-bought apples, choose Golden Delicious or Cameo.

> 5 pounds (about 12 medium) tart apples
> 1 cup water
> Juice of 1 lemon
> ¼ cup sugar

Sterilize 4 pint canning jars in a kettle of boiling water and keep them simmering over low heat while you prepare the applesauce. Wash the apples and put them on a cutting board near the stove. In a large, heavy-bottomed preserving kettle with a close-fitting lid, heat the water with the lemon juice and sugar over medium-high heat. While the water mixture is heating, cut the apples into fairly large chunks, discarding the cores with the seeds. Put the cut-up apples into the boiling water and sugar mixture as soon as they are cut. This prevents the cut apples from turning brown and gives your finished applesauce a lovely pale color. Cook, covered, for 15 minutes, stirring every 3 minutes or so to prevent sticking. Pass the apples through a food mill, then return the applesauce to the pan. Reheat and when it's simmering hot, transfer it to the sterilized jars. Using a canning funnel, fill the jars with hot applesauce, leaving ½ inch head space. Seal the jars with new lids according to the manufacturer's instructions. Process the jars for 15 minutes in a boiling water bath. Remove and let stand, undisturbed, for several hours or overnight. Any jars that fail to seal can be used right away or kept in the refrigerator. Sealed jars will keep in a cool, dark place for at least 1 year.

Makes 4 pint jars

Spicy Pear Chutney

Pear chutney is more than just a garnish for curried dishes. It is a basic condiment, as useful in its own way as sweet relish or ketchup. I like to put a little pear chutney on a turkey sandwich. This chutney is dark golden brown and the spices lend it considerable warmth. Crystallized ginger from Australia, softer and more pungent than the Asian brands, is the best. I buy it already diced.

 8 large, firm, underripe Anjou or Bartlett pears
 3 ½ cups dark brown sugar
 3 ½ cups apple cider vinegar
 3 cups chopped onion
 2 cups dried currants
 6 ounces (about 1 cup) crystallized ginger, finely chopped
 3 cinnamon sticks, broken in half
 12 whole cloves

In a preserving kettle, sterilize 6 pint jars in boiling water and keep the jars simmering while you prepare the chutney. Peel and core the pears and cut them into ½-inch pieces. You should have about 8 cups. In a large preserving kettle over medium-high heat, combine the brown sugar and vinegar and bring the mixture to a boil. Add the chopped onion, dried currants, crystallized ginger, cinnamon sticks, and cloves. Cook the mixture, stirring regularly to prevent sticking, for 30 minutes, or until pears are soft and syrup is slightly thickened. Transfer the chutney to sterilized jars. Seal the jars with new lids and process in a boiling water bath for 10 minutes. When jars are removed from the hot water bath, allow them to stand, undisturbed, for several hours. Any jars that do not seal can be stored in the refrigerator for several weeks. Sealed jars can be kept in a cool, dark pantry for at least 1 year.

Makes 6 pints

Salmon

*I*t was summer, the height of summer, and the sun had set so very late the night before and was rising so early this morning that we felt as if it had never gone down. All night long, the fiery orb had hung, motionless, just below the horizon, and now that it was rising again, the eastern sky turned the brilliant blue-green color of verdigris. Brilliant pink clouds heralded the day's arrival.  The same colors were reflected on top of the tiny waves that covered the surface of the water like scales. Just then, the sun broke over the horizon in a blaze of fluorescent orange and its rays flashed

Salmon

off the water like lightning. Just as the sun rose, a very large salmon leaped from the water in front of our little boat, and the sun shone through the plume of water in his wake. He sparkled and shook as he fell back into the water, like a row of silver dollars tumbling from an unseen hand.

We were young and childless, up before dawn and out on the water in an aluminum boat as close to the water as we could be without being in it. We had, as they say, a moment, a moment that was so colorful and definitive that it has stayed with me for years.

Once, I suppose, when salmon were more abundant than they are now, a sight like that might have been commonplace, just as beautiful but not as striking. For most of human history, salmon have been abundant to the point of surfeit, and following those now recognized laws of supply and demand, their abundance rendered them almost worthless in the eyes of many of their beholders. In colonial times, Atlantic salmon was so common that the fish were considered food for the poor. A standard clause in the contracts of indentured servants stipulated that they would have to eat salmon no more than once a week. Lewis and Clark, when they reached the waters of the Columbia River saw Indians eating salmon, but rather than partake themselves, they bought the Indians' dogs for meat. Even as late as the Victorian era, Dickens wrote that salmon and poverty went together.

Now, salmon is threatened, and it is almost as dear to modern Northwest cooks as it once was to the pre-Columbian Americans who prayed annually for its return to our rivers. "Few societies," wrote Waverley Root, "have been so closely wedded to a single food as the Indians of that region were to salmon." Even today, salmon is the food most closely associated with the Northwest, and the health of the salmon runs influences the health of our economy.

What was once a ubiquitous staple has become a precious commodity. For this reason, it seems to me that every scrap of salmon should be handled very carefully and enjoyed thoroughly. If possible, purchase salmon whole and learn to fillet it yourself. The carcass can be used to make a rich broth in which some of the fillets can be poached.

Salmon Varieties

NORTHWEST INDIANS RECOGNIZED FIVE "TRIBES" OF SALMON, EACH WITH ITS own particular virtues. Modern ichthyologists acknowledge the same categories. A sixth Pacific salmon, known as Masu, resides on the Asian side of the ocean, but is generally considered gastronomically inferior to the salmon of the Pacific Northwest.

King or Chinook King or chinook *(Oncorhynchus tshawytscha)* is the salmon favorite of most chefs. It fillets beautifully; it holds up to grilling or poaching; and its delicate flavor inspires creativity. The king also grows to enormous sizes and makes beautiful cuts available that simply wouldn't be possible on a smaller fish. Its range extends from the Sacramento River in California to at least as far north as the Yukon River in Alaska. Young kings, on their way out to sea where they spend up to eight years before returning upriver to spawn and die, are called black mouths. A one-pound black mouth salmon can be cooked like trout.

Silver or Coho In the days before farmed salmon, silver or coho *(O. kisutch),* with its light pink, firm flesh, was the variety most likely to be found on your fishmongers' shelves. Its season is long; it's widely available, and it pleases people who cook and eat it. In many ways, it is indistinguishable from king salmon, but silver never grows as large as king, and its flesh is not quite as firm.

Sockeye or Red Available fresh beginning in late spring with the Copper River run, sockeye or red salmon *(O. nerka)* stays in the ocean almost as long as king salmon and has firm flesh. This fish is the brightest red of all salmon and is good for baking and oven-broiling. Its fillets are thinner and bake faster than other types of salmon.

Pink or Humpie Used mainly for canned salmon, pink or humpie *(O. gorbuscha)* is characterized by soft pink flesh. Its taste is milder than most other salmon, and it is good fresh, though it's not commonly sold that way. Male pinks, as they prepare to return to their spawning grounds, grow a ridge of cartilage at the back of their necks that has earned them the name of humpback or "humpies."

Chum or Dogfish This fish derives its unappealing name, chum or dogfish (*O. keta*), from the fact that it was used as dog food by Alaskan Eskimos and other Northwest Indians. The roe of chum salmon is generally considered the best salmon roe. Its species name, keta, is Russian for "salmon roe." The roe is bright and fine and crunchy, and it makes a good garnish. Unlike tiny sturgeon roe from which caviar is made, salmon eggs are large. They taste like sea water. If caught at the right stage of its life cycle, chum is actually fine food, but its flesh is very pale compared to other types of salmon—very light pink or even yellowish—and many people find this unappetizing.

Buying Salmon

MONIKERS TO LOOK FOR AT THE FISH MARKET ARE ONES THAT DESIGNATE WHERE the salmon came from or how it was handled. Place names like Copper River tell us where the salmon were harvested. This particular place name, which appears late in spring and early in the summer, is assurance that the salmon will be among the best in the world. The flesh of a Copper River salmon is particularly high in fatty acids and has a compelling flavor.

Troll-caught salmon is individually caught on lines and not in a net. The advantage is that salmon caught in a net is often battered and bruised before it's brought on board the fishing boat. Naturally, troll-caught salmon command a higher price.

Frozen-at-sea salmon is very different from ordinary frozen salmon, which is piled into the hold of a fishing boat as it is caught and kept cold until it is taken ashore and gutted and cleaned. While it waits, bacteria have their way with the flesh and sometimes give it a fishy smell or cause its texture to deteriorate. Salmon that's frozen at sea is gutted and cleaned as soon as it's hauled on board. It's plunged into a bath of sugar water, then frozen at a temperature of twenty below zero. The sugar water prevents the formation of large ice crystals that would ruin the texture.

Farm-raised salmon is usually Atlantic salmon (*Salmo salar*), and while it is technically produced in the Northwest, it is arguably not a true Northwest product. The industry is also hazed in controversy. Some people fear that Atlantic salmon will escape and interbreed with the native stock and create genetic havoc. Certainly fish do escape, but there is no evidence that the Atlantic salmon breed here. Sea lions break the nets and feast on the fish as they fly from their pens. Others are concerned about salmon waste and their feed. Culinarily speaking, farm-raised salmon are inferior to wild salmon.

  The Northwest Essentials Cookbook

White king is an anomaly that occurs because of some genetic difference in certain king salmon. Some people say that the white king is white because of its diet, but fishermen assure me that white kings are swimming alongside their brightly colored cousins. Once the bane of a fisherman's catch because canneries wanted brightly colored fish, the ivory-colored fish are now seen as something of a bonus.

Filleting a Salmon

PLACE THE WHOLE, GUTTED FISH ON ITS SIDE AND, WITH A VERY SHARP KNIFE, remove its head. Starting at the head end, wedge the knife between the spine and the flesh above it. Keeping the knife nearly flat against the spine, cut away the fillet that is on top. Turn the fish over and repeat the process, lifting the second fillet from the spine with the knife. Once the fillets are removed, cut away the fins.

To skin a fillet, lay it, skin-side down, on the work surface. Place the blade at a 45-degree angle at the tail end. Hold the knife firmly in one hand, and with the other hand pull the skin toward you. The knife should stay more or less in the same place it started, while the fish is pulled over it. The fillet is now ready to be cooked. The head, bones, skin, and fins are ready for the stockpot.

Perfect Grilled Salmon

No dish captures the Northwest style more than grilled salmon. The secret to success lies in the degree of doneness. In many parts of the country, rare salmon is in fashion; for Northwest tastes, the salmon should be cooked through, but just barely. Dried out salmon is worse than underdone salmon. Timing depends not only on the intensity of the heat, but on the thickness of the fillets. Thin fillets of sockeye will naturally cook more rapidly than thick fillets of king salmon. King is the first choice for grilling. As soon as the juices of the fish begin to coagulate and turn white, it is wise to test the salmon for doneness by poking it with a knife and peeking inside. It should be barely opaque.

Four 8-ounce skinless fillets of salmon, each about 1 to 1½ inches thick
¼ cup vegetable oil or clarified butter
Kosher salt and freshly ground black pepper
Blackberry Butter Sauce or Three Citrus Butter *(see page 41)*, optional

Using commercial charcoal or a flavorful wood such as madrona, apple, or alder, build a fire in your backyard barbecue. Allow the fire to blaze and then settle into a pile of coals. A bed of embers spotted with small, lively flames is the goal. Wipe a rack with an oily cloth and position it about 6 inches above the coals. Coat skinless fillets lightly with oil or clarified butter. Place the fillets, skinned side up, onto the rack and broil for 10 minutes. If the oil lights and causes tongues of flames to taste the fish, cool the flames with a little water, splashing it on or using a squirt gun. With a long spatula, turn the fillets once and broil for 5 minutes more. Transfer from the broiler to a warm platter, season to taste with salt and pepper, and serve with Blackberry Butter Sauce or Three Citrus Butter.

Serves 4

Perfect Oven-Broiled Salmon

Since Pacific Northwest weather is not always conducive to outdoor grilling, the quintessential Northwest dish is often modified to be prepared indoors. Almost any salmon can be oven broiled. Both king and sockeye broil beautifully, and the method is particularly well suited to silvers, which might dry out on the barbecue. I leave the skin on when oven broiling salmon; as the fish cooks, it bastes itself from underneath. Afterward, the salmon can be lifted easily from its skin, which clings to the baking sheet.

> 1 side of salmon (about 2 pounds), or four 8-ounce fillets
> 2 tablespoons vegetable oil
> Kosher salt and freshly ground black pepper
> Blackberry Butter Sauce or Three Citrus Butter *(see next page)*, **optional**

Position a rack 6 inches from the heating element and preheat the broiler. Place salmon on a two-part broiler pan. (I like to line the bottom tray with foil to make clean-up a little easier. The top tray should be lightly oiled to prevent sticking.) Brush the side of salmon or individual fillets with oil and sprinkle with salt and pepper. Place the fish under the heating element and close the oven. After 5 minutes, turn off the heat and let the salmon bake for another 5 minutes without opening the door. If the fillets are of average thickness, they will be cooked to perfection without being dried out. Transfer to a warm platter and serve with Blackberry Butter Sauce or Three Citrus Butter.

Serves 4

Blackberry Butter Sauce

Some cooks know immediately what a certain combination of foods will taste like before they even try it; others cannot know until they try. People sometimes balk at the notion of seafood and berries, but as soon as they taste it, they know it makes sense. The tart flavor of berries is reminiscent of the acidity in the flavor of lemon, and everyone knows what lemon tastes like with seafood, so if anyone you are feeding is shy about berries with fish, explain that the berries are a substitute for lemon.

> ½ cup blackberries
> Juice of 1 lemon
> 2 tablespoons sugar
> ¼ cup white wine
> 1 teaspoon crushed garlic
> Pinch of salt
> Pinch of freshly ground black pepper
> 1½ cups (3 sticks) unsalted butter, cold, cut into 1-inch chunks

In a blender, purée the blackberries with the lemon juice, sugar, wine, garlic, salt, and pepper. Strain the purée into a small saucepan. Boil rapidly over high heat until the purée is reduced to ¼ cup. Quickly stir the butter into the reduced purée a few chunks at a time. Do not let the mixture return to a boil. Serve immediately with Perfect Grilled Salmon (page 39) or Perfect Oven-Broiled Salmon (page 40).

Serves 6 generously

Three Citrus Butter

> 1 lemon
> 1 lime
> 1 orange
> 1 tablespoon sugar
> 1 teaspoon crushed garlic
> Pinch of salt
> Pinch of pepper
> 1½ cups (3 sticks) unsalted butter, cold, cut into 1-inch chunks

With a zester or grater, remove the colorful outer zest from the lemon, lime, and orange, then juice the fruits. Combine the zest, juice, sugar, garlic, salt, and pepper in a small saucepan. Boil the mixture rapidly over high heat until it is reduced to ¼ cup. Quickly stir the butter into the reduced liquid a few chunks at a time. Do not let the mixture return to a boil. Serve immediately with Perfect Grilled Salmon (page 39) or Perfect Oven-Broiled Salmon (page 40).

Serves 6 generously

Baked Salmon with Sorrel and Cream

Baking fillets of salmon skin side down on an ungreased baking sheet renders them moist and flavorful without a lot of fuss. The skin sticks to the baking sheet and the fillets lift off easily. The secret to success is to avoid overbaking the fillets. Sorrel, which contains a fair amount of oxalic acid, is fresh and lemony; cooked with cream and a little freshly chopped garlic, it turns into a complex sauce that perfectly complements simple baked salmon. Both the salmon and the sauce are easy to prepare, but together they constitute an elegant entrée.

> 6 fillets of salmon with skin (7 to 8 ounces each)
> Salt and freshly ground black pepper
> 12 large leaves of sorrel, cut into fine ribbons
> 1 teaspoon chopped garlic
> 1 cup heavy whipping cream

Preheat the oven to 450°F.

Arrange the salmon fillets, skin side down, on an ungreased baking sheet. Sprinkle lightly with salt and pepper and bake for 10 to 12 minutes, or just until congealed juices appear as white spots on the surface of the fish. While the salmon is baking, combine the sorrel, garlic, and cream in a heavy-bottomed saucepan and cook over medium-high heat until the sauce is boiling hard and slightly thickened. Remove from the heat. With a long metal spatula, lift the fillets from the baking sheet, leaving the skin behind. Transfer to warm plates, top with sorrel sauce, and serve at once.

Serves 6

Salmon in Baker's Parchment with Garden Herbs

Since salmon is very often an entrée served for out-of-town guests, the best formula is the one that takes as little time away from the table as possible. The formula that follows can be prepared hours ahead and kept refrigerated until 15 minutes before dinner, at which point it is placed without fuss into the heat of the oven. The recipe is very forgiving and even badly wrapped fillets turn out pretty well. Melted butter brushed onto the paper perfumes the fish with a buttery smell, but most of the fat stays on the paper, and the moist and flavorful salmon, which needs no sauce, remains very light.

> **6 tablespoons melted butter**
> **6 fresh salmon fillets (6 to 8 ounces each)**
> **Salt and freshly ground black pepper**
> **Fresh lemon juice**
> **Sprigs of fresh herb or herbs of choice**

Preheat the oven to 425°F.

For each salmon fillet, cut a heart-shaped piece of parchment paper roughly 12 inches in diameter. Brush each piece of parchment on one side with butter. Place a fillet on the buttered side of the heart and sprinkle with salt, pepper, and lemon juice. Place a large herb sprig on top of each fillet and drizzle on a little more butter or oil. Fold the other side of the parchment heart over the fish and crimp the edges all around to create a sealed packet. Arrange the packets in a single layer on an ungreased baking sheet and bake for 15 minutes. Serve at once. Let each person open his or her own packet.

Serves 6

Poached Salmon with Tarragon

Tarragon is one of those herbs that takes some getting used to. Before it became familiar to me through repeated exposure, I found its taste jarring. Now, its redolence is reassuring. A hint of anise, a note of basil, the simple fresh green of parsley, all these flavors and more are reflected in what I now consider the queen of all garden herbs. Poached salmon is another acquired taste. The first time I tried it, it seemed insipid compared to the rugged flavor of browned salmon off the grill or out of the sauté pan. Now, I appreciate the unadulterated taste of plain salmon cooked in a gentle bath of its own stock. Here, tarragon and fresh salmon play a nice duet. The flavors are highly complementary and uncomplicated.

4 skinless salmon fillets (about 8 ounces each)
1½ cups Salmon Stock *(page 48)*
2 tablespoons butter
2 tablespoons flour
¼ teaspoon salt
½ teaspoon freshly ground black pepper
½ cup cream
3 tablespoons fresh tarragon leaves or 1 tablespoon dried tarragon
Sprigs of tarragon, for garnish

In a large skillet with a close-fitting lid, arrange the salmon fillets, skinned side down, in a single layer. Pour in the stock and place the pan over medium heat. Cover and let the liquid come to a boil. Reduce the heat to low. Poach the fillets gently for 10 minutes. Remove from heat and transfer the fillets to a warm platter. Melt the butter in a saucepan and add the flour, salt, and pepper. Stir until combined. Add the poaching liquid, the cream, and the tarragon. Bring the sauce to a full rolling boil, whisking to keep it smooth, then pour it over the poached salmon fillets. Decorate the salmon with sprigs of tarragon and serve at once.

Serves 4

Turbans of Salmon and Sole

The smooth and delicate texture of quenelles is mirrored in this mousselike dish. The technique is basically the same as for making quenelles (see page 49), but instead of dropping the fish paste into simmering broth, it's poached in individual ramekins, then chilled and unmolded just before serving. The mousses can be made and assembled completely in advance. A fillet of poached sole wrapped around each little salmon mousse gives the dish considerable panache.

> 1 pound salmon fillet
> 2 egg whites
> ¾ cup heavy whipping cream
> 1 teaspoon salt
> ½ teaspoon freshly ground black pepper
> ¼ teaspoon freshly grated nutmeg
> 6 sole fillets (4 ounces each)
> 2 cups Salmon Stock *(page 48)*
> 1 envelope (about 1 tablespoon) unflavored gelatin
> Watercress and Dill Sauce *(page 46)*
> Sprigs of watercress and dill, for garnish

Butter six 4-ounce timbale molds, place them in a baking dish, and set aside. Preheat the oven to 350°F.

With tweezers, remove any bones from the salmon fillet. If you're using fish from near the tail, cut out the white fibrous line that runs down the center of the fillet and trim away the brownish-gray muscle tissue that lies close to the spine. Cut the salmon into 1-inch chunks. Grind the fish in a food processor by pulsing on and off until it is smooth, about 5 minutes. Add the egg whites, cream, salt, pepper, and nutmeg, and process until well combined. Transfer the salmon mixture to the molds and cover each timbale with buttered parchment and aluminum foil. Pour boiling water around the molds to reach halfway up the sides. Bake for 20 minutes. Cool completely. Remove timbales from the molds and keep covered.

Poach the sole fillets in the Salmon Stock, cool, then wrap the fillets around the salmon timbales. Soften the gelatin in 1 cup of the stock, bring the second cup of stock to a simmer, and stir in the cold stock with the gelatin until it is completely dissolved. Let the gelatinized stock cool until it is just beginning to set, then coat the chilled seafood with several layers of the aspic. Serve with a dollop of sauce and put a feather of dill in each little cap.

Makes 6

Watercress and Dill Sauce

This sauce was conceived to serve with Turbans of Salmon and Sole (page 45), but it makes a fine accompaniment to just about any seafood.

> 1 small bunch watercress, roughly chopped (about 2 cups)
> 1 small bunch dill, roughly chopped (about ¾ cup)
> 2 egg yolks
> 2 tablespoons fresh lemon juice
> 1 teaspoon chopped garlic
> ½ teaspoon salt
> ¼ teaspoon freshly ground black pepper
> 1¼ cups light olive oil or vegetable oil

In a food processor, combine the watercress, dill, egg yolks, lemon juice, garlic, salt, and pepper and purée. With the motor running, add oil in a very thin stream to create a smooth emulsion.

Makes 1½ cups

Chilled Salmon Salad

I've never been very enthusiastic about leftovers, but I make an exception for cold salmon. On a bed of greens with a tangy dressing, last night's salmon can become a really great lunch. I like fish on salads so much in fact that I am inclined to bake an extra fillet with the next day's lunch in mind. The same technique applies to cold roast chicken, pulled from the bones. If you have extra steamed or roasted potatoes, toss these with the dressing and serve with the salad.

> 1 head Bibb lettuce
> 1 salmon fillet (about 8 ounces), baked and chilled
> Simple Herb Dressing *(recipe follows)*
> Bread or crackers, for serving

Break the lettuce into individual leaves, rinse, and spin dry. Divide among 4 serving plates, then break the salmon into fairly large chunks over the greens. Pass the dressing separately and serve with bread or crackers.

Serves 2

Simple Herb Dressing

¼ cup rice wine or cider vinegar
1 tablespoon sugar
½ cup mayonnaise
2 tablespoons chopped fresh sorrel, dill, or parsley
1 teaspoon chopped garlic (optional)

In a jelly jar, combine the vinegar, sugar, mayonnaise, sorrel, and garlic, if using, and shake until smooth. Serve with chilled seafood or chicken salads.

Makes ¾ cup

Salmon Sandwich

Someone once told me that his mother managed to serve leftovers every night for thirty years and no one ever saw the original dish. Incorporated into casseroles or transformed into à la king–style sauces to be poured over biscuits, leftovers were once a dreaded staple in American homes. These days, people cook smaller amounts to start with or simply microwave extra portions, so dishes made from leftovers are fading mercifully into the past. I have no wish to revive the golden age of leftovers, but a few classic dishes made with leftovers deserve to be preserved. Here's one of them.

1 baguette
¼ cup mayonnaise
2 tablespoons chopped parsley
1 tablespoon fresh lemon juice
2 teaspoons chopped garlic
10 to 12 ounces grilled or poached salmon fillet, chilled
2 cups shredded lettuce
Salt and freshly ground black pepper

Split the baguette in half lengthwise and toast it, if desired, under a preheated broiler. In a small bowl, stir together the mayonnaise, parsley, lemon juice, and garlic. Spread the inside of the baguette with the mixture. Crumble the cold salmon over the spread, then pile on the shredded lettuce. Sprinkle liberally with salt and pepper, then close the loaf tightly and wrap it. Allow the flavors to mingle for as long as it takes you to reach a scenic spot for a picnic.

Serves 4

Salmon Stock

Many cooks feel that salmon broth is too strong for classic preparations calling for fish stock, but I do not count myself among them. Salmon stock is a rich and satisfying stock with many of the same fine properties that make good chicken stock a kitchen staple. It becomes gelatinous when refrigerated and a layer of bright orange oil forms at the top. This oil is rich in omega-type fatty acids, which medical authorities tell us will prolong life by preventing heart attacks. Certainly the stock and the rich oil that forms on top constitute a wonderful medium for poaching salmon or making salmon stew. In a pinch, fish bouillon may be substituted for homemade fish stock.

> Bones, tail, fins, and head of an 8- to 10-pound salmon
> 1 onion, unpeeled and sliced
> 2 stalks celery, roughly chopped
> ½ teaspoon fennel seed
> ½ teaspoon whole or coarsely ground black peppercorns
> 1 bay leaf
> 1 cup white wine
> 8 cups water

With a large chef's knife, cut the bones, tail, and fins of the salmon into pieces that will fit easily into a stockpot. Cut the head lengthwise in half to expose more of the interior to the boiling water. Put the pieces into a heavy stockpot and add the onion, celery, fennel seed, peppercorns, bay leaf, and wine. Pour in the water and cook over high heat until the mixture comes to a boil. Reduce the heat to low and press the contents of the pot with a wooden spoon to submerge any fish parts rising above the level of the water. Simmer for 20 minutes, or until the pieces have just begun to disintegrate. Strain the stock into a clean pot and discard the solids. The stock may be used immediately or refrigerated or frozen for future use.

Makes about 2 quarts

Quick Salmon Stew

When we fillet a whole salmon at my house, the best cuts from the fillets are set aside for the broiler or the grill and the thinner portions near the tail are cut into strips for salmon quenelles or for a quick salmon stew like this one. Very often the salmon comes to us when fresh green peas are available and the green peas seem to go hand in hand with the celebration of summer. If sweet green peas are not available, snowpeas cut into julienne strips may be substituted.

> 3 tablespoons butter
> 3 tablespoons flour
> 3 cups Salmon Stock *(page 48)*
> ½ cup heavy whipping cream
> 1 pound skinless salmon fillet, cut into ½-inch strips
> 1 carrot, cut into matchsticks
> ½ cup fresh green peas or julienned snowpeas
> Salt and freshly ground black pepper
> 2 tablespoons chopped fresh dill

In a medium saucepan over medium heat, melt the butter. Add the flour and stir until combined. Add the stock and bring the mixture to a boil. Add the remaining ingredients, stir, and simmer for 10 minutes. Serve hot.

Serves 4

Salmon Quenelles in Saffron Broth

I buy saffron, an extravagant ounce at a time, in a fancy little tin that comes from Spain, and I've seen similar tins on the spice shelf in most serious restaurant kitchens. Decorated with zebras or crocuses or scenes from royal Spanish courts, the playfully colored boxes serve a sober purpose. Exposed to light and air, the delicate threads that constitute the world's costliest spice would lose their potency, and their considerable value. The tin keeps the spice in the dark so it can lend its light to the dishes that could not exist without it. Once the spice comes out of the tin and into something good to eat, I like to see it. The tiny red threads serve as a garnish as well as a powerful flavoring agent. In this soup, tiny threads of saffron wiggle through a clear salmon broth, stained brilliant yellow from the spice, and billowing dumplings of salmon mousse float by like clouds.

6 cups Salmon Stock *(page 48)*, well chilled
1 generous pinch of saffron threads
1 pound salmon fillet
1 tablespoon finely chopped fresh dill
1 egg
¾ cup heavy whipping cream
Kosher salt

Spoon off any fat that has congealed on top of the salmon stock. Scoop the gelatinous stock into a saucepan. Leave any particles of fish or seasoning behind. Simmer the stock over medium heat with the saffron threads for 15 minutes, or until the stock takes on a brilliant yellow color and smells strongly of the spice.

Meanwhile, prepare the salmon quenelles. With tweezers, remove any bones from the salmon fillet. If you're using fish from near the tail, cut out the white fibrous line that runs down the center of the fillet and trim away the brownish-gray muscle tissue that lies close to the spine. The idea is to have all pink fish. Cut the salmon into 1-inch chunks. Put it in a food processor with the dill, egg, cream, and 1 teaspoon salt. Process, pulsing the motor on and off for 5 minutes, or until the mixture forms a smooth paste. Using two tablespoons dipped in cold water, shape the fish paste into ovals, dropping them into the simmering broth as soon as they are formed. Poach the quenelles in the broth for 6 to 8 minutes. Serve hot in a bowl of broth.

Serves 6

Alder-Smoked Salmon

Alder-smoked salmon is one of the fundamental flavors of the Northwest kitchen and numerous professional smokers produce fine products that can be used in recipes calling for smoked salmon. However, there is nothing quite as satisfying as salmon that you have smoked yourself. Like baking bread, smoking requires a little know-how and an investment of some time, but the results are so flavorful, aromatic, and gratifying, that any serious home cook would do well to develop the skill. A simple home-smoking kit can be had at almost any hardware or sporting-goods store in the Northwest for well under a hundred dollars and at a garage sale for considerably less. The wood chips needed to stoke the smoker are sold in the same outlets.

Smoked salmon always seemed like a mystery to me until I tried it myself. Then, without losing any of its magic, it became very simple. The fish is soaked in a brine of salt and sugar

until it becomes firm and slightly translucent, then it's held in a very warm, very smoky place until it dries out somewhat and takes on a mahogany-colored glaze. While producing smoked salmon takes a day or two of on-again off-again attention, actual hands-on time is minimal. The salmon is ready to eat after an overnight bath in brine and 6 to 8 hours in the smoker. If inclement weather interferes with your smoking project, the box that the smoker came in may be used as a shelter for the thin aluminum-sided smoker. A prolonged power failure could be disastrous though, so avoid starting a batch of smoked salmon if a serious storm is brewing.

Most Northwest smoked salmon enthusiasts have their own favorite formulas for brine. Some include soy sauce, herbs, or spices; some include more or less sugar than others; all contain salt. Some cooks simply salt the fish overnight with a kind of dry rub and forgo real brine. This simple formula works very well for me. I like to smoke half of a fish and use the other half fresh.

> **One 3-pound salmon fillet, skin intact**
> **¾ cup (packed) brown sugar**
> **¾ cup kosher salt**
> **2 cups very hot water**
> **4 cups cold water**
> **Vegetable oil, for greasing the rack**
> **4 cups alder chips or other hardwood chips, such as apple or maple, for smoking**

Cut the salmon fillet into 6 portions, rinse, and set aside. In a 13 x 9 x 2-inch glass baking dish, stir together the sugar, salt, and hot water until the sugar and salt are dissolved, then stir in the cold water. Float the salmon portions, skin side up, in the brine for 8 hours or overnight.

Remove the salmon from the brine and pat dry with paper towels. Rub the racks of the smoker with a paper towel dipped in vegetable oil and place the brined salmon, skin side down, on the oiled racks. Plug in the smoker and fill the pan with wood chips. Put the salmon in the smoker. Every 90 minutes or so, stir the wood chips and replace them, if necessary. After 3 hours, rotate the racks, top to bottom and bottom to top. When the salmon has smoked for 6 hours, the surface of the fish will have acquired a rich shiny brown finish, and some of the juices may have begun to congeal white, as in cooked salmon. Depending on the weather and the temperature of your smoker, the salmon will be ready after 6 to 8 hours. Remove salmon from smoker, cool it for 30 minutes, then wrap each piece in plastic wrap and refrigerate. Smoked salmon keeps, refrigerated, for 2 weeks.

Makes six 6-ounce pieces

Smoked Salmon Pâté

This rich, buttery spread makes a little smoked salmon go a long way. It can be formed into logs and served in thin slices with toast or crackers as an hors d'oeuvre. The slices may also be served on top of a bed of greens in a salad.

12 ounces fresh salmon fillet
¼ cup water
¼ cup white wine
1 bay leaf
¾ cup (1½ sticks) butter, softened
12 ounces smoked salmon
Salt and freshly ground black pepper
Sprigs of herbs, for garnish
Toast or crackers, for serving

Remove bones from the salmon fillet with tweezers, and then remove the skin and cut the salmon into 4 pieces. In a small saucepan over high heat, combine the water, wine, and bay leaf and bring to a boil. Reduce heat to medium, add the fresh salmon and cook, uncovered, for 10 minutes, or until the salmon is barely cooked through and most of the water has evaporated. Remove from the heat and discard the bay leaf. In a stand mixer fitted with a paddle, combine the cooked salmon, any remaining cooking liquid, and the butter on low speed until the salmon is broken up and the butter is incorporated. Remove skin from the smoked salmon, break it into 1-inch pieces, and drop it into the bowl. Continue mixing just until the smoked salmon is incorporated into the poached salmon and butter mixture. Lay two pieces of plastic wrap on the counter and divide the salmon mixture between them. Shape each into a 10-inch log and refrigerate for several hours or overnight.

To serve, peel away the plastic wrap and cut the logs into slices. Season with salt and pepper, garnish with herb sprigs, and serve with toast or crackers.

Serves 12

Smoked Salmon and Cream Cheese Quiche

Combining smoked salmon and cream cheese is almost a reflex, so natural and pleasant is the combination. Baked together in a pie shell, the salmon and cream cheese are wedded in a delicate custard and their bed is a crisp and delicate butter pastry. I used to bake this quiche to serve at a bed and breakfast: I prepared the pastry the night before and refrigerated it in the pie pans overnight; I also stuck the cream cheese in the freezer so that it would be easier to cut into bits in the morning. There, wild fennel grew in lavish abundance not far from the kitchen door, so chopping a few leaves to scatter over the filling was almost obligatory; the herb gave the quiche a wonderful aroma. Fresh dill could be used instead. In winter though, when the fennel was gone, I made the cheesecake without it and no one ever missed it.

CRUST

2 cups flour

1 teaspoon salt

½ cup (1 stick) butter, cold, cut into ½-inch bits

⅓ cup ice water

FILLING

8 ounces smoked salmon, skin and bones removed, crumbled

8 ounces cream cheese, frozen

2 tablespoons chopped fresh fennel leaves (optional)

4 eggs

2 cups light cream or half-and-half

½ teaspoon salt

¼ teaspoon freshly ground black pepper

Preheat the oven to 400°F.

To make the crust, combine the flour and salt in a food processor or mixing bowl. Add the butter and process or combine with a fork until uniformly crumbly. Transfer mixture to a clean, dry work table or a mixing bowl and add the water all at once. Handling as little as possible, press the mixture into a dough.

Divide the dough into thirds and roll each third into a 12-inch circle. Transfer to a 10-inch tart pan and line with foil or parchment paper. Fill with dried beans or rice to weigh it down and bake for 12 minutes. Remove the weights and lining and cool before filling.

Preheat the oven to 375°F.

To make the filling, spread the smoked salmon over the partially baked tart shell. With a cold, wet knife, cut the frozen cream cheese into bits and sprinkle over the smoked salmon. If using fresh fennel leaves, scatter them over the cream cheese. Beat the eggs in a mixing bowl. Add the cream, salt, and pepper. Pour over smoked salmon and cream cheese and bake for 35 minutes. Serve hot.

Makes one 10-inch tart

Fettuccine with Smoked Salmon and Cream

When it's paired with the flavors of tarragon and cream, smoked salmon assumes a whole new character. Avoid any temptation you may feel to garnish this dish with cheese. Relish instead the subtle flavors of the seafood and pasta.

> 1 pound fresh or 12 ounces dried fettuccine
> 3 quarts boiling water
> 1 tablespoon salt
> 1 cup dry white wine
> 1 tablespoon chopped fresh tarragon leaves or 1 teaspoon dried tarragon
> 1 cup heavy whipping cream
> 6 ounces smoked salmon, skin and bones removed
> Salt and freshly ground black pepper
> Fresh sprigs of tarragon for garnish (optional)

In a large pot over high heat, cook the fettuccine in boiling water with salt for 10 minutes, or until just tender. Meanwhile, boil the wine with the tarragon in a heavy saucepan over high heat for 5 minutes, or until reduced to half its original volume. Add the cream and boil hard for 3 or 4 minutes more, or until slightly thickened. Crumble the smoked salmon into the boiling cream mixture and cook for 1 minute, or until the salmon is heated through. Drain the pasta and stir it into the smoked salmon sauce. Season with salt and pepper and serve at once, garnishing each portion with sprigs of fresh tarragon, if desired.

Serves 4

Stone Fruits

$\mathcal{M}$y first home in the Northwest was in Bellingham, Washington, and during my five years there, I lived in five different houses, each in its own way a little better than the one before. The first place was a dismal gray house too close to downtown and to the reeking pulp mill. Only a glimpse of Mount Baker from the bedroom window made the place tolerable. Then came a time in a rented room, about which all I can say is that it was mercifully brief. ✑ The third house, the one I stayed in longest, was another rented room where I shared the kitchen and living room with the owner.

Stone Fruits

Most of my time there was spent in the big sunny garden where I grew good vegetables and read good books in the nook of an old apple tree. ✑ Memories of the fourth house may have been romanticized because it was there that I first entertained my wife, and the place has become, at least in memory, the quintessential Bellingham house. Nothing more than a converted old motel cottage, it should not have been as nice a place as it was. Still, the little roadside cottage was well built with broad archways connecting its three tiny rooms, and its living room walls curved into the ceiling in a clever twist of masonry that gave the place the feeling of a crafted country house. While the front of the house stared mercilessly out at a busy street, the windows along the back opened onto a small field flanked by a crumbling old carriage house.

The first summer I was there, I ripped out the horsetail ferns that grew in profusion along the south wall of the cottage and made a raised bed. A friend brought annuals as a housewarming gift and filled the little flower bed with color and a few vegetables. Another friend made green striped curtains to replace the torn plastic roll-up blinds. I painted the walls. I laid tile in the floor of the shower. I borrowed a wooden card table from my landlady and some broken antique chairs from the basement of the restaurant where I worked.

The day I moved in, a couple of my co-workers gave me a basket of cherries. The cherries were almost transparent red, sharp and sour, the kind that hardly anyone grows anymore. The couple lived in a rented house on what was once a farm and was on its way to becoming the site of a condominium complex. That basket constituted the better part of an old tree's last harvest. I canned some and determined to make something interesting with the rest. So I looked up cherries in *Larousse Gastronomique,* the dictionary of French cooking that has never failed to instill in me an urge to get into the kitchen and cook.

What caught my eye was a brief paragraph under the heading "Danish Cherry Tart or Flan." "Fill a flaky pastry shell or flan case with stoned cherries soaked in sugar and sprinkled with a pinch of cinnamon." Typical of the brief format of *Larousse,* no formula for the flaky pastry or measurements for the cherries or sugar were given. Somewhat more precise instructions followed.

"Cover the cherries with a prepared mixture of 6 tablespoons of softened butter, 6 tablespoons of sugar, ½ cup of powdered almonds and 2 eggs. Cook the tart or flan in the oven at a moderate temperature. Leave it to cool, and then cover it with gooseberry jelly and glaze with rum."

Having neither access to nor interest in the gooseberry jelly, I proceeded as best I could with the dish and had a fine tart to serve my friends from the restaurant when we gathered after work for an impromptu housewarming. The formula I devised, modeled after the one in *Larousse,* is on page 75.

I improvised other tarts in that house too. In the backyard was a plum tree that yielded enough fruit to make dozens of tarts, and for two weeks running I made several double batches of Cinnamon Plum Tarts (see page 76). The tree also taught me to make plum jelly, and to roast plums with chicken, and to try my hand at homemade plum wine.

As for the fifth house in Bellingham, I inhabited it more or less at the same time I inhabited the fourth one, for my wife-to-be lived there and I spent as much time there as I ever did at home. That house had no plum tree, but wild cherry trees covered the bank behind the house. The blossoms rained down on us in the spring, and in summer, while we wove our commitment to one another, the cherries ripened and wild birds gathered to devour them.

The way stone fruits are made, two halves woven around a kernel in the center, is like a marriage. And the fruits are undeniably romantic. Their provocative shapes and their sweetness are downright libidinous, and the all-too-brief season during which they ripen is a reminder of the transience of our own season in the sun.

Cherries

EVEN IN THE PACIFIC NORTHWEST, WHERE THE SEASON OF THE CHERRY (*Prunus arium*) is longer than it is in most parts of the world, there is an urgency and a boisterousness about cherry season that sends us rushing to the market to buy cherries while we may. Cherries are a fleeting pleasure. There is nothing like fresh cherries, and many attempts to put them by for the off season meet with sad results. Unlike other stone fruits, cherries don't take well to canning. Canned in syrup they are as eerie as specimens preserved in formaldehyde, and cherry preserves can be chewy and cloying.

Cherries do dry well and some of my recipes call for dried cherries. But dried cherries are as different from fresh as raisins are from grapes. Fresh cherries, like fresh grapes, are perhaps best enjoyed very simply, warmed by the sun on a picnic, or from a bowl of ice water on a shady porch, but basically unadorned. Still, when their season is upon us, who can resist making something with them?

Cherries are typically grouped into two general categories: sweet and tart. Traditionally, the sweet ones are eaten raw and the tart ones are used for cooking. Cherry growers in Washington, Oregon, Idaho, and Utah, who market their produce collectively, grow sweet cherries almost exclusively, and Northwest cherries account for 80 percent of all the cherries grown in the nation. (Farmers in Michigan produce 70 percent of the tart cherries.) I tend to cook with sweet cherries, and I use dried tart cherries, which are sweetened, interchangeably with naturally sweet dried Bing cherries.

Northwest cherry growers produce almost exclusively sweet cherries, but among the sweet cherries grown in the Northwest, important distinctions are made.

The basic criterion is size. Large cherries command a higher price than small ones. Cherries are graded according to row size. In the early days of commercial cherry farming, cherries were packed into standard-size boxes and the number of cherries that could be packed in a row determined their market value.

The largest cherries could be packed at no more than nine rows per box. Smaller, twelve-row cherries could not command the same price. Beyond distinctions among various sizes of cherries are differences among individual varieties.

Rainier Cherries In many people's minds, the real star of cherry season is the golden, rosy-cheeked Rainier. With 20 to 25 percent sugar compared to 17 to 19 percent for dark red cherries, the Rainier is sweeter than other cherries. Some people associate it with the similar looking Royal Ann cherry, which used to be grown pretty widely in Northwest backyards. Actually it bears no relation to that cherry, which is now grown for producing maraschino cherries. Oddly, the Rainier variety sprang from a cross between two dark varieties, the Van and the Bing. Since it ripens over a period of weeks, requiring pickers to comb the same trees several times over, and since it is very easily bruised, the Rainier cherry is more difficult than other cherries to harvest, hence the very high price this cherry commands. Most Northwest cooks never tamper with Rainier cherries. These are simply served the way God and His farmers made them, pure and unadorned in the warm sunshine.

Bing Cherries For cooking, we turn to the most abundant cherry in the Northwest, the Bing, a variety named for the Chinese worker who identified it where it volunteered in an Oregon orchard. With its sweet, mahogany-red flesh as dark as the wine-dark sea, the Bing has a relatively long season, appearing as early as mid-June and lasting well into the second week of August. Like all sweet cherries, Bings are considered best eaten raw—they are generally too sweet and soft for pies—but they perform well in certain tarts and in savory relishes to be dolloped on top of grilled meat or seafood. Uncooked dark cherries can also be piled on top of cakes.

Other Black Cherries To the untrained eye, other varieties of sweet red cherries are almost indistinguishable from the standard Bing, but a closer look will reveal subtle differences. The earliest cherries to appear in Northwest markets are of the Chelan variety, not quite as sweet as Bings but welcome because they are the first. Among the last cherries of the year to ripen are the dark Lapins. Their season overlaps the Bing but extends several weeks beyond it. Another late cherry is the lipstick-red Sweetheart variety whose heart-shaped body probably inspired its cutesy name. The Sweetheart is a glorious cherry that lends itself to chocolate desserts.

Plums

THE PLUM I ASSOCIATE MOST WITH THE NORTHWEST IS THAT DARK OVAL VARIETY commonly referred to as the Italian prune *(Prunus domestica)*. It ripens late and delivers the most brilliant plum flavor. But what makes it so practical and so irresistible is its sheer abundance. Whenever I have lived in the proximity of one of these trees, and that is to say as long as I have lived in the Northwest, I have been presented each fall with more fruit than I know what to do with.

Other plum varieties seem destined, I think, to be simply eaten out of hand, but this one lends itself to all sorts of preparations. I have roasted them and laid them to rest on beds of salad greens where their bright warm juices became a kind of salad dressing. I have boiled and strained the plums to produce a thick juice, which I put up in jars and opened up for winter breakfasts. I have baked it in tarts, roasted it with pork and chicken, and transformed it into chutney and jelly. I never get tired of these plums.

Peaches

THE DIFFERENCE BETWEEN A REALLY GOOD PEACH *(Prunus persica)* AND A MEDIOCRE one is so great that anyone who has had only one would be hard pressed to imagine the other. A really good peach yields to the slightest pressure when it's held in the hand. Even before it enters the mouth, the sensual experience begins. For one thing, a really good peach is never cold; it's warm to the touch because really good peaches are only available at the height of summer, and once a peach is refrigerated, it is no longer really good. Peaches change when they are chilled. It's as if something inside the cells of the fruit senses the change in temperature and shifts the cells' efforts from producing an irresistible fruit, a vehicle for coaxing animals to carry the pit far from the tree, to a survival module. The texture changes from voluptuous custard to packing foam and the flavor from nectar to preserving fluid.

Really good peaches are a gift from well-tended trees living in good soil. Their essence is fleeting and should be enjoyed like ripe strawberries in the moment of their perfection.

When peach season hits in the Northwest, several long weeks after the first hard, underripe peaches have appeared in stores, I shift into a kind of hyperdrive. I go out of my way to find the really good ones, happily driving across town to see if the best peaches are on the shelves at the few stores I can trust to stock the really good ones. I have also been known to drive across the state to visit the peach orchards of Eastern Washington and buy peaches right off the farm. The same farms sell their fruit to distributors who carry it to stores on my side of the state, but by the time it reaches me, the fruit is usually a disaster. Either it's been picked too green and it never ripens, or it's packed in refrigerated trucks and transformed into something other than the sensory delight it should be.

Once a peach is picked, it ceases to ripen. Of course every produce seller will tell you that fruit continues to ripen off the tree, but this is not quite true. Ripening is a complex process. Part of that process is simply softening. As the complex structure of the fruit begins to break down, hard green peaches will continue to soften after they're picked, but this is not ripening in the true sense of the word. A picked peach will become softer but not sweeter, and certainly not more fragrant. On the tree, where true ripening occurs, a peach will grow increasingly sweeter and more aromatic as it approaches a state of true ripeness. The color of its skin will change from a pale yellow blushed with pink, to a full deep yellow, golden as the light of a late-August afternoon, with streaks and bursts of pure wild rose red.

One time, a neighbor who sensed that I might appreciate truly good peaches persuaded me to follow her across the mountains to Yakima, where she had once built a home and run a peach farm with her husband. I packed up my family and drove behind her. On a plateau above Cashmere, we stopped at a rest stop and shared a picnic lunch. She described the way the land had been when she first came to Washington during the Great Depression.

"There were no real roads then," she said, "not like there are now. And our car wasn't much to speak of. We camped out in the desert and made fires out of sagebrush. I'll never forget it." Acre by acre, they transformed a portion of that desert into an orchard. By mid-afternoon, we were at her old farm. "There's the house," she said. "You can't really see it behind the hedges they planted, but I laid those bricks one on top of the other. I can see it hedge or no hedge. Our land came to here. Now you can't see where one farm ended and the other began."

The warehouse was on the neighboring farm and the grandson of the man to whom she had sold her farm was running the show. Outside the warehouse, crates of fruit were piled on pallets. "This is the fruit you want," she told me. "These are the peaches that are picked ripe, too ripe to ship." The varieties were myriad. There were pure white-fleshed peaches, peaches with pale yellow flesh, and peaches with dark orange flesh, but they all shared the qualities of perfection. Each was fully ripened, bursting with sugar and perfume. Firm until the moment they were bitten into, then soft as silk and positively dripping with juice.

A few farmers have changed the way they handle peaches so that they can bring fully tree-ripened fruit like that into supermarkets. Packed in single layers instead of piled into crates, and shipped quickly without refrigeration from farm to consumer, premium peaches really need no recipes. They demand to be eaten unadulterated. But of course really good peaches tempt us to buy them by the carload. So we make peach preserves and peach chutney and put the fruit up in syrup and glass. Even preserved, really good peaches are better than mediocre peaches eaten fresh.

While not much attention is paid to varieties of peaches, it is worth noting that late-season peaches are generally better than early-season varieties, especially for cooking. Early season peaches may be sweet and good for snacking, but for cooking, the varieties that ripen later are easier to handle. Typically, late-season peaches are freestone varieties, that is, their stones or pits slip out easily, unlike cling peaches in which the fibers of the fruit are bound to the pit.

Apricots

IN MOST PARTS OF THE COUNTRY, A FRESH APRICOT *(Prunus armeniaca)*, WHICH may be thought of as a small, strong cousin of the peach, is seldom seen. Most Americans happily resign themselves to dried apricots or the occasional apricot preserves without a clue as to what they're missing. Here we know that a tree-ripened apricot is a thing of beauty. The most productive apricot-growing regions lie south of the Pacific Northwest in California, but the fruit prospers here to a degree that makes its production commercially feasible, and every summer the orchards of Eastern Washington and Oregon deliver a host of these golden apples of the sun.

Eaten like a peach or a plum right out of the hand, a fresh apricot lulls you into a timeless place where golden fruits hang on mythical trees, and the notes from some long forgotten stringed instrument vibrate in the air of an exotic Middle East where these plum-shaped beauties originated. Some translators say that apricots and not apples grew in the walled garden immortalized in the Song of Solomon. Persephone's golden apples were probably apricots, and some have even dared to suggest that Eve offered Adam not an apple, but an apricot. Certainly this fruit would be more seductive.

Like Rainier cherries and perfect peaches, the best specimens, the really exceptional fruits bursting with flavor, need no adornment. More often than not, though, the fresh apricots we find in stores are less than perfectly ripe and are more suited to the preserving kettle than to the fruit basket. Even when they are ripe, we are sometimes compelled to cook with them anyway. If the apricots are less than explosive with flavor, a little added sugar and acid in the form of lemon juice or cider vinegar can enhance their naturally sweet-tart flavor. If the apricots are very flavorful, the amounts of lemon juice and sugar I call for in these apricot recipes may be reduced accordingly.

Sliced in half and planted, cut side down, on the grill, fresh apricots become a sublime companion to meat cooked on the barbecue. As the grilled surface of the fruit caramelizes into a concentrated crust of flavor, the inside develops a soft, custardy texture. In the oven, apricots make excellent crisps and pies. On the stove, apricots melt into vitalizing nectar and what may be the finest fruit jam known to man.

Cooking with Stone Fruits

IN MANY OF THE RECIPES THAT FOLLOW, ONE STONE FRUIT WILL HAPPILY REPLACE another. Apricots can stand in for plums, plums for cherries, or plums for peaches. Still, each fruit has its own distinctive character. Adventurous cooks will flip and flop these fruits as they please.

Cherries, apricots, peaches, and plums all seem to have in common some ancient ancestor that also apparently sired the almond, a nut closely related to all these fruits and one with which they share an affinity. While in most instances where nuts are called for I opt for the indigenous Northwest hazelnut, where these fruits are involved, I am more inclined toward almonds.

Freezing Stone Fruits

PEACHES, PLUMS, APRICOTS, AND CHERRIES CAN BE FROZEN SUCCESSFULLY IF A few simple steps are taken to ensure that they freeze quickly and uniformly.

PEACHES Dip peaches in boiling water to loosen the skins (see page 78) and then peel, slice, and pit them. Place the slices on a baking sheet lined with parchment or wax paper in a single layer without touching one another. Put the pan in the freezer for at least 1 hour. Pack the slices in heavy-duty, self-sealing plastic bags.

PLUMS AND APRICOTS Split plums and apricots in half lengthwise and pit them. Place the halves on a lined baking sheet in a single layer. Put the pan in the freezer for at least 1 hour. Pack in heavy-duty, self-sealing plastic bags.

CHERRIES Pit cherries and arrange them on a lined baking sheet in a single layer without touching. Put the pan in the freezer for 1 hour or until cherries are frozen solid. Pack in heavy-duty, self-sealing plastic bags.

Sautéed Prawns with Apricot Nectar

Whenever I have apricot nectar in the house, I know I have a flavorful way to brighten up not only breakfast but lunch and dinner as well. Aside from drinking the nectar straight for a tonic, I can use it in much the same way that I use wine to deglaze a pan in which I have browned meat or chicken to create an impromptu sauce. In this recipe the sweet-tart nectar adds zing to a quick sauté of prawns.

> 1 pound spot prawns or jumbo prawns (16 to 20)
> 2 tablespoons olive oil or butter
> ½ cup Apricot Nectar *(page 80)*
> ¼ teaspoon freshly ground black pepper

With a sharp knife, split the back of each prawn and slip off the shell, reserving only the bit at the tail. Rinse under cold running water and set aside. In a large sauté pan over medium-high heat, sauté the prawns in olive oil, turning once, for 5 minutes, or until they turn pink. Add the Apricot Nectar all at once and stir to coat the prawns. Transfer the prawns to serving plates and allow the nectar to boil for another minute or two to thicken it. Pour the reduced nectar over the prawns, season with pepper, and serve hot.

Serves 2

Flame-Broiled Arctic Char
with Cherry Salsa

Like any fresh fruit, dark, sweet cherries provide an astringent counterpoint to broiled fish. Rich king salmon or sturgeon would benefit from this salsa, but the large salmonlike ocean-going trout known as char seems especially amenable to this summer condiment. Served against a background of steamed or sautéed leafy greens like kale or mustard or chard, this makes a memorable entrée.

> 6 skinless fillets of Arctic char (8 ounces each)
> Salt
> 6 tablespoons light olive oil or corn oil
> Fresh Bing Cherry and Jalapeño Salsa *(recipe follows)*

Using a flavorful wood such as madrona, apple, or alder, build a fire in your backyard barbecue. Allow the fire to blaze and then settle into a pile of coals. A bed of embers spotted with small, lively flames is your goal. Wipe the grill rack with an oily cloth and position it about 6 inches above the glowing coals.

Sprinkle the fish with salt, coat lightly with oil, and place the fillets, skinned side up, onto the rack. Broil for 7 to 10 minutes. With a long spatula, turn the fillets once and broil for 5 minutes more. Transfer the fillets to plates and top each fillet with about ⅓ cup of salsa. Serve at once.

Serves 6

Fresh Bing Cherry and Jalapeño Salsa

> 2 tablespoons apple cider vinegar
> 2 tablespoons sugar
> 1 teaspoon kosher salt
> 1 or 2 jalapeño peppers, very thinly sliced
> 2 cups ripe Bing cherries

Stir together vinegar, sugar, and salt in a bowl, then add jalapeños. Pit the cherries, split them lengthwise in half, and toss them with the vinegar mixture. Salsa may be made several hours ahead and kept, covered, at room temperature.

Makes about 2 cups

Chicken Salad with Apricots and Almonds

This salad makes great use of cold roast chicken, and may sound like just a way to use left-overs, but three of my favorite flavors—apricots, almonds, and roast poultry—are so merrily combined here that I would happily roast a chicken just to make the salad. Dried apricots, plumped in just enough boiling water to cover them, can be substituted for fresh. In November the salad can be easily adapted to cold turkey and dried apricots.

> 2 tablespoons apple cider vinegar
>
> 1 tablespoon sugar
>
> 1 teaspoon salt
>
> ½ teaspoon freshly ground black pepper
>
> ¼ cup light olive oil or corn oil
>
> 2 pounds fresh apricots, pitted, or 8 ounces dried apricots, plumped in boiling water and drained
>
> 2 cups (bite-size pieces) cooked roast chicken or turkey, cold
>
> 1 head Bibb lettuce, rinsed and spun dry
>
> ½ cup slivered almonds, lightly toasted
>
> ¼ cup chopped green onion (optional)

In a salad bowl, whisk together the vinegar, sugar, salt, and pepper. Still whisking, stream in the oil to make a smooth emulsion. Slice the apricots and toss them with the dressing in the salad bowl. Add the chicken and toss to coat. Divide the lettuce among salad plates and spoon a generous amount of the chicken mixture onto each bed of lettuce. Top with toasted almonds and green onions, if desired; serve at once.

Serves 4 to 6

Chicken Baked with Plums and Olives

The combination of sweet and salty is almost always appealing to me. In this dish, the gentle goodness of plums is slightly intensified in the heat of the oven, and the powerful punch of strong dark Mediterranean olives is toned down a notch or two. Together, the plums and the olives create a playful exchange of flavors around baked chicken pieces. The recipe can be easily doubled. It's good hot, warm, or cold and makes a great contribution to a potluck.

One 3-pound chicken

9 ripe Italian prune plums, halved and pitted

¾ cup pitted Saracena or Niçoise olives

1 tablespoon chopped garlic

1 teaspoon salt

¼ teaspoon freshly ground black pepper

1 cup white wine

Preheat the oven to 375°F.

With a sharp chef's knife, cut the chicken in half lengthwise. Remove the backbone, saving it for the stockpot, and cut each half into 4 pieces: leg, thigh, wing, and breast. (If you are uncomfortable cutting up your own chicken, you may use a cut-up bird, but the pieces will be uneven.) Arrange the pieces in a single layer in a 9-inch square glass or ceramic baking dish with the plums and the olives. Sprinkle the chicken with the garlic, salt, and pepper and pour on the wine. Bake for 50 minutes. With tongs or a slotted spoon, transfer the baked chicken pieces with the plums and olives to a platter and pour the pan drippings into a small saucepan. Boil over high heat, stirring with a wire whisk until slightly thickened. Pour over the chicken and serve hot.

Serves 4

Breasts of Duckling with Tart Cherry Sauce, Caramelized Onions, and Grilled Polenta Rounds

The combination of duckling and cherries is a very good one. In summer, when cherries are ripe, try this same dish made with fresh, pitted Bing cherries. Any other time of year, dried tart cherries from Eastern Washington add a piquant counterpoint to the rich and flavorful breasts of duckling. Ask your butcher for breasts of duckling, or remove them from whole ducklings with a sharp boning knife and save the hind quarters for Confit of Duckling (page 227). Make the polenta ahead, so it has time to set.

3 whole boneless breasts of duckling, split in half

Salt and freshly ground black pepper

Grilled Polenta Rounds *(page 70)*

Caramelized Onions *(page 70)*

Tart Cherry Sauce *(page 71)*

Using a flavorful wood such as madrona, apple, or alder, build a fire in your backyard barbecue. Allow the fire to blaze and then settle into a pile of coals. A bed of embers spotted with small, lively flames is your goal. Wipe the grill rack with an oily cloth and position it about 6 inches above the glowing coals.

Season the breasts of duckling with salt and pepper. Arrange the breasts on the rack in a single layer, skin side down. Cook for 8 minutes, or until most of the fat has cooked off and the skin is well browned. Meanwhile, slice the polenta into 1-inch rounds and dip in oil. Grill the polenta rounds next to the duck breasts. Place a grilled round of polenta on each warm serving plate. Slice the duck breast and fan over polenta. Pile onions on top of the polenta and ladle sauce over the duckling, letting cherries tumble down in a loosely formed ring at the base of the duck slices.

Serves 6

Grilled Polenta Rounds

> 3 cups water
> 2 teaspoons kosher salt
> 1 cup cornmeal

In a saucepan over high heat, bring the water to a rolling boil. Add the salt and stirring with a wire whisk, slowly stream in the cornmeal. Cook, stirring constantly for 10 to 15 minutes, or until the polenta is very smooth and thick and leaves the sides of the pan. Transfer hot polenta to two clean 12-ounce metal cans reserved from frozen juice concentrate or any clean 3-cup container. Let cool, then refrigerate until firm before slicing. Slice polenta into rounds and grill or sauté in butter or olive oil.

Serves 6 as a side dish

Caramelized Onions

> 3 onions, thinly sliced
> ¼ cup olive oil
> 1 tablespoon sugar
> 1 teaspoon dried thyme leaves
> Salt and freshly ground black pepper

In a kettle over high heat, cook the onions in olive oil, stirring for 10 minutes, or until tender and golden brown. Stir in the sugar and dried thyme leaves and cook, stirring, 10 minutes more, or until the onions are very browned and soft. Season to taste with salt and pepper.

Serves 6 as a side dish

Tart Cherry Sauce

1 cup red wine
1 cup chicken broth
1 cup dried tart cherries
1 teaspoon crushed black pepper
1 bay leaf
1 tablespoon cornstarch dissolved in 1 tablespoon water

In a saucepan over medium-high heat, bring the wine and chicken broth to a boil. Add the cherries, pepper, and bay leaf, and cook 10 minutes, or until the cherries are plumped over the level of the wine. Stir a little of the boiling sauce into the dissolved cornstarch, then stir the cornstarch mixture all at once into the sauce. Remove the bay leaf. Serve at once or keep warm until serving time.

Makes about 1 1/2 cups

Grilled Pork Chops with Apricots and Sage

By a happy coincidence, the great fruits of summer ripen just in time for the outdoor grilling season. All the stone fruits make good accompaniments to barbecued meats, and warmed through on the grill, their sun-drenched flavors are enhanced and intensified. Something about the combination of grilled pork and apricots is especially compelling. Fresh sage leaves lend a savory note to the dish, but dried sage is a fine substitute.

3 tablespoons olive oil
12 leaves of fresh sage, or 1 teaspoon dried sage
2 teaspoons kosher salt
1 teaspoon freshly ground black pepper
6 pork loin chops, about 1 inch thick (8 ounces each)
6 ripe apricots, halved and pitted

In a shallow baking dish, combine the olive oil, sage, salt, and pepper. Add the pork chops and turn to coat. Set aside.

Using a flavorful wood such as madrona, apple, or alder, build a fire in your backyard barbecue. Allow the fire to blaze and then settle into a pile of coals. A bed of embers spotted with small, lively flames is your goal. Wipe the grill rack with an oily cloth and position it about 6 inches above the glowing coals.

Place the chops on the rack, and if using fresh sage, press a leaf onto each side of each chop. Grill, basting with the marinade for 5 to 7 minutes. Turn and continue to grill and baste until the chops are done, 5 to 7 minutes more. Just after you turn the chops, dip the halved apricots in the remaining marinade and grill them for 2 minutes on each side, or until browned and heated through. Serve the grilled apricots with the grilled chops.

Serves 6

Chocolate Almond Apricot Cake

Apricot Jam is great on toast, on biscuits and scones, and spread on just about any bread in the house, but my real agenda for making this jam involves baking with it. It can be spooned into thumbprint cookies or spread over a pan of shortbread and drizzled with melted chocolate. It can also be used in assembling this cake, which is reminiscent of Sachertorte. I use a rectangular baking sheet known in professional circles as a half sheet pan, which measures 15½ x 11½ x ½ inch. Pans like these are available in all good kitchen stores and many department stores.

> 1 cup whole almonds
> 1 cup flour
> 1 cup chocolate chips
> ½ cup unsweetened cocoa powder
> 9 eggs
> 1½ cups sugar
> ½ cup (1 stick) butter, melted
> 1 teaspoon vanilla extract
> ½ teaspoon salt
> 1 cup Apricot Jam *(page 80)*
> Chocolate Glaze *(recipe follows)*

Preheat the oven to 375°F. Grease and flour the sides of a half sheet pan and line the bottom with parchment paper. Set aside.

In a food processor, chop the almonds very fine. Add the flour and process until the almonds are ground as fine as cornmeal. Add the chocolate chips and cocoa and chop fine. Separate the eggs. Place the whites in the bowl of an electric mixer or in a deep mixing bowl and set aside. In another large mixing bowl, whisk the yolks with ¾ cup of the sugar, then stir in the melted butter, vanilla, and salt. Beat the egg whites until they hold soft peaks. Stream in the remaining ¾ cup of sugar and beat until the whites hold firm peaks. With a rubber spatula, fold one third of the egg whites into the yolk mixture with half the almond mixture. Fold in another third of the egg whites with the remaining almond mixture. Fold in the remaining egg whites and transfer the batter immediately to the prepared sheet pan. Spread the batter evenly over the pan. Bake for 18 to 20 minutes, or until the cake springs back when pressed lightly in the center. On a rack, cool the cake to room temperature.

Trim the crusts and cut lengthwise into thirds to form three rectangles, each measuring 10 x 5 inches. Spread half the apricot jam on one layer and top with the second layer. Spread the remaining apricot jam on the second layer and top with the third layer. Prepare the chocolate glaze and spread it over the layered cake.

Serves 8

Chocolate Glaze

> 1 cup heavy whipping cream
> 1 cup semisweet chocolate chips

In a saucepan over medium-high heat, heat the cream to a simmer. Remove from the heat and stir in the chocolate bits. Continue stirring until smooth. Use at once to cover the cake.

Kirschwasser Chocolate Cake with Dark Cherries

As a kid, I always loved the idea of Black Forest cake, but I never actually got close to one. By the time I was free enough to choose a cake like that for myself, it no longer made sense. The too-red maraschino cherries and the dubious whipped topping had lost their appeal. But when, as an adult, I learned to make souffléed chocolate cake, I started altering the ingredients and toppings to match the seasons until I came up with this take on the old Black Forest theme. It satisfied that childhood craving at last. This cake calls for a splash of Kirschwasser, a cherry eau de vie. If you cannot find it, use cherry-flavored brandy or Cherry Bounce (page 79).

¾ cup sugar
¾ cup flour
1 cup semisweet chocolate chips
¾ cup (1½ sticks) butter
2 tablespoons boiling water
¼ cup Kirschwasser or cherry brandy
6 eggs, separated
1 teaspoon vinegar
¼ teaspoon salt
Boiling water, for water bath
2 cups heavy whipping cream
2 tablespoons powdered sugar
1 tablespoon vanilla extract
2 cups pitted dark cherries

Preheat the oven to 325°F. Line a 9-inch springform pan with parchment paper and place it in a larger baking pan.

Mix the sugar and flour and set aside. In the top of a double boiler over simmering water, combine the chocolate and butter and stir until just melted. Add the boiling water and Kirschwasser. Whisk in the egg yolks, one at a time, then whisk in the flour mixture and stir until smooth. In a clean, dry bowl beat the egg whites with the vinegar and salt until they hold soft peaks. Gently fold the egg whites into the chocolate mixture. Transfer batter to the pan and pour boiling water in the baking dish around the pan to reach halfway up the sides. (This prevents a crust from forming on the cake and makes it uniformly tender right to the edge of the pan.) Bake for 35 minutes. Cool the cake on a rack before removing from the pan.

Whip the cream and stir in the powdered sugar and vanilla. Transfer the whipped cream to a pastry bag or a self-sealing food storage bag and pipe the whipped cream onto the cooled cake, then pile on the cherries.

Serves 6

Danish Cherry Tart

My favorite college apartment had a tiny kitchen. Within easy walking distance there were blackberry vines, and empty lots filled with apple trees and cherry trees dripping with fruit that no one else seemed to want. Whenever I could squeeze in time between tests and papers, I could be found gleaning food to make wine and pickles and preserves and baked goods for my friends. I spent at least as much time cooking as I did studying. The first thing I ever prepared in that kitchen was this tart, inspired by Larousse Gastronomique, *and it has since become a part of my standard repertoire.*

PASTRY

1½ cups flour
¼ cup sugar
½ teaspoon salt
¾ cup (1½ sticks) butter, cold, cut into 1-inch pieces
1 egg yolk

CHERRY FILLING

6 cups pitted cherries, halved
2 tablespoons fresh lemon juice
1 cup whole almonds
¾ cup sugar
1 teaspoon ground cinnamon
2 eggs
1 teaspoon vanilla extract

Preheat the oven to 400°F.

To make the pastry, combine the flour, sugar, and salt in a food processor. Add the butter and process until the mixture resembles crumbs. Add the egg yolk and process, pulsing on and off, until the dough comes together to form a crumbly ball. Turn the dough out onto a floured surface and roll into a 10-inch circle. Transfer to a 9-inch tart ring and fill.

To make the filling, toss the cherries with lemon juice, then pile them into the pastry-lined tart pan and set aside. In a food processor, combine the almonds, sugar, and cinnamon. Process until the almonds are finely ground. With the motor running, add the eggs, one at a time, then the vanilla, and process until smooth. With a rubber spatula, spread the almond mixture over the cherries. Bake for 30 to 35 minutes, or until the tart is browned and beginning to crack on the surface. Cool thoroughly on a rack, then remove from the pan. Serve warm or at room temperature.

Makes one 9-inch tart

Cinnamon Plum Tarts

When summer fruits are abundant, several of these tarts can be assembled, wrapped tightly in plastic wrap and aluminum foil, and frozen, unbaked, to be pulled out and baked in the winter. A thin single layer of plums melts into a smooth filling with no need for a thickener. The crisp and crumbly cinnamon topping brings it all together.

CINNAMON TOPPING
¾ cup flour
¾ cup (packed) brown sugar
1 tablespoon ground cinnamon
½ cup (1 stick) butter

CRUST
2¼ cups flour
¼ cup sugar
1 teaspoon salt
¾ cup (1½ sticks) butter, cold, cut into 1-inch pieces
⅓ cup cold water

36 Italian prune plums, halved and pitted

To make the topping, combine all the topping ingredients in a food processor or a bowl and mix thoroughly to create a smooth paste. Chill.

Preheat the oven to 350°F.

To make the crust, combine the flour, sugar, and salt in a food processor or a large mixing bowl. Add the butter and process or cut it in until the mixture resembles coarse meal. Add the water all at once and process or stir the dough quickly together, without overhandling.

Divide the dough into two equal portions. Turn out one portion onto a smooth, floured surface and roll the dough into a 12-inch round. Keep the second portion covered with plastic wrap. Transfer the dough to a 10-inch pie pan and trim the edges. Repeat with the second portion of dough.

Arrange the plum halves, skin side down, in the crusts. Divide the topping mixture evenly in two, and on a well-floured surface roll the paste into two circles just large enough to cover the tarts. Cover each tart with one of the circles. Bake for 45 minutes and serve hot or cold.

Makes two 10-inch tarts

Peach Pie

Long before apple pie became synonymous with wholesome American food, peach pies were made and eaten in American homes. In colonial times, peach trees were actually more common than apple trees on American farms.

The secret to great peach pie is starting with good ripe peaches and then peeling them. Another step that makes peach pie extraordinary is a woven lattice top. Blackberry, blueberry, or apricot pie can also be made with the same crust. Use 6 cups of berries or pitted and sliced apricots with the same amount of sugar, lemon juice, and cornstarch called for in the filling.

BUTTER PASTRY

> **2 cups flour**
> **1 teaspoon salt**
> **1 cup (2 sticks) butter, cold, cut into bits**
> **6 tablespoons cold water**

PEACH FILLING

> **6 large freestone peaches, peeled** *(see Note on page 78)*
> **2 tablespoons fresh lemon juice**
> **¾ cup sugar**
> **¼ cup cornstarch**

To prepare the pastry, combine the flour, salt, and butter in a food processor or large mixing bowl and process or work with a fork until the mixture is uniformly crumbly. Add the water all at once and pulse the food processor on and off until the mixture comes together to form a ball of dough. Do not overprocess. Without handling the dough any more than necessary, divide in half and press each half into a disk. Wrap them in plastic wrap and refrigerate while preparing the fruit.

Preheat the oven to 350°F.

To prepare the pie filling, split the peaches in half, remove the pits, and cut each half into six slices. In a mixing bowl, toss the sliced peaches with the lemon juice, sugar, and cornstarch and set aside. On a well-floured surface, roll out one disk of the pastry into a 12-inch circle, fold it in quarters so that it can be lifted without tearing, and unfold it into a 10-inch pie pan. Press the pastry into place without stretching, which renders a pie crust tough. Pile in the filling. Roll the second disk of dough into a 12-inch square, and with a sharp knife, cut the pastry into 12 strips. Weave the strips into a lattice pattern on top of the fruit and pinch the corners into place. Bake for 1 hour or until crust is golden and filling is bubbling hot. Cool thoroughly on a rack.

NOTE: To peel peaches, fill a large saucepan with water, place over high heat, and bring to a boil. Fill a clean sink or large bowl with cold water. Drop the peaches into the boiling water and let them bob for 1 minute. With a strainer, lift the peaches from the boiling water and transfer them to the cold water bath. The skins will slip right off.

Makes one 10-inch pie

Peach Ice Cream

Peach ice cream is the essence of summer. In its healthy decadence, it transcends the category of mere food and borders a realm of luxury attainable only by grace and good fortune.

> 1 vanilla bean
> 2 cups milk
> 6 egg yolks
> 1½ cups sugar
> 1 cup heavy whipping cream, cold
> 4 cups ripe peaches, peeled *(see Note, above)* and chopped

Split the vanilla bean lengthwise and scrape the insides with the edge of a knife to free the seeds. Place the seeds and pod in a saucepan over medium-high heat, stir in the milk, and heat until steaming hot but not boiling. Remove from heat and set aside. In a mixing bowl, whisk together the egg yolks and sugar until light and fluffy. Stir the milk mixture slowly into the yolk mixture, then pour it all back into the saucepan and cook, stirring gently, until steaming hot and slightly thickened. Do not boil. Remove from heat and chill for several hours or overnight. Add the whipping cream and peaches, and freeze in an ice cream machine according to the manufacturer's instructions. For soft ice cream, serve immediately; for firmer ice cream, transfer to a tightly covered container and freeze for several hours or overnight to set.

Makes about 2 quarts

Cherry Bounce

Within just a few days of moving into the Bellingham apartment that had once been a motel unit, I was invited to help myself to the fruit of an old and magnificently productive pie-cherry tree. I had recently read about something called "Cherry Bounce," in which the cherries were secreted away in a jar with a cinnamon stick and enough cheap vodka to cover them. In winter, the essence of the cherries, captured in a sweet, potent drink, is released in the company of friends. The same drink may be made with brandy instead of vodka, and any sort of cherry will work. They don't have to be pie cherries.

> 4 cups cherries, rinsed
> ½ cup sugar
> 1 cinnamon stick
> 2 cups vodka

In a 1-quart canning jar with a lid, combine the cherries, sugar, cinnamon stick, and vodka. Every day for 2 weeks turn and gently shake or swirl the jar. Strain the liqueur into a clean dry pint jar and discard the solids. Keep in a cool dark place until Christmastime.

Makes 2 cups

Apricot Nectar

The pure goodness of a real apricot nectar reveals itself more clearly with each sip, and a few jars tucked away on a pantry shelf are insurance against the winter blahs.

>   4 pounds very ripe apricots, halved and pitted
>   1 cup sugar
>   3 cups water
>   ¼ cup fresh lemon juice

In a kettle of boiling water, sterilize 4 pint canning jars and keep them simmering over low heat while the nectar is prepared. Combine the apricots, sugar, water, and lemon juice in a large heavy-bottomed pot over medium-high heat. Cook, stirring, for 5 minutes, or until the mixture is boiling hot. Reduce the heat to low, cover, and simmer for 10 minutes, stirring once or twice to prevent the mixture from sticking. When the apricots are completely soft, pass them through a food mill into a clean saucepan. Heat the purée to boiling.

Using a canning funnel, transfer the purée to sterilized jars. Seal with new lids according to manufacturer's instructions. Process the jars for 15 minutes in a boiling water bath. Remove and let stand to cool, undisturbed, for several hours. Any jars that fail to seal can be used at once or refrigerated for several days. Sealed jars will keep in a cool, dark place for at least 1 year.

Makes 4 pints

Apricot Jam

It may be that the apricot season is very short and I am compelled to try to make it last, or it may be that I am so enthralled with ripe apricots that the sight of them prompts me to buy more than I can possibly use. For one reason or another, I often buy more apricots than I really need, and then I hasten to preserve them before they go to ruin. This is fortunate because apricots take very well to canning. The kernels of apricots contain a trace of strychnine, but the strong almond scent of these kernels makes them a compelling addition to apricot preserves and the trace amount of the poison is harmless. The truly cautious may wish to forgo this addition or replace it with a drop or two of pure almond extract.

3 pounds barely ripe apricots, halved and pitted
¼ cup fresh lemon juice
5 cups sugar

In a kettle of boiling water, sterilize 6 half-pint canning jars and keep them simmering over low heat while the jam is prepared. With a nutcracker, open six of the apricot pits and reserve the kernels inside. Put the apricots into the workbowl of a food processor and chop them into a coarse purée. In a preserving kettle over high heat, combine the purée with the lemon juice and cook, stirring, until the mixture comes to a full rolling boil. Add the sugar all at once and stir until the mixture returns to a boil. Drop in the reserved apricot kernels. Insert a candy thermometer if you have one and cook until the temperature reaches 220°F, or until drops of the jam rolling off the back of a spoon fall in two separate streams that come together to form a sheet. With a slotted spoon, remove the kernels and place them in the sterilized jars. Pour in the jam and seal the jars with new lids. Turn the jars upside down for 5 minutes then turn them right side up and let them stand, undisturbed, for at least 1 hour to seal.

Makes 6 half pint jars

Plum Jelly

Ripe plums are good for tarts or for snacks, but for jelly-making choose only firm, barely ripe or not quite ripe plums. (If you suspect that the plums you have are too ripe to produce a firm jelly, use pectin, following the proportions for sugar and plum juice given in the package.) Through some alchemy, the purple skin and greenish amber flesh of Italian prune plums become a sparkling burgundy-colored liquid when the fruit is cooked and strained through a jelly bag. In lieu of a jelly bag, I use a pillowcase and tie the long end of the case to the handle of a cabinet door. My wife finds this annoying and recommends that I purchase a real jelly bag and some kind of device for suspending the jelly bag over a bowl. I recommend that you do the same. However you extract it, the juice of plums cooked for jelly-making is remarkable enough in and of itself. More than once I have canned jars of plum juice just to have it on hand as a kind of elixir. Simply bring the extracted juice to a simmer and pour it into sterilized canning jars. Put lids on the jars and process them in a boiling water bath for 20 minutes.

4 pounds barely ripe Italian prune plums, halved and pitted
2 cups water
Juice of 1 lemon
3 ¾ cups sugar

Put the plums in a large heavy-bottomed pot, add the water, and cook over medium-high heat, stirring constantly to prevent sticking, until the plums begin to disintegrate. Reduce the heat to low, cover, and cook for 5 to 10 minutes more, or until the plums are reduced to a pulpy mush. Rinse a jelly bag or a clean pillowcase in cold water and wring it out. Drape the bag inside a large mixing bowl and pour the contents of the pot into the bag-lined bowl. Lift the bag from the bowl and suspend the bag above the bowl. Allow the juice to drip uninterrupted into the bowl for several hours, or until you can't stand it any-more, or until you have 4 cups of juice. Do not squeeze the bag to force out the juice or it will get cloudy; it should be perfectly clear.

When you have a sufficient quantity of juice, sterilize 6 half-pint jars in a kettle of boiling water and keep them simmering over low heat while the jelly is prepared.

Measure 4 cups of the plum juice into a clean dry pot and add the lemon juice. Over high heat, bring the liquid to a full rolling boil and add the sugar. Stir until the mixture returns to a boil, then insert a candy thermometer if you have one, or watch the jelly closely. Cook the jelly until it reaches 220°F or until it forms a sheet as it drips off the back of a spoon. Transfer the jelly to the sterilized jars and seal with new lids. Turn the jars upside down for 5 minutes, then turn right side up and let stand, undisturbed, for at least 1 hour to seal.

Makes 6 half pint jars

Preserved Peach Chutney

18 ripe peaches, peeled *(see Note on page 78)*, pitted, and sliced
3 cups (packed) brown sugar
2 cups apple cider vinegar
1 cup dried currants
3 cinnamon sticks, split lengthwise
¼ cup crystallized ginger, chopped

In a large, heavy-bottomed pot, over medium-high heat, combine the peaches, brown sugar, vinegar, currants, cinnamon sticks, and crystallized ginger. Bring the mixture to a boil, reduce the heat to medium low, and cook, stirring occasionally with a wooden spoon, for 35 to 45 minutes, or until the mixture is slightly thickened.

Meanwhile, sterilize 6 pint jars in a kettle of boiling water and keep them simmering over low heat until the chutney is ready.

Using a canning funnel, transfer the chutney to the sterilized jars. Seal the jars with new lids according to the manufacturer's instructions. Process the jars for 20 minutes in a boiling water bath. Remove and let stand, undisturbed, for several hours or overnight. Any jars that do not seal can be stored in the refrigerator for several weeks. Sealed jars will keep in a cool, dark pantry for at least 1 year.

Makes 6 pint jars

Plain Plum Chutney

I call this chutney plain because it has none of the raisins, onions, or spices found in most recipes for chutney. Its vibrant flavor, reminiscent of Asian plum sauce, is anything but plain. Serve it with pork or chicken.

> **4 pounds plums, halved and pitted**
> **3 cups cider vinegar**
> **3 cups (packed) brown sugar**

Sterilize 6 half-pint jars in a kettle of boiling water, and keep them simmering while you make the chutney.

Combine all the ingredients in a large pot. Bring the mixture to a boil over high heat, reduce the heat to medium, and cook, uncovered, stirring occasionally to prevent sticking, for 35 minutes, or until the chutney is somewhat thickened and syrupy. Transfer the chutney to the sterilized jars, leaving ½-inch head space. Seal the jars with new lids and process in a boiling water bath for 10 minutes. Allow jars to stand, undisturbed, for several hours before storing. Sealed jars will keep in a cool, dark pantry for at least 1 year.

Makes 6 half pint jars

Chocolate-Dipped Frozen Sweetheart Cherries

When the passing of cherry season seems too sad to bear, it helps to prolong it just a little by stashing some cherries in the freezer. One good way to enjoy these is to sneak them out of the freezer a few at a time and gobble them, still frozen, while standing in the kitchen wondering what to do next. As soon as they thaw, they tend to lose their charm, but they do serve well in place of fresh cherries in baked goods like Danish Cherry Tart (see page 75). Perhaps the best way to indulge in cherries after the season has ended is to dip frozen ones one by one into melted chocolate. Frozen black cherries are available year round in the freezer sections of most supermarkets. These chocolate-dipped cherries can be pulled out of the freezer after a special dinner when you wish the evening would never end.

> **12 ounces semisweet chocolate**
> **4 cups (12 ounces) frozen pitted cherries** *(see page 66)*

Line a baking sheet with parchment paper and set aside. In the top of a double boiler or stainless steel bowl set over a pan of barely simmering water, melt the chocolate. Dip the frozen cherries, one by one, into the melted chocolate and place them on the lined pan. Put the baking sheet in the freezer for 20 to 30 minutes. Transfer the chocolate-dipped cherries into an airtight container, seal it, and keep the cherries frozen until serving time.

Makes about 50 pieces

Herbs

When my wife and I bought our first home, we planted a low-growing variety of mint around the stepping stones. We imagined that coming and going, we would catch its delicate scent. I can't say we ever did; we came and went at a pretty rapid clip, and the stepping stones were behind us before we could take a breath. Still, the tiny green leaves looked sweet around the big lentil-shaped river rocks we used for stepping stones, and it was nice to know that the scent of mint was there if we took time to take it in. 🌿 We have moved away from that house, but I suspect that the

Herbs

mint is still thriving. Mint always thrives in the Northwest. In fact, local gardening books advise keeping mint in pots because the herb can be so invasive in its happy opulence here. More than one Northwest garden has morphed into a mint patch.

Consequently, Washington, Oregon, and Idaho mint farmers, harvesting between four and five million pounds a year, make our corner of the country the mint production capital of the world. Mint is grown extensively in the irrigated river valleys east of the mountains, and while the wetter west may seem more amenable to this water-loving herb, it is the intense sunshine of the arid eastern regions that causes the plants to produce marketable quantities of menthol, its valuable essential oil.

Herbs

Herbs

Mint According to Greek mythology, mint *(Mentha* species*)* originated in the sunny Mediterranean, where a seductive nymph named Minthe was apprehended in the arms of Pluto by his jealous wife, Persephone. The goddess promptly transformed Minthe into a plant, which she angrily crushed under her feet, but the plant released a seductive scent and survived. Alexander the Great maintained that mint still carried some of the charm of the temptress, and he forbade his soldiers to chew it on the grounds that it would turn their thoughts from fighting to romance.

Even though mint leaves are no longer commonly chewed as they were in the days of Alexander, Minthe's spell is reflected in many products to which the herb lends its essential oil. Candy, gum, and toothpaste are the ultimate destination for 90 percent of all the mint oil produced in this country.

Menthol, the essence of mint, is found in the fine, hairy fibers that cover the leaves of this valuable plant. It has the unique property of triggering temperature receptors in our skin. Menthol tricks us into experiencing sensations of coolness or warmth, depending on the concentration. A little mint feels cool; more mint produces a warming sensation.

Most familiar culinary herbs, while they lack the unique cooling and warming properties of mint, are closely related. Oregano, lavender, sage, and thyme, are, like mint, members of the Labitae family. Each has its own unique essential oil contained in the hairy fibers that line its leaves and stems. Like mint, all these herbs thrive in the maritime climate of the Pacific Northwest. The character these plants add to our cuisine is immeasurable. They add more than flavor, they introduce a kind of vitality into our food—and into our lives—that goes beyond taste and smell. Powers that are at least medicinal and sometimes even magical have been attributed to almost every herb.

Rosemary According to *Banckes's Herbal* of 1525, smelling rosemary *(Rosmarinus officinalis)* will keep a person young. I would venture to say that sometimes the scent of rosemary could keep you sane. Our friend Joy, who used to housesit for us from time to time, told me that our rosemary bush once helped her keep her wits about her. She was making soup and feeling cooped up, when she decided she just had to get out. It was one of those short winter days when morning seems to rush headlong into evening and the light is never bright enough to promote real wakefulness.

"Standing in your yard, trying to muster enough enthusiasm to take a walk," she told us, "I noticed your rosemary bush was blooming, so I broke off a sprig and took a deep whiff and for the first time that day, I felt really awake." She took the sprig with her, and continued to breathe in its scent from time to time as she walked. "I felt lighter and happier with every whiff, and when I got back to the house, I dropped the sprig in the soup and it made the whole house smell good."

A single sprig of rosemary does have the capacity to fill an entire house with its scent. In fact, I have been known to toss sprigs of rosemary into an empty oven simply to enjoy the incenselike aroma. But even if the smell of rosemary is pleasant and its effects are beneficial, a little goes a long way. Rosemary, as with all fresh herbs, should be used judiciously.

Wild Fennel As my own appreciation of fresh herbs grew, I encountered common threads between certain herbs. The same aniselike scent that gives wild fennel (*Foeniculum vulgare*) its distinctive character can be detected in basil. A restaurant critic once described a dish I made using lots of basil as being flavored with tarragon. There was no tarragon in the dish, but the critic wasn't ignorant or careless. In the finished dish, the basil did taste like tarragon. Both herbs contain a chemical that tastes faintly licoricelike.

Most herb gardens in the Northwest can boast at least one wild fennel plant. In fact, the plant can be found growing wild along highways, even in neglected urban areas. Quick growing fennel plants sprang up along many roads where its seeds were scattered to prevent erosion of the hillsides. Its strong roots grow deep and allow it to thrive in seemingly adverse conditions.

With feathery fronds that look like dill and large, umbelliferous flowers that bear clusters of fragrant seeds, the herb is a tall, graceful, and sweet-smelling addition to any yard. Because of its sweet scent, the seeds and even the leaves of this herb can be overpowering, so few gardeners actually put it to use in the kitchen. But its strength can be a great advantage, and once a cook becomes accustomed to using this herb, it seems almost indispensable.

Fennel is a great seasoning for fish and shellfish. Salmon, tuna, and crab especially benefit from the presence of this herb. The light, aniselike scent counteracts the strong smell of seafood and elevates the overall dish.

A friend of mine who is a chef gathers fennel seeds from his garden and uses them to make crackers, which he serves with seafood appetizers. Chefs often tuck fennel leaves and stems inside a fish before baking it, and they sometimes burn branches of dried fennel when they grill fish. I wrap fennel leaves with fillets of fish in parchment packets so that their fragrance is bound together as the fish bakes inside the paper. Fennel leaves can also be steeped like tea leaves to make spirited tonics, which can be served as a nonalcoholic aperitif or an afternoon refresher.

Sorrel The tender perennial known as sorrel is appreciated for its fresh green flavor more than for any aromatic oil. Between the rows of spinach in my first garden in Bellingham, Washington, I was happy to discover a weed I called purple clover. It looked like a three-leafed version of a shamrock, but its tiny foliage was a deep crimson-violet, and its long, crisp, translucent stems were filled with a tangy and familiar sap. Actually the plant is not clover at all, but wood sorrel *(Oxalis acetosella),* a wild potherb and salad plant whose flavor closely resembles French sorrel *(Rumex acetosa),* the lance-leafed denizen of medieval herb gardens, which looks completely different.

In Washington, I learned, another wild sorrel, more closely related to French sorrel, inhabits the ground between woodlands and grassy areas. Its tiny green leaves are piquant and good, but it would be too tedious to gather enough for even a small salad. For any cooking or salad making, I turn to domesticated French sorrel.

Bay Leaves One herb that does not thrive here is sweet bay *(Laurus nobilis),* but a little pampering is a small price to pay for a living source of its fragrant leaves. Some gardening experts say this part of the country is just too cold for the bay tree and perhaps it is. But, even though most of the Northwest lies as far north as New England, the warm winds of the Pacific keep the maritime parts of our region bathed in a kind of Mediterranean microclimate, which allows some cold-sensitive plants like the bay laurel to prosper.

Once I had a small bay tree in a pot on my porch, and on a particularly cold autumn night, it froze. For a while I superstitiously feared catastrophe for I had heard that the death of a bay tree was a bad omen. For my ancient Mediterranean ancestors, bay leaves were the symbol of Apollo, and their prosperity reflected his favor. Soon enough, I realized that the only misfortune resulting from the death of my bay tree was the loss of its leaves for cooking. Dried bay leaves are fine, but they are not the same as fresh.

I especially appreciate the less conventional uses of the leaves. Homemakers of old, who for too many months out of the year had to go without fresh foods, used dried bay leaves to brighten plain cottage foods like Hasty Pudding, and I suspect that I am not the first cook to consider hiding a bay leaf in a cake pan or a batch of shortbread to impart its delicate scent to the finished baked good.

Lavender Perhaps the most fragrant of all herbs is lavender *(Lavendula* species). The word lavender is derived from the Latin word for wash, so it isn't surprising that we associate this herb with bathing. To this day it is used extensively in soaps and sachets for its clean, fresh scent. For centuries, it has cleansed the flavors of ripened cheeses and freshened the taste of game. Lavender is a member of the mint family and a vital component of that staple of southern French cooking known as *herbes de Provence*.

The Northwest has no monopoly on herbs, but it is hard to imagine any place where herbs could thrive as well as they do here. Most of our herbs come from the Mediterranean region, but they often grow lusher in the rich soil and ample moisture of the Northwest. This doesn't make them better—in fact, herbs are often less potent when they grow quickly as they do here—but it does make them more abundant. Virtually all the culinary herbs are easily naturalized here, and cooks as well as gardeners take blissful advantage of the easy relationship between the weather and the fragrant plants that give our food so much color and flavor.

Fresh Mint Purée

A purée of fresh mint is a grand accompaniment to roasts, especially if the use of sugar is avoided in its preparation. Equal parts vinegar and water in the blender become the base, and fresh mint leaves are added a few at a time until the sauce is thick and green. Strip the mint leaves from the stems and pick through, discarding any brown or yellow leaves.

> 3 tablespoons white vinegar
> 3 tablespoons water
> 2 shallots, sliced
> ⅛ teaspoon salt
> ⅛ teaspoon freshly ground black pepper
> 2 cups (packed) mint leaves

In a blender, combine the vinegar, water, shallots, salt, and pepper. With the motor running, begin adding the mint, a few leaves at a time, allowing them to become thoroughly ground before adding more. Continue adding mint until the mixture becomes too dry. If the mixture will not flow, add a few drops of water to loosen, then continue adding mint and an occasional drop of water, if necessary, until all the leaves are incorporated. After adding the last bit of mint, allow the motor to run for a minute or so to insure a smooth paste. Serve with curried vegetable dishes or roast lamb.

Makes about ½ cup

Fresh Mint Ice Cream

Nothing captures the cooling power of mint like this subtle ice cream does. Do not confuse this herbal-infused confection with the strong peppermint candy ice cream that's popular at Christmastime. This is a summer food. A scoop of fresh mint ice cream is the ideal accompaniment to many of the fresh fruit tarts and pies that Northwest cooks love to make. I like to serve mint ice cream instead of vanilla with Peach Pie (page 77) and with my Hazelnut Tart (page 247).

> ¾ cup (packed) chopped fresh mint
> 2 cups milk
> ⅔ cup sugar
> 4 egg yolks
> 2 cups heavy whipping cream, cold

Combine the mint and the milk and bring to a boil. Remove from heat and let steep for 10 minutes. Meanwhile, combine the sugar and the egg yolks and whip them to a smooth, ribbony consistency. Strain the milk through a wire strainer into the egg yolk mixture, pressing hard to extract all the juices. Discard the mint. Cook over medium heat, stirring constantly, until it just begins to boil. Remove from heat, transfer to a bowl, and chill. Add the cream and freeze in an ice cream maker, following the manufacturer's directions.

Makes about 6 cups

Rosemary Flatbread

The very name has a scent, a pungent, evergreen, sharp-needled, wake-up call of a scent. To me, it smells like fir trees in the wind on the shores of San Juan Island. To the ancient Romans, it must have recalled ocean breezes that blew over its branches on the shores of the Mediterranean where the plant took root.

Cast into a dry oven, or laid to rest on top of the wood stove, a sprig of rosemary can work like incense, lifting our spirits and raising our hopes. Pressed into a flattened round of bread dough before it bakes, it produces the same livening effect on the air and provides the substantial bonus of something memorable to eat.

1 package active dry yeast
1 cup warm water
2½ cups unbleached flour
1 teaspoon sugar
1 teaspoon salt
3 sprigs of rosemary

In a large measuring cup, dissolve the yeast in warm water. Place 1 cup of flour in the workbowl of a food processor. With the motor running, add the yeast-water mixture all at once and process until smooth. Whirl in the sugar, salt, and remaining flour. Process until the mixture forms a soft dough that leaves the sides of the workbowl. Allow dough to rise in the workbowl of the food processor for 45 to 50 minutes, or until doubled in bulk.

Preheat the oven to 400°F and line an 11 x 9-inch baking sheet with parchment paper. Transfer the risen dough from the food processor to a well-floured counter top, and divide the dough into thirds. With floured hands, press and stretch each piece of dough into a rough circle about 6 inches in diameter and poke a few holes in each one. Press the rosemary sprigs into the surface of each round. Bake for 20 minutes, or until well raised and browned. Serve at once.

Makes 3 small round loaves to serve 6

Fennel Limeade

Fennel and other licorice-scented herbs have flavored everything from before-dinner drinks to after-dinner cordials for centuries. It is the key flavoring ingredient in licorice-flavored liqueurs such as Pernod, which are known generically as pastis. It is also the base for Sambuca. Such beverages were originally devised as medicinal infusions of herbs, and one modern herbal cites fennel as "antispasmodic, diuretic, expectorant, galactagogue, stimulant, and stomachic," whatever all that means. About the simple formula for fennelade that follows, I make no such claims, but it does seem to help people who are feeling disgruntled to feel better.

4 tablespoons fennel seed
1 cup boiling water
¾ cup honey
1 cup fresh lime juice (about 8 limes)
7 cups ice water
Sprigs of fennel (optional)

  The Northwest Essentials Cookbook

Crush the fennel seeds with a mortar and pestle, or by placing them on a cutting board and breaking them with the back of a knife. In a small saucepan, stir the seeds into boiling water and boil for 1 minute. Remove from the heat and let stand for 10 minutes. Strain the infusion into a 2-quart pitcher. Stir in the honey and lime juice. Add water and ice to fill the pitcher and serve at once with sprigs of wild fennel leaves, if you have them.

Makes 2 quarts

Sorrel Soup

With a tangy snap suggestive of lemon, sorrel stands out among greens. Unlike other herbs, it is attractive not for any aromatic oils but for its tart flavor. When the first sorrel becomes available in the spring, I like to make my annual batch of sorrel soup. Like asparagus, or wild morels, it's a tonic. Even as summer waxes and the tips of the leaves turn bronze from the sun, the leaves continue to unfold, and I often make another batch or two of this light, refreshing soup for an easy summer supper.

> 1 medium onion, thinly sliced
> 3 tablespoons butter
> 4 cups cut-up potatoes (1-inch pieces)
> 3 cups sorrel chiffonade (¼-inch ribbons)
> 6 cups chicken broth
> 1 tablespoon chopped garlic
> Salt and freshly ground black pepper
> 1 cup heavy whipping cream, whipped
> Shredded fresh sorrel, for garnish

In a large, heavy saucepan over medium-high heat, cook the onions in butter, stirring often, for 10 minutes, or until they begin to brown. Add the potatoes and cook for 2 to 3 minutes more, stirring. Add the sorrel chiffonade, broth, and garlic, cover the pan, and bring to a boil. Stir, reduce the heat to low, and cook for 15 minutes, or until the potatoes are fork tender. Remove from the heat. Transfer the soup in small batches to a blender. Drape a dishtowel over the blender to prevent soup from splashing out from under the lid while the motor is running, then purée. Season to taste with salt and pepper. Serve hot with generous dollops of whipped cream and shredded fresh sorrel for garnish.

Serves 6

Bay-Scented Shortbread

Fresh bay leaves can stand in for vanilla beans in simple custards, and a single leaf slipped into the pan will infuse an entire batch of shortbread or pound cake with its intriguing perfume. Dry bay leaves can be substituted for fresh, but select the greenest, most carefully packaged brand and buy only a few at a time. The scent deteriorates considerably after a few months in the cupboard.

> 1 fresh bay leaf
> 1 cup (2 sticks) butter
> ½ cup powdered sugar
> ½ teaspoon salt
> 2 ¼ cups flour

Preheat the oven to 375°F. Place the bay leaf on the bottom of a 9-inch pie pan. In a mixing bowl, cream together the butter, powdered sugar, and salt. Add the flour all at once and stir briefly, just until the flour is absorbed. Press the dough into the pan on top of the bay leaf. Bake for 20 minutes, or until golden brown. Cut the shortbread while still hot into 12 wedges, then let cool. Peel away the bay leaf when the cookies are served.

Makes 12 large cookies

Lavender Ice Cream

Even before I'd ever been to Provence and seen lavender used in this way, it occurred to me that it could stand in for vanilla beans in homemade ice cream.

> ½ cup lavender flowers
> 2 cups milk
> ⅔ cup sugar
> 4 egg yolks
> 2 cups heavy whipping cream

Combine the lavender flowers and the milk and bring to a boil. Remove from the heat and let steep for 10 minutes. Meanwhile, combine the sugar and the egg yolks and whip them to a smooth, ribbony consistency. Strain the milk through a metal strainer into the egg yolk mixture, pressing hard to extract all the juices. Discard the flowers. Cook until it just begins to boil. Quickly remove from heat and let cool. Add the cream and chill. Freeze in an ice cream maker, following the manufacturer's directions.

Makes about 6 cups

Lavender Jelly

Lavender, a vital ingredient of herbes de Provence *and a popular component of homemade pomanders and potpourris, is increasingly available at specialty food stores. Years ago, when I realized that lavender is a member of the mint family, it occurred to me to serve it with lamb. Of course, this had already been done for centuries in France. But I wanted something more specifically lavender than the traditional herb blend. In the middle of the night, I woke up from a dream that I was sprinkling lavender flowers into boiling water to make the water into jelly. In the morning I went out and bought a few boxes of pectin, and after only one or two false starts, I had my first successful batch of lavender jelly. Serve the jelly with biscuits or with savory roasts like Rack of Lamb, Roasted with Herbs (see below).*

> 3½ cups water
> 1 cup dried lavender flowers
> Juice of 1 lemon
> 1 (1¾-ounce) box powdered pectin
> 4 cups sugar

Bring the water to a boil, stir in the lavender, remove from heat, and let steep for 10 minutes. Strain into a deep preserving kettle, discarding the solids. Stir in the lemon juice and pectin and continue stirring until the pectin is dissolved. Over the highest possible heat, bring the mixture to a boil and add the sugar. When the solution returns to a hard rolling boil, time it for 2 minutes, stirring constantly. After 2 full minutes, transfer the jelly to hot, sterilized glasses and seal according to manufacturer's suggestions.

Makes 5½ pints

Rack of Lamb, Roasted with Herbs

A rack of lamb is an expensive cut, but if it's handled correctly, it's worth every cent. Generally speaking, domestic lamb tastes better than the less expensive lamb imported from New Zealand. If the rack of lamb is part of a meal in which several courses are served, two chops per person, with an interesting vegetable accompaniment is a reasonable portion. If the lamb is the main event, four chops per person are recommended, and there is something romantic about an herb-crusted rack of lamb for two.

1 rack of lamb (8 to 9 ribs)
1 tablespoon chopped garlic
1 tablespoon olive oil
Salt and freshly ground black pepper
2 tablespoons Provençale Herb Blend *(recipe follows)*
Lavender Jelly *(page 97)*

Preheat the oven to 400°F.

Trim excess fat from the rack of lamb and with a sharp boning knife, cut out the fat between the ribs. Combine the garlic and olive oil and spread the mixture evenly over the meat. Sprinkle generously with salt and pepper, then with the herb blend. Place the rack, fatty side up, on a rack in a roasting pan and roast for 10 minutes. Reduce the heat to 350°F and continue to roast for 15 minutes more. If desired, test with a meat thermometer: 130°F is rare; 150°F is well done. Transfer the rack to a carving board and let the meat rest at room temperature for 6 to 8 minutes before carving. Carve the meat between the bones and serve with the jelly passed separately.

Serves 2

Provençale Herb Blend

2 tablespoons dried lavender flowers
¼ cup dried oregano
2 tablespoons fennel seed
3 tablespoons dried rosemary leaves
¼ cup dried thyme leaves

Combine the lavender, oregano, fennel, rosemary, and thyme. Store the mixture in an airtight jar and use it to season lamb, chicken, or pizza. It will keep, covered, in a dark, dry place for several months.

Makes about 1 cup

A Salad of Herbs and Flowers

Northwest chefs are guilty of excess in many areas. The sheer abundance of good things we have to work with drives us to experiment with combinations that would be merely ridiculous in regions with a smaller variety of fresh local produce. Raspberries garnish grilled salmon, and in the summer when basil becomes almost ubiquitous, it is slipped into everything from salads to desserts. Somehow, in this Oz-like setting where rainbows are as regular as rain, and hundreds of acres of brilliant red and purple tulips grow against a backdrop of majestic mountain ranges, we feel comfortable serving and eating outrageously colorful things.

So salads are regularly filled with tiny violas, yellow and orange nasturtiums, and the occasional petals of a day lily. In spring, don't put it past a Northwest chef to serve the petals of unsprayed tulips in a salad. They taste like snow peas and have the texture of the best butter lettuce. Experiment with other edible flowers in season, but be sure to use only unsprayed garden flowers and avoid experimenting with blossoms that are of dubious edibility.

> 6 to 8 cups mixed salad greens, washed and dried
> 2 to 3 tablespoons Fresh Raspberry and Basil Vinaigrette *(page 100)*
> 24 to 36 basil leaves
> 6 tulips (in spring) or day lilies (in summer)
> 18 nasturtium blossoms
> 18 violas, Johnny-jump-ups, or pansies
> 3 chive blossoms
> 1 cup fresh raspberries

Pick through the salad greens, removing any undesirable leaves. Pile in a large salad bowl and toss with the vinaigrette. Add the basil leaves and toss lightly to avoid bruising the basil. Arrange the petals of the tulips or day lilies on each of 6 chilled salad plates, then divide the dressed greens evenly among them. Tuck 3 whole nasturtium blossoms into each salad, scatter the petals of the violas over the greens, then pluck the petals from the chive blossoms and scatter those over as well. Finally, sprinkle each salad with a few raspberries and serve at once.

Serves 6

Fresh Raspberry and Basil Vinaigrette

Ordinarily a raspberry vinaigrette is made with raspberry-flavored vinegar. This dressing incorporates whole raspberries, and the pulp of the berries allows the oil and vinegar to emulsify to a creamy consistency.

½ cup raspberries
3 tablespoons rice vinegar
1 tablespoon sugar
⅔ cup light olive oil or vegetable oil
1 teaspoon kosher salt
½ teaspoon freshly ground black pepper
12 leaves fresh basil

In a blender, combine the raspberries, rice vinegar, sugar, oil, salt, and pepper and purée the mixture at high speed. Force the purée through a fine strainer to remove seeds. Cut the basil into fine ribbons and stir in. Use 2 to 3 tablespoons for each salad. Dressing keeps, refrigerated, for at least 1 week.

Serves 6

Oysters

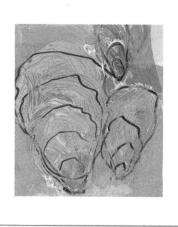

Since the first time I seriously tasted oysters, I have loved to eat them. That was when I was still a child and lived in Florida, and the oysters were from Apalachicola. They tasted like the cool dark rivers and the bright, clear Gulf of Mexico and like the sun. When I came to Washington, I learned to love Pacific oysters and especially the sweet cold oysters from Westcott Bay on San Juan Island where I lived and cooked for a dozen years. 🖋 Not long after I moved my family from San Juan Island to Bainbridge Island to be closer to my work in Seattle, my family in Florida

Oysters

sent me a large, framed photo from my childhood. It was taken in 1964, and my brothers and sisters and I were on the beach in Florida. The picture made me happy because I have so many bright memories of living on the beach. Now my boys were living on a beach, and I felt, looking at the picture, that I had done the right thing by moving.

In the picture, my three brothers, my two sisters, and I were all looking away from the camera toward the Gulf of Mexico, walking from east to west along the shore. The sand is pure white, and the gulf an iridescent blue-green. We are framed like characters in a Charlie Chaplin movie, positioned halfway between the top and bottom of the frame, entirely visible from head to toe. On Bainbridge, my boys spend a lot of time on the beach, gazing out at the water, trailing sticks along the sand, looking a lot like we looked in that picture.

Then one day I got a call from home. I was at work when my wife answered the phone, and when I came home, she was crying. I wanted to know if the boys were all right. "If the boys are all right," I said to God, "then I can handle anything else. Please let the boys be all right."

"It's your brother Flip," she said. "He had a heart attack." We have always called my brother Phillip Flip.

"Is he all right?" I asked, but I knew he wasn't. "Is he in the hospital?" She couldn't look at me. She hid her face in her hands. "Is he dead?" She nodded into her hands.

A few minutes later when I finally believed it and thought I might be able to cry, I said I wanted to go outside, to walk along the beach, to look up at the stars, and remember when it was daytime and we were children and we all walked along the beach together, when we were all still alive. In the picture from home, Flip is in the lead. He's wearing shorts and a striped T-shirt. He's barefoot, and his right hand is out in front as if he were holding a walking stick. But there is nothing there, just the edge of the frame.

"I love you," said my wife. I felt a howl rise up in me, and I knew I would be inconsolable and I said, "But I'm not all there anymore." And that's how I've felt ever since, like I'm not all there. A part of me is gone. "He was the best one," I said, "the best of all of us." Then I cried until my tears were like the water on the beach. I called my brothers who survived and I called my parents and I called the airlines, and I prepared to go home.

The next day, while I tried to pull everything together so that I could be gone for a while, we ate oysters. I steamed a big pot full of dozens of oysters and made a little pot of sweet wine butter sauce and I sat at the table in the kitchen on Bainbridge with my wife and my youngest son, Erich. My older boy, Henry, was off at school. I opened the steamed oysters and dipped them in the butter sauce.

"Do you know what Erich said," asked my wife, "when I told him your brother had died? He looked at Henry, and he looked at me, and he said, 'Oh no! Losing your brother is like losing a piece of your heart.'" We laughed at the pure sweet innocence of his remark, and we cried at the truth of it, and we ate more oysters.

The oysters tasted like tears, the tears tasted like oysters, and I felt like it was the end of the world. But the oysters tasted very good, even little Erich thought so, and we laughed about how the oysters tasted like our tears and we laughed about how good they were, how good it was to be alive. I tried to remember if my brother liked oysters, and I think he did, but I couldn't remember.

In Florida, we huddled together and stood awkwardly apart at Flip's restaurant, in my mother's kitchen, and in the church where my mother's cousin Henry said Mass, and where my brother had seldom darkened the door since he was old enough to have anything to say about it. Then we went to the beach. My surviving brothers and sisters and their children and my parents and I formed a procession and drove to the western end of the island where we grew up together, and there we stood on the edge of the world and remembered Flip. The wind was blowing cold out of the west and the water was dark gray and wild with the incoming tide. Navy jets flew overhead and the children forgot why we were there and started laughing and playing on the shore.

A few of us walked out into the water up to our knees. Flip's widow opened the can of his ashes and moaned and cried while she scattered his remains in the water. My oldest brother sang a kind of chant and shook a bundle of burning sage. Flip would have wanted this. Then my other brother and I held Flip's widow so she wouldn't be bowled over by the waves, and we splashed water over the ashes so they wouldn't fly up into the faces of the rest of the family standing on the shore. We were laughing and crying, and freezing, and it was as if he was there with us.

Since then, when I eat oysters, I taste the tears I cried when my brother was gone, and I feel very much alive.

Oyster Varieties

WITH THICK SHELLS AND FIRM, PLUMP, SWEET-TASTING FLESH, THE OYSTERS grown on the East Coast are Atlantic oysters *(Crassostrea virginica)*. These account for some 85 percent of the oysters grown in the United States, but they represent a much smaller fraction of the oysters served on the half-shell. Most Atlantic oysters are processed in some way before anyone has a chance to eat them.

Where I grew up, the oysters bore the faint smell of something we used to call bayou muck—not a fishy smell, but the vegetal and salty smell of sediment at the bottom of southern bays. This sounds less appealing than it was. When I moved to the Northwest, I came to know the sharper, cleaner, almost metallic flavor of Pacific oysters *(Crassostrea gigas)*, and at first, I wasn't sure I liked them. I missed the faint seaweed smell and the plump sweetness of the southern oysters. But over time, I warmed to the new tastes. Most people do. Fully half of the oysters sold in the shell in this country are grown in Washington, and most people who contemplate such matters consider Washington oysters to be among the finest half-shell oysters in the world.

Olympia Oyster

The only oyster truly native to the Northwest, the Olympia oyster *(Ostrea lurida)* is possessed of a sweet flavor and never grows to be much larger than a grown man's thumbnail. It was gathered almost to the point of extinction by the turn of the twentieth century, but now it's successfully farmed, and is protected wherever it has kept a foothold in the wild. Since this oyster is unique, it is usually marketed under the name Olympia, regardless of where it's grown. Since cooking causes oysters to shrink and since Olympias are so tiny to begin with, these oysters are eaten almost exclusively on the half shell.

Pacific Oyster

Almost all of the Pacific oysters grown commercially on the West Coast, and most of the oysters growing wild here, are a type known as Miyagi. From central Honshu, the large island of Japan, Miyagi is one of four types of oysters from

Japan. All four are technically *Crassostrea gigas,* but each has characteristics distinct enough that oyster connoisseurs can tell them apart. The Pacific oyster is the most widely cultured in the world. It is mildly flavored and easily propagated—so easily that it often escapes to the wild and naturalizes itself.

Like wine grapes, oysters reflect the environment in which they grow. No two oyster farms produce exactly the same oysters, even if they grow the same variety. Depending on the type of algae they eat, the temperature of the water, and the way in which they are handled by their growers, oysters vary, and there are myriad flavors and textures to be found among Northwest oysters. So Pacific oyster growers and distributors name each of their products after its home turf, or surf as the case may be. And the Northwest is blessed with some very appealing place names for oyster growers to adopt.

Consider the Dosewallips River, on the Olympic Peninsula, at whose mouth are harvested oysters as light as the gentle rain that feeds the river itself. Or Totten Inlet at the south end of Puget Sound, where shellfish farms produce full-flavored oysters as bold as the big fir trees that surround the water. Then there are Judd Cove, Penn Cove, and Willapa Bay. It's no wonder Northwest diners order so many oysters; we just like to say the names.

Kumamoto Oyster A Japanese cousin of the Miyagi, the Kumamoto is almost as small as the Olympia oyster. It originated on Kushu in southern Japan and is celebrated for its deep cup, its sweet flavor, and its buttery texture. Some oyster slurpers think of this as the perfect beginner's oyster; some simply think of it as the perfect oyster. I like the Kumamoto, but my favorite oyster is the Westcott Bay.

After a twelve-year sojourn on San Juan Island, I developed a special fondness for this sweet hybrid. A cross between the Miyagi and Kumamoto, Westcott Bays grow in hanging lantern nets in a deep, clean bay surrounded by ancient fir trees. With a delicate flavor inherited from the Kumamoto and the ample size of a Miyagi, the Westcott Bay also carries some intangible quality of the San Juan Islands from which it sprang, a taste as elusive and compelling as any oysters I have ever eaten anywhere.

European Flat Oyster Commonly known as the Belon, the European flat *(Ostrea edulis)* is distinguished by its flat shell and coppery taste. Belon is a name that should really be reserved for oysters that come from a particular region in France. Instead, the name is often used to describe any oysters of the *Ostrea edulis* variety. These oysters once formed a great reef that stretched from Scandinavia down the Atlantic coast and into the Mediterranean. These days only patches of the great reef remain, but seed from those oysters is cherished and cultivated here in the Northwest. The briny metallic flavor of these oysters may be an acquired taste, but once acquired it is compelling, and no other oyster is quite as satisfying. "Your oysters taste like copper pennies," says the American to the Frenchman. "At least my oysters taste," replies the Frenchman.

Oysters Mignonette

In winter, when they are at their sparkling best, oysters should be appreciated with nothing more than a squeeze of lemon or a splash of this very simple, very refreshing sauce.

> 12 live oysters, shucked
> 3 tablespoons white wine vinegar
> 3 tablespoons cold water
> 1 tablespoon finely chopped shallot
> A generous grind of black pepper

Arrange the shucked oysters on chilled plates or a tray lined with crushed ice. Combine the vinegar with the remaining ingredients and spoon over oysters.

Serves 2 as a first course

Barbecued Oysters

Many Northwest oyster lovers claim that this is the only way to eat oysters. Certainly it is the most traditional. Middens from Indian encampments give us reason to believe that oysters have been enjoyed in this manner for thousands of years. Barbecued oysters can be eaten au naturel, with Wasabi and Soy Sauce, with a butter sauce, or with ordinary cocktail sauce.

> 24 medium-sized oysters in their shells, scrubbed
> Wasabi and Soy Sauce *(recipe follows)* or Sweet Wine Butter Sauce *(page 110)*

On a backyard barbecue grill, arrange the oysters with the curved side of the shell down and the flat side up. Cook over hot coals for 8 to 10 minutes, or until the liquid inside the shells is boiling and the "lids" pop open. Serve the oysters immediately with a teaspoon of sauce on top of each one, if desired.

Serves 4 as a main course

Wasabi and Soy Sauce

A simple combination of lemon juice and soy sauce can enhance any seafood, grilled or steamed. A touch of the powerful green Japanese horseradish known as wasabi makes the sauce even better. Wasabi can be found in the Oriental food section of most grocery stores.

2 teaspoons wasabi powder
2 tablespoons lemon juice
¼ cup natural soy sauce

In a small dish, stir the wasabi powder with the lemon juice and then stir in the soy sauce. Serve the sauce sparingly with oysters or any fresh seafood.

Makes ⅓ cup

Oysters Baked with Basil and Parmesan

In winter, oysters are perfect on the half shell, but in summer, oysters may be milky. (When oysters spawn, their flesh is softer and their flavor is not as clear.) Baking or steaming firms them up. Since fresh basil is most widely available in summer, this dish is the perfect solution for summer oysters. They may be served as a passed hors d'oeuvre or as an elegant first course.

12 basil leaves
12 live oysters, shucked and held in their shells
¾ cup grated Parmigiano-Reggiano cheese
Freshly ground black pepper
2 tablespoons olive oil

Preheat the oven to 450°F. Lay a basil leaf over each shucked oyster, sprinkle on 1 tablespoon of grated cheese, season with pepper, and drizzle with olive oil. Bake for 10 minutes and serve immediately, hot in the shells.

Serves 2 to 4

Basic Steamed Oysters

The easiest and most versatile way of cooking oysters is steaming. Since the tight-lipped shells open themselves, cooks who don't like shucking will appreciate that steamed oysters are the foundation for many of my favorite oyster recipes. A soup or a bisque practically makes itself with steamed oysters, and the steaming liquid, also known as oyster liquor, may be transformed into a sauce to go on top of the opened oysters just before they are reheated in a hot oven.

> **12 oysters**
> **1 cup water**

In a large covered kettle over high heat, steam the oysters in the water for 10 minutes, or until the oysters begin to open. Remove from the heat and serve at once. Or use the oysters in a bisque or baked dish. (Oysters may be steamed and held, refrigerated, for several hours or overnight.)

Serves 2 to 4

Oysters with Sweet Wine Butter Sauce

Hot salty steamed oysters dipped in sweet butter sauce can be a meal in themselves. Serve them right out of the pot with a bowl of the butter sauce and a basket of crusty bread as a casual main course, or offer them on plates, three per person, resting in their half shells with a tablespoon of sauce drizzled over each one for a first course at a holiday dinner.

> **½ cup sweet wine, such as late-harvest riesling**
> **Pinch of freshly ground black pepper**
> **1 tablespoon heavy whipping cream**
> **½ cup (1 stick) butter, cut into 1-inch pieces, cold**
>
> **12 Basic Steamed Oysters** *(see above)*

While the oysters are steaming, prepare the butter sauce. Combine the wine and pepper in a saucepan over high heat and boil the mixture rapidly until it is reduced to ¼ cup. Add the cream and boil. Stir the butter pieces rapidly into the reduced wine and cream, whisking the sauce all the while.

Serve the sauce in little bowls and have big bowls ready to receive the empty oyster shells.

Serves 2 to 4

  The Northwest Essentials Cookbook

Oysters Baked with Spinach and Savory Sherry Sabayon

Served in sparkling stemware with fresh summer fruits or little cookies, sabayon, the French version of zabaglione, is usually thought of as a dessert. But this fluffy custard of sweet wine and egg yolks just happens to make a delectable sauce for oysters. I reduce the amount of sugar and add a bit of garlic, salt, and pepper. The finished dish is luxurious, but every step is simple. If you're preparing the oysters for company, all of the work can be done ahead of time.

24 Basic Steamed Oysters *(see preceding page)*
8 ounces fresh spinach, cut into fine ribbons
Savory Sherry Sabayon *(recipe follows)*
Freshly ground black pepper, to taste

Preheat the oven to 450°F. Remove oysters from shells and put a pinch of cut spinach into each shell, reserving half the spinach for garnish. Place each oyster on top of the spinach and top with a generous tablespoon of sabayon. Bake for 5 minutes, or until the sabayon is just beginning to brown. Divide the reserved spinach ribbons among 4 serving plates and place the oysters on top of the spinach. Grind pepper over the oysters and serve at once.

Serves 4

Savory Sherry Sabayon

4 egg yolks
½ cup amontillado or cream sherry
1 teaspoon chopped garlic
½ teaspoon kosher salt
A generous grind of black pepper

In a heavy-bottomed pan over medium-high heat, beat the egg yolks, sherry, garlic, salt, and pepper with a wire whisk for 2 minutes, or until light, fluffy, and just beginning to set. Continue beating vigorously as long as the mixture is in the pan or the egg yolks will scramble. As soon as the sabayon thickens into a stable foam, transfer it to a bowl and set aside. Sabayon may be used at once or refrigerated and used up to 4 hours later.

Makes about 1½ cups

Fried Oysters

Perhaps no way of serving oysters has more universal appeal than this homey and comforting preparation. Properly fried, oysters are firm but moist, sealed in a soft-crisp coat. The following steps ensure success:

- Apply the seasoned flour just before the oysters are plunged into the oil.
- Have the oil at the proper temperature.
- Avoid overcrowding the pan.

If frying oysters for more than just a close circle of two or three friends, fry the oysters in batches, holding them in a warm oven on a cookie sheet lined with paper towels or a brown paper bag.

> 12 shucked oysters
> ½ cup flour
> ½ teaspoon baking powder
> ½ teaspoon freshly ground black pepper
> Oil, for frying

Rinse the shucked oysters in cold water to remove any bits of shell, then drain them in a single layer on paper towels. In a small bowl, stir together flour, baking powder, and pepper. Heat the oil in a cast-iron skillet over medium-high heat to 375°F, or until a cube of bread dropped in floats immediately to the surface and browns in 1 minute. Roll the oysters in the flour mixture and fry for 2 to 3 minutes, turning once. Drain on paper towels or a brown paper bag. Serve immediately or use them to make an oyster loaf or an oyster salad.

Serves 2

Fried Oyster Salad

Somehow, a bed of cold, clean leafy greens exonerates any guilt I might feel about eating fried foods. Here the juxtaposition of hot crisp oysters and tender leaves is brought together with a light, oil-free dressing.

> 24 Fried Oysters *(see above)*
> 6 to 8 cups mixed salad greens, washed and dried
> Rice Wine Vinaigrette *(recipe follows)*
> Freshly ground black pepper

Fry the oysters in small batches, keeping them warm on a paper-lined tray in a 250°F oven. When all the oysters are fried, dress the greens with about ¾ cup of the dressing and divide them evenly among 4 to 6 salad plates. Divide the oysters evenly among the plates and top each salad with a grind of black pepper. Serve immediately.

Serves 4 to 6

Rice Wine Vinaigrette

> 1 cup rice wine vinegar
> ½ cup corn syrup
> ¼ cup water
> ¼ cup sugar
> 1 tablespoon salt

In a small bowl, whisk together vinegar, corn syrup, water, sugar, and salt. Use about 2 tablespoons per serving to dress mixed greens. Dressing keeps, covered and refrigerated, for several weeks.

Makes about 1½ cups

Oyster Loaf

On the Gulf Coast, especially in New Orleans, fried oysters were once packed into hollowed-out loaves of French bread and sent home with late-night revelers as a snack to be shared with the spouse who stayed at home. In New Orleans, the oyster loaf earned the name médi-atrice, or peacemaker, for its power to diffuse any marital spats. Here in the Northwest, a sandwich is just a sandwich, but this one makes an uncommonly romantic dinner for two.

> 1 loaf French bread
> 12 Fried Oysters *(see preceding page)*
> 1 cup shredded iceberg lettuce
> 3 tablespoons olive oil
> 1 tablespoon red wine vinegar
> Kosher salt and freshly ground black pepper

Cut the bread lengthwise in half and hollow it out without damaging the crust. Set aside. Arrange the fried oysters on the bottom half of the bread. Combine the lettuce, oil, vinegar, and salt and pepper to taste in a small bowl, then pack the dressed lettuce into the loaf with the fried oysters. Serve the sandwich at once.

Serves 2

Oyster Bisque

A winter tradition at my house, this rich soup is tonic. On New Year's Eve or Valentine's Day, it makes a wonderful celebration dinner for two, but it also serves to open a grand dinner for guests around Christmastime. Unlike most oyster bisques, the soup contains no whole oysters; instead they are puréed to the consistency of a sauce with no thickener required. The pure taste of oysters and cream comes shining through.

> 12 **Basic Steamed Oysters** *(page 110)*
> 2 **shallots, sliced**
> 2 **tablespoons butter**
> ¼ **teaspoon freshly ground black pepper**
> 1 **cup heavy whipping cream**

Strain the steaming liquid from the oysters into a blender. Remove the oysters from their shells and put them in the blender. Blend until smooth. Sauté the shallots in the butter in a saucepan until soft and transparent, about 5 minutes. Add the pepper and cream and bring the mixture to a boil. Stir in the puréed oysters, and when the soup returns to a boil, serve hot.

Serves 4 as a starter or 2 as a main course

Spinach and Oyster Soup with Coconut Milk

Faced one afternoon with an abundance of raw oysters, a garden full of spinach, some canned coconut milk, and the need to produce a soup, I came up with this concoction, which has become a standard in my repertoire.

> **24 small oysters**
> **½ cup water**
> **2 tablespoons butter**
> **1 small onion, thinly sliced**
> **1 pound spinach, stemmed**
> **1 (15-ounce) can coconut milk**
> **½ teaspoon freshly ground black pepper**
> **¼ teaspoon freshly grated nutmeg**
> **Salt**

In a covered kettle over high heat, steam the oysters in the water for 10 minutes, or until they just begin to open. Remove oysters from their shells and set aside. Strain the steaming liquid and set aside. In a clean pot over medium-high heat, melt the butter and add the onion. Cook, stirring, for 5 minutes or until the onion is soft and just beginning to brown. Add the spinach, coconut milk, pepper, and nutmeg. Bring the mixture to a boil, add the reserved oysters and their steaming liquid, and season to taste with salt. Serve hot.

Serves 4

Prawns & Crab

The first time I saw our local shrimp, they were swimming freely in the black water below a dock, and they left phosphorescent stars in their wake. I wondered what they were. With a flashlight, my wife, Betsy, spotlighted the little crustaceans darting back and forth between the pilings; their armored bodies shone iridescent green, a color that vanishes when they are brought into the light.　✐　"Do you see those shrimp?" she asked. Sure I did. "When we were kids," she said, "my sisters and I would come down here at night and gather these shrimp with a net."　✐　"Do you still have

Prawns & Crab

the net?" I asked, and fifteen minutes later, we were back on the pier, lying flat on our bellies and scooping shrimps from the water. I held the light while my more nimble partner manipulated the net.　✐　"You'll love these," she said with confidence, drawing in the net with two or three lively shrimps flipping around inside. She was right, of course. As soon as we had a fair number, we took them back to the kitchen and boiled them in spiced water. Then we peeled them one by one and dipped their little bodies in cocktail sauce. Later I learned that the shrimps we ate that night were called coon shrimps after their stripes.

Spot Prawns

LARGER COUSINS OF THE COON SHRIMP LIVE IN DEEPER WATER AND ARE KNOWN as spot prawns *(Paudalus platyceros)*. They have the same sweet flavor, and like coon shrimp they need no deveining. If spot prawns are unavailable, farm-raised tiger prawns or gulf shrimp can be substituted in recipes, but they will need deveining and they will produce slightly different results.

Availability of spot prawns follows a schedule that I have never been fully able to fathom. Occasionally they will appear in fish markets in Seattle in the middle of the winter. Availability in winter is sporadic, though, because the weather sometimes prevents fishermen from going out and limits the catch of those who do. The season seems to peak in springtime, when in Washington's San Juan Islands coon shrimps and spot prawns can be purchased live on the docks.

One fishmonger in Friday Harbor holds the spot prawns in pens so that they can be purchased live, and, when it comes to these delicate creatures, live is definitely best. Like lobster, they rapidly deteriorate as soon as they are killed. I used to walk down to the dock from the restaurant where I worked and collect enough live spot prawns to sell in the restaurant that night. In summer, and in fact throughout the year, frozen spot prawn tails from Alaska can be purchased. Without their spiny heads, and without the spark of animation, they are not half as exciting, but they are still a desirable commodity.

Dungeness Crab

THE SAME PLACE THAT SELLS LIVE SPOT PRAWNS IN FRIDAY HARBOR ALSO SELLS live Dungeness crab *(Cancer magister)*, and in fact so do many fish markets. Like the spot prawns, Dungeness crab is best cooked while it is still alive. It is, in fact, not possible to buy one unless it is either living or already cooked. Out of water, it dies quickly, and dead crab is not fit to cook.

Commercial and recreational openings for Dungeness crab, like those for spot prawns, follow clandestine rules. Each year a test run is conducted to determine the state of the crab population and to establish harvest limits. Then the harvest limits are divided between recreational and commercial interests. A certain percentage of the commercial share is then allocated for the tribal catch, further narrowing the harvest limits.

Most of the time, even when crab traps are banned, less effective techniques, like ring nets, are still legal for recreational crabbers. Anyone interested in harvesting live crabs can check the bulletin board at a sporting goods store where licenses are sold or contact the office of the Washington State Fisheries.

Large numbers of Alaska Dungeness crab are cooked and quickly frozen to be shipped to fish markets all over the country. According to the Alaska Seafood Commission, these cooked and frozen specimens may be handled more or less like live crab. To be served hot, they are simply reboiled or steamed for a few minutes. In all honesty, though, I have never reheated a whole cooked crab. When I buy cooked crab, I usually remove the meat from the shell and use it in recipes. Sometimes, cooked crab from Alaska has better flavor than live crab cooked at home because if the crab we buy live at the market has been held in tanks for several days, it will have lost the clean, fresh flavor of the sea.

Many Northwest crab connoisseurs reject dishes made with crabmeat on the principle that crab is well enough left alone. The purists hold that all attempts to serve it with anything other than plain melted butter, or perhaps a little mayonnaise, are at best misguided attempts to gild the lily, and at worst sheer stupidity. There is some sense in this abstinent approach to eating crab. Fresh Dungeness crab, cooked and eaten lickety-split with a simple dip is perfect. Nevertheless, crab concoctions abound, and most Northwesterners have favorite formulas for crab cakes and crab bisques. That strange and wonderful thing known as crab dip is a guilty pleasure for even the most diehard advocates of plain crab, even though it sometimes contains a list of ingredients as long as their arms.

Crab *is* best eaten plain (see page 129), and there is considerable diversity in the way people do that. If you put half a boiled crab down in front of each of several hungry people and provide them all with bibs and nutcrackers and little dishes of melted butter or mayonnaise, interesting aspects of the character of each person will be revealed. There are those who head straight for the meaty claws, cracking, peeling, dipping, and eating in a whirl of passion. Others will crack and eat various parts in succession. Still others will carefully remove every bit of meat from the entire crab before they allow a single morsel to pass their lips. Then, when the eager crack-and-eat types are getting down to a struggle with the last meager bits of meat left in the smallest legs, the crack-it-all-first types will be just dipping the first large morsel of claw meat.

Spicy Boiled Spot Prawns or Dungeness Crab

Some might say the spices and the cocktail sauce overwhelm the delicate flavor of local shrimp and prawns, and perhaps they do. I have had them cooked other ways and indeed, I have cooked them in other ways myself—I am particularly partial to spot prawns cooked over hot coals—but at least once a year, I am called to spice up a gallon of water and cook them in the way we cooked them the first time I had them.

> 1 gallon water
> 1 tablespoon salt
> 2 bay leaves
> 1 teaspoon mustard seeds
> 1 teaspoon crushed red pepper flakes
> 1 teaspoon thyme leaves
> 3 or 4 whole cloves
> ½ teaspoon fennel seeds
> 2 pounds live spot prawns or one 2-pound live Dungeness crab
> Ice (optional)

In a large kettle, combine the water, salt, and spices. Bring the mixture to a rolling boil, then drop in the live prawns or crab. Return to a boil and cook for 3 to 5 minutes for prawns, or 10 minutes for crab. Pour into a colander and serve at once. Or cover with ice and chill before serving.

Serves 2

Butterflied Spot Prawns Sautéed with Red Chilies and Lime

The short list of ingredients and quick cooking time belie the depth of flavor and the sheer delight that this dish evokes. Served with sautéed spinach and steamed rice, spot prawns cooked this way constitute a simple but thoroughly epicurean delight. The wine used in the dish should be the same wine poured to drink with it. A good sémillon from Eastern Washington would be my first choice. For a radical twist, replace the wine both in the pan and at the table with a pale ale from one of the Northwest's celebrated microbreweries. There is no need to devein the spot prawns, and the shells impart a terrific flavor to the sauce, so sauté them intact, then serve them with finger bowls and extra napkins, or those wonderful, hot, wet washcloths that the Japanese call oshi-buri.

1 pound spot prawn tails
2 tablespoons olive oil
2 teaspoons chopped fresh garlic
1 teaspoon crushed red pepper flakes
¼ cup white wine or pale ale
Grated zest and juice of 1 large lime
2 tablespoons butter

Cut each prawn down the length of the back without cutting all the way through, so the shrimp will unfold, butterfly style, when cooked. Heat the oil in a large sauté pan. Add the garlic and red pepper flakes and stir for a few seconds until the seasonings are sizzling hot. Add the prawns and cook for 2 minutes on each side, or just until the shells are bright pink. Add the wine and the lime juice and zest and cook for 1 minute. Swirl in the butter and transfer the prawns immediately to serving plates, pouring the pan drippings on top. Serve hot with finger bowls and extra napkins.

Serves 2 generously

Pan-Seared Prawns and Scallops with Tomato Butter Sauce, Sautéed Spinach, and Crispy Garlic

While this recipe may sound difficult, it really isn't. The dish comes together quickly but seems wonderfully complex because of the contrasts on the plate. I like to serve it as a first course in lieu of a salad at an important dinner.

12 large prawns
12 large scallops
Tomato Butter Sauce (page 126)
12 cloves thinly sliced fresh garlic
6 sprigs of fresh thyme
¼ cup olive oil
1 teaspoon salt
1 teaspoon freshly ground black pepper
1 pound spinach, washed and stemmed

Peel the prawns and set aside the peels. If the prawns have heads, set aside the heads as well. With a sharp knife, cut each prawn down the length of the back without cutting all the way through. Set aside. Rinse the scallops and pat them dry with paper towels. Set aside. Prepare the sauce and keep it barely warm while proceeding.

Cook the garlic and thyme sprigs in olive oil in a large sauté pan over medium-high heat just until the garlic is golden. With a slotted spoon, lift the thyme and garlic from the oil and set aside on a paper towel to drain. Cook the prawns and scallops for 3 minutes on each side. On 4 dinner plates, arrange the cooked shellfish, 3 of each, in a circle around the center of each plate. Add salt and pepper to the hot pan and sauté the spinach in the remaining oil for 1 minute, or just until it is dark green and wilted. Divide the spinach between the 4 dinner plates, placing a mound in the center of each circle of shellfish. Drizzle about 3 tablespoons of butter sauce around each portion of shellfish. Sprinkle the fried garlic slices on top of the spinach and sprinkle leaves of fried thyme around the edges of the butter sauce.

Serves 4

Tomato Butter Sauce

This sauce is tailor-made to match the sauté of prawns and scallops served with spinach, but it can easily be put together without the prawn shells and used as a sauce with halibut or other white fish.

> Reserved prawn shells and heads, if any
> 6 sprigs of fresh thyme
> ¾ cup vermouth
> 1 tablespoon tomato paste
> ½ cup (1 stick) cold butter, cut into 1-inch pieces

In a saucepan over medium-high heat, combine the prawn shells, thyme, and vermouth. Cook at a gentle boil for 10 to 15 minutes. Strain the liquid into another pan, discarding the solids. Bring the strained liquid to a rolling boil over high heat and reduce to ¼ cup. Whisk in the tomato paste and butter to form a smooth sauce. The sauce may be held over a pan of barely simmering water, or simply set aside near a warm stove. Do not reboil, or it will separate.

Makes about ³/₄ cup

Spot Prawn Étouffée

Smothered shrimp and crawfish as they are prepared on the Gulf Coast are almost Provençale in their reliance on tomatoes and garlic for flavor. For this Southerner turned Northwesterner, substituting local spot prawns for Gulf shrimp was not a problem. Traditionally an étouffée is served with cooked rice, an abundant crop in Louisiana. Here in the Northwest, crusty bread may be served instead.

4 cups water
3 bay leaves
3 sprigs of thyme
1 teaspoon salt
2 pounds live spot prawns
2 tablespoons butter
2 tablespoons oil
¼ cup flour
1 medium onion, sliced
2 stalks celery, diced
1 green bell pepper, diced
4 cloves garlic, finely chopped
6 tablespoons tomato paste
6 green onions, finely chopped
Pinch of cayenne
Pinch of freshly ground black pepper
Cooked rice or French bread, as an accompaniment

In a kettle over high heat, boil the water, bay leaves, thyme, and salt. Add the prawns, cover, and cook for 5 minutes. Drain the prawns, reserving the broth. As soon as they are cool enough to handle, peel the prawns and put the heads and peels into the broth. Let simmer while preparing the sauce.

Cook the butter, oil, and flour in a saucepan over medium heat until the flour is lightly browned. Add the onion, celery, bell pepper, and garlic and cook for 10 minutes, or until the vegetables are soft. Add the tomato paste, green onions, peeled prawns, cayenne, and black pepper. Strain the simmering prawn broth into the mixture and stir until the sauce is smooth. Simmer for 15 to 20 minutes to allow flavors to develop, then serve at once over hot rice.

Serves 4

Spot Prawn Jambalaya

Elizabeth David, the English cookbook author who brought an appreciation of French and Italian culinary arts into English kitchens during the second half of the twentieth century, once said, "The French have never found out how to cook rice," but she had never encountered the Louisiana French. A fanciful twist on the French word jambon, *which means ham, jambalaya in Louisiana means a pot full of perfectly cooked rice teeming with ham, shrimp, sausages, chicken, and whatever else family tradition demands. Each family's version is different. Since we live in the Northwest, my family's version usually includes spot prawns. When I can get them, I use live spot prawns and brew a flavorful broth from the heads. Then I use the broth to cook the rice. I sometimes use a stock made from a ham bone. In a pinch, I use chicken broth.*

> 1 pound spot prawns, preferably live
> 1 chicken, cut into 8 to 10 pieces
> ¼ cup olive oil
> 1 medium onion, sliced
> 2 stalks celery, chopped
> 6 cloves garlic, chopped
> 1 large, red bell pepper, diced
> 1 pound smoked ham, cut into ½-inch strips
> 2½ cups long-grain rice, preferably basmati or converted
> 4 cups broth, shrimp or chicken or a combination
> 1 cup chopped peeled tomatoes
> 1 bay leaf
> 1 teaspoon coarsely ground black pepper
> ¾ cup finely chopped parsley or green onions
> Lemon wedges
> Hot pepper vinegar

If using live spot prawns, make a broth by boiling the prawns in 4 cups of water for 5 minutes. With a slotted spoon, lift the prawns from the boiling water and set them aside until cool enough to handle. Snap the heads off and set aside. Peel the tails and set aside the meat. Return the heads and shells to the water, reduce heat to low, and boil for 10 minutes, then strain the broth, discarding the heads and shells. Measure the broth and add enough chicken broth to make 4 cups total.

Sauté the chicken pieces in the oil in a large heavy-bottomed stew pot for 5 minutes on each side, or until nicely browned. Remove the chicken pieces from the pot and set aside. Sauté the onion, celery, garlic, and bell pepper, stirring, for 5 minutes, or until the onions are translucent. Add the ham and cook, stirring gently, for about 1 minute, or until heated through. Stir in the rice and cook for 1 minute more. Pour in the broth and tomatoes. When the mixture boils, add the chicken, bay leaf, and black pepper. Cover and reduce the heat to low. Cook, undisturbed, for 20 minutes. Remove from heat, stir in the parsley and the prawns, and let stand for 5 minutes before serving. Pass lemon wedges and hot pepper vinegar separately.

Serves 6 to 8

"Plain Crab"

Like many Northwesterners, my father-in-law believes that the internal organs of a crab are too strongly flavored, and so he removes the crab's innards before the critter is cooked. A live crab is placed on its back on the dock, on a chopping block, or in some cases, on the patio or deck, and a large knife or cleaver is applied to the crab's midsection. A triangle of flesh is removed from the center of the animal, then its side portions, containing all the edible meat, are cooked in the same manner that I cook the whole crab. Since this method is difficult to teach without an actual live demonstration, I offer the option of cooking the crab whole. Live Dungeness crab can be handled like lobster: Keep the live crab well chilled until just before cooking and drop it into boiling water. The crab will perish almost instantly from the shock.

> 3 quarts water
> 3 tablespoons salt
> One 2-pound live Dungeness crab, well chilled
> Melted butter or mayonnaise, for dipping

In a 4-quart kettle over high heat, bring the water and salt to a full rolling boil. Drop in the live crab and cover the pot. When the water returns to a boil, and steam is spewing from under the lid, crack the lid and reduce the heat to medium. Begin timing. Cook the crab for 12 to 15 minutes, or until the shell turns bright orange.

While the crab is boiling, melt as much butter as you think you will need or fill up little bowls of mayonnaise for each person. Lift the crab from the boiling water with tongs and split it in half. Remove the feathery lungs, the liver, and other internal organs and holding each half with the tongs, give it a quick plunge into the boiling water to rinse. Serve at once or use the crabmeat and broth in another dish.

Serves 2

Crab Burgers

One of my favorite crab dishes rivals the sheer luxury of eating crabmeat unadulterated by other ingredients. It comes to me from family friends who spend several weeks every summer in a cabin on Sequim Bay in Washington, not far from the Dungeness Spit. The flavor of the crab is not altered by the simple ingredients, but the texture is. Instead of individual fibers, the meat comes together to form a delicate whole. Following the family tradition, crab burgers should be eaten on soft white rolls with tartar sauce and leaves of iceberg lettuce. Bucking tradition, they may be served on a bed of mixed baby lettuces as an elegant first course.

> 1 pound cooked Dungeness crabmeat
> 2 egg whites
> ¾ cup heavy whipping cream
> ½ teaspoon kosher salt
> Freshly ground black pepper
> 2 tablespoons butter
> 4 large soft rolls
> Iceberg lettuce
> Tartar Sauce *(page 209)*

In a small mixing bowl, with a fork, stir together the crabmeat, egg whites, cream, salt, and pepper to taste, breaking up the crabmeat as you stir. With the fork, divide the mixture into 4 parts. Melt a tablespoon of the butter in a skillet over medium heat or on an electric griddle. Wet your hands under cold running water and pat one fourth of the crab mixture into a patty about 4 inches in diameter. Place the patty in the pan, rinse your hands, and repeat the process to form 4 patties. Cook the patties for 6 to 8 minutes, or until well browned on the bottom (attempts to turn them sooner will result in sticking). Turn and cook 5 minutes more, adding the remaining tablespoon of butter to the pan to prevent sticking. Serve on rolls with lettuce and tartar sauce.

Serves 4

Dungeness Crab Wrapped in Sole with Fennel

Wild fennel leaves, often grown in Northwest herb gardens, have a great affinity for seafood, especially crab. They have a pronounced anise flavor not unlike crushed fennel seeds. If the wild variety is unavailable, replace it with the feathery green tops of fennel bulbs from the grocery store. The somewhat milder leaves of bulb fennel will still provide enough of the essential oil of the herb to bring its pronounced flavor to the dish. A sumptuous sauce made from a mixture of wine and cream in which the fish and crab are baked bring the flavors all together.

> **4 ounces cooked Dungeness crabmeat**
> **¼ cup fresh fennel leaves, chopped, plus 4 sprigs for garnish**
> **1½ pounds fresh Petrale sole fillets, larger fillets cut in half**
> **2 cups white wine**
> **2 cups heavy whipping cream**
> **Salt and freshly ground black pepper**

Preheat the oven to 400°F.

Pick through the crabmeat to remove any bits of shell, then stir chopped fennel leaves into the crabmeat. Lay the fillets, skin side up, on a flat surface and divide the crab mixture evenly among them. Roll each fillet to enclose the crabmeat mixture. Arrange the rolls in a single layer in a flameproof baking dish. Pour in the wine and cream. Bake for 10 to 12 minutes, or until fish fillets are opaque and firm to the touch. Transfer baked fillets to a warm platter or plates. Put the baking dish on the stovetop if flameproof, or pour the liquid from the fillets into a sauté pan or saucepan. Boil over high heat until reduced by half and slightly thickened. Pour the reduced liquid over fillets, season with salt and pepper, garnish with the reserved sprigs of fennel, and serve hot.

Serves 4

Dream Enchiladas with Bacon and Orange Sauce

During five of my on-again off-again college years, I worked as a cook at a Mexican restaurant in Bellingham, Washington, north of Seattle and south of the Canadian border. For years after I left the restaurant, the kitchen and the people I worked with there haunted my dreams. One of the great things about the restaurant was the bacon and orange enchilada sauce served with beef, cheese, and chicken enchiladas. I borrowed the formula for that sauce and prepared the dish with crabmeat. These enchiladas are truly the stuff dreams are made of.

> 12 corn tortillas
> Corn oil, for frying
> Bacon and Orange Sauce *(recipe follows)*
> 8 ounces cream cheese
> 1 pound freshly picked crabmeat
> ½ cup grated Parmesan cheese
> 4 cups shredded iceberg lettuce

In a skillet over medium-high heat, fry the tortillas, one at a time, in hot oil, for 30 to 45 seconds, turning once. As the tortillas are fried, stack them on a plate; when all are fried, set aside.

Preheat the oven to 375°F.

Combine ½ cup of the enchilada sauce with the cream cheese in a small bowl. Stir the crabmeat into the cream cheese mixture. Divide the filling evenly among the 12 fried tortillas and roll each one into a cigar shape. Pour 1 cup of the sauce into a 12 x 9-inch baking dish and arrange the rolled enchiladas in a single layer on top of the sauce. Ladle the remaining sauce over the enchiladas, making sure that the ends are covered. Sprinkle on the Parmesan cheese and bake for 15 minutes, or until sauce is bubbling and cheese is beginning to brown. Serve hot with shredded iceberg lettuce.

Makes 12 enchiladas to serve 4 to 6 people

Bacon and Orange Sauce

4 ounces bacon, chopped

6 tablespoons flour

¼ cup finely chopped onion

1 teaspoon ground chili powder

½ teaspoon ground coriander

¼ teaspoon freshly ground black pepper

2 cups crab broth, seafood bouillon, or chicken broth

½ cup fresh orange juice

1 tablespoon grated orange zest

1 teaspoon crushed garlic

In a saucepan over medium-high heat, cook the bacon until crisp. Lift out the bacon with a slotted spoon, then stir in the flour and cook for a minute more. Stir in onion, chili powder, coriander, and pepper, and cook for 1 minute more. Whisk in the crab broth, orange juice, orange zest, and garlic and continue stirring until the mixture is smooth. Continue stirring until the sauce comes to a boil, then remove from heat, and stir in cooked bacon bits.

Makes 2 ½ cups

Dungeness Crab Gumbo

The gumbo that follows contains no okra. Even if good okra could be grown in the Northwest, which it cannot, I would not include it here. Rather, I use filé, or pulverized sassafras bark, another classic ingredient of gumbo. All gumbos, whether they contain that peculiar seasoning, or okra, are characterized by the presence of a roux. To preserve the delicate flavor of Dungeness crab, in this version of gumbo, the roux is barely browned; it serves merely to thicken the crab-scented broth in which chunks of Dungeness crabmeat are suspended.

One 2-pound live Dungeness crab, well chilled
3 quarts boiling water
1 tablespoon salt
3 bay leaves
½ teaspoon dried thyme or sprigs of fresh thyme
½ cup (1 stick) butter
½ cup flour
1 teaspoon filé powder
Salt and freshly ground black pepper

In a large kettle, cook the crab in boiling water seasoned with salt, bay leaves, and thyme for 12 to 15 minutes or until shell turns bright orange. Remove the crab from the water and as soon as it is cool enough to handle, pick out the meat and set it aside; drop the shells back into the boiling water. Cook the butter and flour in a heavy saucepan over medium heat for 3 to 5 minutes, or just until flour begins to turn golden. Strain 6 cups of the crab broth into the roux and whisk smooth to create a creamy soup base. Add the reserved crabmeat, the filé powder, and salt and pepper to taste. Serve at once.

Serves 4

A Feast of Shellfish

Both crab and spot prawns respond well to a bath of boiling water infused with herbs and spices. So for that matter do ears of corn and small Yukon Gold potatoes. In imitation of that great Gulf Coast tradition known as a crab boil, the amount of water and spices called for in the recipe for Spicy Boiled Spot Prawns or Dungeness Crab (page 124) may be adjusted to accommodate some of both crustaceans and some vegetables. The only requirement is a very large pot, and an abundance of both kinds of shellfish. Most rental agencies offer crab cookers that are very large indeed. The kettles hold about 20 gallons and come attached to a propane burner that gives off sufficient heat to raise the whole kettle to boiling temperature in very short order. For a large gathering, scale the proportions of this recipe up to serve as many as you wish.

6 gallons water
6 tablespoons salt
12 bay leaves
2 tablespoons mustard seeds
2 tablespoons crushed red pepper flakes
2 tablespoons thyme leaves
About 20 whole cloves
1 tablespoon fennel seeds
2 pounds Yukon Gold potatoes
Three 2-pound live Dungeness crabs, well chilled
6 ears corn
4 pounds live spot prawns
¾ cup butter, or to taste

In a very large kettle over high heat, bring the water, salt, and spices to a full rolling boil. Add the potatoes. After 5 minutes, add the crabs. After another 5 minutes, add the corn, and after another 5 minutes, add the spot prawns. As soon as the prawns are cooked, serve everything at once with plenty of butter to melt over the corn and potatoes.

Serves 6

Wild
Mushrooms

The first time I ever cooked for Betsy, the woman who eventually became my wife, I went all out. All out in those days did not mean expensive food; it meant effort. I could not afford fine wine, so I made my own crude wine and mead from berries and plums, honey and herbs. The humble foods I managed to procure were transformed by my efforts into the most tantalizing things I could manage. I grew my own vegetables and baked my own bread. I made homemade pasta with eggs I gathered from my neighbor's hen house. (She traded me fresh eggs for the outer leaves of

Wild Mushrooms

lettuce that would have otherwise been discarded from the restaurant where I worked. The chickens ate the lettuce, and I ate some of their eggs.) So fettuccine-like strands of handmade pasta were hanging from the kitchen curtain rods when my date arrived. ✐ For an appetizer I stuffed the caps of some ordinary supermarket mushrooms with diced carrot, celery, and onion sautéed in olive oil. Sometimes, when Betsy is trying to justify why she married me, she recalls that dinner, and especially the stuffed mushrooms. Since I scored such high marks for cooking mushrooms once, I am forever trying to win them again.

Betsy claims that I can never take a walk in the woods without thinking about mushrooms, and she's right. Lab rats who have once pressed a bar and received a treat will go on pressing the bar as long as they are able, hoping there will be another treat. Having once found chanterelles and morels in the bracken along the sides of the trail, I keep an eye to the side of the trail every time we walk through the woods, searching for the savory prizes I know I might find again.

In the spring, I am on the lookout for morels. These conical prizes stand anywhere from two to six inches tall and their caps are covered with convoluted ridges. Once having seen one, a mushroom picker will always be able to spot one again. In markets, the mushrooms pop up in early April and are usually available until mid-June. Dried morels, which can be quickly reconstituted in boiling water, are available all year long.

In summer and into the fall, I watch for the chanterelle. This golden beauty was the first wild mushroom I learned to recognize with any certainty, and it remains my favorite. Finding a patch of chanterelles is like spotting a wild deer. Like that totem animal, these fungi stand for something.

In open areas, I occasionally spy the close cousins of the button mushroom known as *Agaricus campestris,* and that meaty champion known as the Prince *(A. augustus)*. Several varieties of boletus, easily identified by the spongy undersides of their caps, also catch my eye; the best of these is that great king boletus that the French call *cèpes* and the Italians call *porcini*.

In most of the recipes that follow, one mushroom can be substituted for another. This is not to say the dish will be the same; it won't. But Beef Filet Steaks Sautéed with Shiitakes and Madeira (page 148), can be made with morels or chanterelles, or even button mushrooms in place of the shiitake, and the recipe will still yield good results. Similar substitutions can be made in the other recipes. The recipes for Mushroom Duxelles (page 150) and Mushroom Bisque (page 156) will work with any kind of mushrooms.

The fruiting bodies of certain fungi, mushrooms are often only a small, visible portion of a larger system growing underground or in a mass of wood. Mushrooms come to us in some fifty thousand forms, most of which are—

technically speaking—edible. But many are "edible" only because they are not poisonous, not because they are particularly pleasant. Some two thousand species of mushroom are eaten regularly throughout the world, but only a handful of these are familiar to us, and only a small percentage are actually possessed of any epicurean value.

The nutritional components of mushrooms are almost incidental. They are made up of water, protein, and carbohydrates, but the protein and carbohydrates are bound together in such a way that they are not very accessible to our systems. Mushrooms also contribute small amounts of the B vitamin riboflavin and the mineral potassium. Still, nutritionally speaking, they're not much. Their most advantageous component is gastronomic, a mineral salt akin to monosodium glutamate, the MSG of Chinese restaurant fame. Mushrooms in combination with other foods act as a flavor enhancer, and their own subtle flavor is something of an appetite stimulant. Mushrooms make excellent appetizers when served stuffed, sautéed, or marinated. They also lend tremendous impact to otherwise ordinary main dishes like baked or sautéed meats.

Just a few years ago, most American sources recommended avoiding wild or exotic mushrooms in favor of the familiar button mushroom, a mushroom that the French writer Colette described as "an insipid creature born in the dark and incubated in humidity." Recently, though, a broader acceptance of more flavorful varieties has prevailed.

Mushroom Varieties

Chanterelle Escoffier, who chronicled half a dozen formulas for preparing morels and several recipes for cèpes, had little to say about the chanterelle *(Cantharellus cibarius)*. "These varieties of edible fungi are not well known or well liked in the United States," he said "but are much appreciated in the Scandinavian and Central European countries. The best way to prepare them is to toss them quickly in butter." It's hard to know from this passage if the master liked them or not. In our own time, chanterelles are very well known and very much appreciated in the United States, especially here in the Northwest, where they lend considerable mystique to our regional cooking. One thing has not changed much though. The best way to prepare them is still to sauté them in butter. Personally, I like to use a combination of butter and olive oil and finish them with a splash of white wine.

King Boletus The grand fungus of the forest, king boletus *(Boletus edulis)* is known as cèpe in France, porcino in Italy *(porcini* is the plural in Italian), and Steinpilz in Germany *(Steinpilzen* is the plural in German). It is universally regarded as one of the best mushrooms, and since it bears no resemblance to any poisonous mushrooms, it is one of the safest. Its huge stems are every bit as delectable as the cap, but flies often lay their eggs in the stem before we have a chance to pick the mushrooms, so watch for worms. Boletus grows all over the Northwest and enjoys a long season, appearing from spring through summer and into fall if conditions are right. In the market it commands a high price, but if it's available, it will substitute nicely for any of the other mushrooms.

Lobster Mushroom The lobster mushroom *(Hypomyces lactiforum)* is the victim of a parasitic mold that renders its host deformed and unrecognizable. Most often the original mushroom was a delectable Milky Cap *(Lactarius deliciosis),* found in the fall under second-growth Douglas firs. But field guides warn that the host mushroom may have been poisonous, and once the lobster mold has had its way with a mushroom, its origins are unidentifiable. I have eaten and served these mushrooms with gusto and impunity when the source was a friend who had enjoyed the same mushrooms from the same spot for several years. Lobster mushrooms from a reliable source are a treat, but be very wary of any you find in the forest. If you find them at a market, sauté them in butter, or make them into soup.

Matsutake The matsutake *(Tricholoma ponderosum),* also known as the Japanese pine mushroom, bears a disturbing similarity to one of the most poisonous mushrooms around, *Amanita ocreata,* also known as the Destroying Angel. So never hunt this mushroom without absolute confidence in your ability or your guide's ability to identify it. Fortunately, the poisonous *amanita* grows almost exclusively under oak trees and seldom appears north of California, while the coveted matsutake grows only under conifers and in thickets of wild huckleberry and rhododendron. The two mushrooms have different seasons too. The poison one comes in winter or early spring, while the good one comes in the fall. Matsutake has a strong, affable scent and a firm, meaty texture that make it irresistible to those who have come to know it.

Meadow Mushroom and the Prince Found in open fields, the meadow mushroom *(Agaricus campestris)* and the Prince *(A. augustus),* two closely related species, are similar to the button mushrooms we buy in supermarkets, but they are not the same. During spring, summer, and fall, these mushrooms pop up in open fields, on lawns, and on golf courses; they do not grow in the forest. The Prince is distinguished by its enormous size. It can grow up to twelve inches high and seventeen inches across. The more modest meadow mushroom never gets over six inches across, but otherwise is very similar. Both mushrooms have creamy caps with pale, purplish brown gills that turn darker after the mushrooms are picked. These mushrooms are most appealing the day they are picked, before the gills turn charcoal gray. Their flavor is mild, but unmistakably mushroomy.

Morel A harbinger of spring, the morel *(Morchella esculenta)* is quite unlike any other mushroom. It has no gills; instead its head is made up of convoluted folds that form a little cone-shaped cup. Its texture is somewhat firmer than other mushrooms, and it stands up very well to stuffing. The flavor is very mild and enhances the flavor of anything with which you serve it or fill it. I have eaten morels filled with a forcemeat of fois gras and enjoyed them very much. When I cook morels, though, I generally go for a simpler preparation, sautéing them to be tossed with pasta, stirring them into a risotto, or building a sauce around them to accompany a cut of meat they've been cooked with.

Oyster Mushroom The oyster mushroom *(Pleurotus ostreatus)* is easily cultivated, and so we see it most often in its domesticated form, which is grown on wood chips in a relatively sterile environment. In the forest, it sprouts from the sides of decaying alder trees and other deciduous logs in the spring and early fall. The younger specimens are best because as the mushroom matures, the stems grow too fibrous to eat.

Shaggy Mane The unmistakable sight of these mushrooms standing in huddled clusters, usually along driveways and quiet roads, always makes me happy. Shaggy mane *(Coprinus comatus)* is white when first picked but quickly becomes dark on the underside. My wife often celebrates the discovery of a patch of shaggy manes with an impromptu gratin, combining the mushrooms with a small amount of mayonnaise and a rather large amount of Parmesan cheese, then baking the gratin until it is crusty on top.

Shiitake A quintessential forest mushroom, the shiitake *(Lentinus edodes)* is native to Asia and does not appear in the wild at all in the Pacific Northwest. It is so widely cultivated though, and such an integral part of our cuisine, that most of us think of it as a Northwest ingredient. The dark brown mushrooms are available year round and they stand up to just about any treatment a creative cook can dish out. I use them whenever wild mushrooms are unavailable, and sometimes, I cook them along with wild mushrooms to extend the amount or to enhance the dish.

Preparing Forest Mushrooms

TO PREPARE FOREST MUSHROOMS FOR THE STOVE, BRUSH AWAY ANY SOIL OR debris with a soft kitchen towel. If they are very dirty, rinse them briefly, but don't soak them or they will absorb too much water. Shiitakes and large oyster mushrooms should have their tough stems removed. If the mushrooms are larger than a silver dollar, slice them. If they are very small, leave them whole. Large morels should be cut in half lengthwise, or if they are very large, quartered. Very small morels may be left whole, but if there is evidence of any creatures hiding inside, cut them so that the creatures can be removed.

Reconstituting Dried Mushrooms

IF FRESH FOREST MUSHROOMS ARE UNAVAILABLE AND THEIR FLAVOR IS SOUGHT, dried mushrooms are a viable alternative. Cover dried mushrooms in boiling water, and by the time the water has cooled (about 10 minutes), the mushrooms should be soft. To drain the reconstituted mushrooms, don't pour them through a sieve; instead, lift them out of their soaking liquid, leaving any grit behind. Then strain the soaking liquid to use in soup or in a sauce for the dish in which the mushrooms appear. Cook the mushrooms as you would fresh ones.

Marinated Chanterelles

Typically prepared by blanching mushrooms in boiling water then tossing them with a vinaigrette, marinated mushrooms are a splendid addition to an antipasto platter along with olives, cheeses, and crackers as an appetizer. Or toss them with cooked pasta. This technique can be applied to almost any mushroom, and even ordinary button mushrooms seem like something special when they're handled in this way. Chanterelles are even better. Layered with sliced provolone and shredded lettuce, they make an incredible sandwich filling.

    2 quarts water
    2 tablespoons salt
    1 pound chanterelles
    ¼ cup white wine vinegar
    ¼ cup chopped Italian parsley
    3 cloves garlic, thinly sliced
    1 tablespoon crushed red pepper flakes
    ½ cup olive oil

In a large pot over high heat, bring the water and salt to a full, rolling boil. Pick through the mushrooms, removing any debris. Leave the smallest ones whole, cut medium ones lengthwise in half, and quarter the largest ones. Plunge the mushrooms into the boiling, salted water and cook for 5 minutes. Meanwhile, in a large mixing bowl, whisk together the vinegar, parsley, garlic, and red pepper flakes, and whisking constantly, stream in the olive oil to make an emulsion. Drain the boiled chanterelles and toss them immediately with the vinaigrette. (The broth in which the mushrooms were boiled may be reserved and used for soup stock.)

Makes about 2 cups

Sautéed Mushrooms

No cooking method does more for mushrooms than cooking in a shallow pan with butter or oil. Water trapped inside the mushrooms evaporates, and in the high heat of the butter or oil some of the starch in the mushrooms caramelizes to provide a hint of sweetness. The method is universally applicable to all varieties of mushrooms, but works especially well with large forest mushrooms, such as chanterelles, oyster mushrooms, or shiitake caps. (Always remove shiitake stems; they are tough and do not soften readily when cooked.) Some mushrooms, like morels, might benefit from slower sautéing at a lower temperature.

3 tablespoons butter or olive oil or a combination
1 pound domestic or wild mushrooms, cleaned and cut
¼ cup white wine
1 teaspoon kosher salt
Freshly ground black pepper

In a large sauté pan over medium-high heat, warm the butter and/or oil. Add the mushrooms. Shake the pan or stir gently with a wooden spatula to keep the mushrooms in motion. Cook for 5 minutes, or until the edges begin to brown. Pour in the wine and shake or stir until the liquid has almost evaporated. Season with salt and pepper to taste and serve hot.

Serves 4

Savory Stuffed Mushroom Caps

Most mushrooms are structured in a way that allows them to be filled with something savory. My favorite filling is this aromatic blend of sautéed vegetables. It makes ordinary button mushrooms shine, special mushrooms even more so. Cutting the carrot into tiny, uniform dice affords a great opportunity to sharpen your knife skills and makes for a handsome finished dish.

12 large mushrooms, cleaned
Salt and freshly ground black pepper
½ cup finely chopped onion
1 carrot, cut into ¼-inch dice
2 stalks celery, cut into ¼-inch dice
3 tablespoons olive oil
1 teaspoon chopped garlic
1 teaspoon dried thyme leaves
½ teaspoon salt
¼ teaspoon pepper
⅛ teaspoon freshly grated nutmeg
¼ cup bread crumbs

Remove stems from the mushrooms and set aside. Sprinkle the inside of the caps with salt and pepper. Arrange the caps in a buttered baking dish large enough to hold them in a single layer and set aside.

Preheat the oven to 400°F.

Cut the mushroom stems into ¼-inch dice. In a sauté pan over medium-high heat, sauté the diced mushroom stems, onion, carrot, and celery in olive oil for 5 minutes, or until the vegetables are soft. Add the garlic, thyme, salt, pepper, and nutmeg and cook for 1 minute more. Add the bread crumbs. Let cool briefly. Pile the mixture into the mushroom caps, rounding off the top with a tablespoon. Mushrooms may be made ahead up to this point and refrigerated for several hours or overnight. Bake for 12 minutes, or until lightly browned and bubbling hot. Serve at once.

Makes 12

A Gratin of Potatoes and Chanterelles

Mushrooms have a great affinity for pasta and other starchy foods, like potatoes, polenta, and rice. In this preparation, the earthy flavors of potato and mushroom are combined, and the contrasting textures of the two make a wonderful backdrop for a roast of chicken, beef, or lamb. Or pair it with steamed broccoli or green beans, and it is substantial enough to stand on its own as an entrée.

> 1 pound chanterelles
> 3 tablespoons butter
> ¼ cup white wine
> 2 pounds russet baking potatoes, peeled and sliced ½ inch thick
> 3 tablespoons olive oil
> 1 teaspoon kosher salt
> Freshly ground black pepper
> 2 cups chicken broth, simmering hot

Preheat the oven to 350°F and butter a ceramic oval baking dish.

Clean the chanterelles. If they are small, leave them whole. If they are large, cut them lengthwise into ½-inch slices. Heat the butter in a sauté pan over medium-high heat. Sauté the mushrooms for 5 minutes, add the wine, remove from heat, and set aside. Lay a third of the potato slices in a row along one side of the pan and spoon one third of the sautéed mushrooms on top. Arrange a second row of potatoes overlapping the first row and top with the next third of the mushrooms. Repeat with the remaining potatoes and mushrooms. Drizzle with olive oil, sprinkle with salt and pepper to taste, and pour on the broth. Bake for 35 to 40 minutes or until potatoes are tender and liquid is almost completely evaporated.

Serves 6 as a side dish or 4 as a light main course

Pork Tenderloin Sautéed with Morels

Sautéed mushrooms can do more than amplify the flavors of a dish with which they are served; they can become an integral part. Here, morels are sautéed in the same butter and oil in which medallions of pork tenderloin have been browned. Once the basic technique is understood, a cook can apply it to other combinations like chicken with chanterelles, sturgeon with oyster mushrooms, or even tofu and shiitake.

> 2 pork tenderloins (about 1 pound each)
> 1 teaspoon kosher salt
> Freshly ground black pepper
> 2 tablespoons olive oil
> 2 tablespoons butter
> 1 pound fresh morels, sliced and rinsed briefly in cold water
> 1 cup chicken broth

Cut each pork tenderloin against the grain into 6 medallions and sprinkle them with salt and pepper. In a large sauté pan over medium-high heat, warm the olive oil and butter. Add the meat and cook for 5 minutes, or until browned. Turn and cook for 5 minutes more. Remove the meat from the pan and add the mushrooms. Sauté for 5 minutes, return the browned meat to the pan, and pour in the broth. Reduce the heat to medium and cook, uncovered, for 15 minutes, or until the liquid has almost evaporated and the meat is cooked through. Serve hot.

Serves 4

Beef Filet Steaks Sautéed with Shiitakes and Madeira

Like sherry, Madeira enhances the flavor of mushrooms. And its subtle sweetness accentuates the caramelized qualities of pan-seared filet of beef. The shiitake mushrooms contain mineral salts that, like monosodium glutamate, enhance our ability to taste other foods. Here, the shiitakes absorb the beef juices and the Madeira and bring them together into an almost explosive flavor bonanza. I like to serve this dish without potatoes or rice, which might dull the effect. Instead, I serve winter squash and a dark green vegetable like broccoli or kale.

4 beef tenderloin filet steaks (8 ounces each)
Salt and freshly ground black pepper
3 tablespoons olive oil or butter or a combination
8 ounces fresh shiitake mushrooms
1 teaspoon fresh thyme leaves or ½ teaspoon dried thyme
⅔ cup Madeira

Season the steaks with a generous sprinkling of salt and pepper. In a large sauté pan over medium-high heat, warm the butter or oil, then add the steaks. Cook for 5 to 7 minutes, or until browned. Turn and cook for 5 to 7 minutes more. While the steak is cooking, remove the stems from the mushrooms, and cut the caps into ½-inch slices. Remove the meat from the pan and add the mushrooms and thyme. Cook the mushrooms for 1 to 2 minutes in the pan juices left from the steaks, then pour in Madeira and cook, uncovered, for 3 to 5 minutes more, or until the liquid has almost evaporated and the mushrooms are cooked through. Return the steaks to the pan and turn briefly to coat. Serve hot.

Serves 4

Chicken Breasts Baked with Mushroom Duxelles

In the old days when French cooks found a bounty of mushrooms, they would chop them very fine, cook them with chopped shallots in butter, and store the treasured paste in a crockery jar. They called the conserved mushroom paste duxelles. Later, a spoonful of this concentrated mushroom purée could be tucked inside a hollowed-out tomato to form a simple stuffed vegetable garnish. Mixed with a little white sauce and baked in a pastry shell, the mixture made an excellent savory tart. I like to tuck a spoonful of duxelles under the skin of chicken breasts and then bake them with wine and cream. The wine and cream thicken into a flavorful sauce that comes together with a stroke or two of the whisk.

4 chicken breasts, boned with skin left on
¾ cup Mushroom Duxelles *(page 150)*
1 cup white wine
½ cup heavy whipping cream
Freshly ground black pepper
Soy sauce (optional)

Preheat the oven to 425°F.

Tuck 2 or 3 tablespoons of the duxelles under the skin of each chicken breast and arrange the stuffed breasts in a single layer in a 13 x 9-inch roasting pan. Pour in the white wine and cream and sprinkle with pepper. Bake for 15 minutes, or until the skins are slightly browned. Transfer the chicken to a warm platter or serving plates. Pour the pan drippings into a small saucepan over high heat. Boil for 2 minutes, whisking once or twice, or until smooth and slightly thickened. Pour the sauce over the chicken or pass separately. Serve hot.

Serves 4

Mushroom Duxelles

> 1 pound mushrooms, cleaned and trimmed
> ¼ cup (½ stick) butter
> 2 large shallots or ¼ onion, finely chopped
> 1 teaspoon salt
> ½ teaspoon freshly ground black pepper
> ½ teaspoon freshly grated nutmeg
> 1 tablespoon butter, melted (optional)

In a food processor, chop the mushrooms very fine, pulsing on and off. Melt the butter in a large sauté pan over medium-high heat and add the shallots, salt, pepper, and nutmeg. Add the mushrooms and cook, stirring constantly, for 10 minutes, or until the mushrooms are fairly dry. The steam will subside. Transfer to a clean, dry plate, spread flat for quick cooling, and refrigerate. When thoroughly chilled, pack into a clean, dry bowl and cover. For longer storage cover with melted butter.

Makes about 1 cup

Mushroom Ravioli

For those who enjoy making their own pasta, there is no kitchen project more satisfying than assembling a batch of homemade ravioli. I sometimes fill mine with a mixture of ricotta cheese and eggs. In winter I like to fill them with puréed squash, but the most intriguing filling is a duxelles of wild mushrooms. Before they are cooked, the ravioli are fragile and excess moisture tends to soften them, so be sure the surface on which they rest is coated well with flour, and don't allow the ravioli to touch.

1 pound Hand-Rolled Pasta *(recipe follows)*
1 egg, beaten
1 cup Mushroom Duxelles *(preceding page)*
¼ cup butter, melted

Divide the rolled pasta in half. Brush one half with beaten egg and keep the remaining sheet under a damp kitchen towel or plastic wrap. Place rounded teaspoons of Mushroom Duxelles at 2½-inch intervals over the surface of the pasta sheet. Cover with the remaining sheet of pasta and press well between each dollop of duxelles to create little pillows. With a pastry wheel or a sharp knife, cut between the pillows to create individual filled pasta shapes. Keep the pasta shapes separate and protect from moisture. Cook in boiling salted water for 2 to 3 minutes, or until barely tender. Serve hot with melted butter.

Makes about 36 ravioli

Hand-Rolled Pasta

3 eggs
2 cups flour

In a food processor or a bowl, make a dough of the eggs and flour and knead until very smooth and elastic. Wrap the dough in plastic wrap or a damp, lint-free towel and set aside for at least 10 minutes.

Sprinkle a clean countertop with flour and then, working with swift, firm strokes of the rolling pin, roll the pasta into a large circle about ⅛ inch thick. Working quickly to prevent the dough from drying out, elongate the circle of dough into a rectangle by stretching it as you roll. Continue rolling and stretching the pasta until it is as thin as you can get it. Use as directed in recipe.

Makes about 1 pound

Penne with Porcini

Porcinis have a compelling aroma that seems almost imperceptible one moment and bliss-fully apparent the next. Some of the excitement brought on by porcini is probably due to pheromonelike compounds present in this mushroom. Pheromones are chemicals that play a role in sexual attraction. Similar chemicals are found in truffles. Resist the urge to add cheese to this simple dish; savor instead the subtle flavor of the mushrooms.

> 3 quarts water
> 1 tablespoon salt
> 8 ounces penne pasta
> 2 tablespoons olive oil
> 1 teaspoon chopped garlic
> 8 ounces fresh porcini mushrooms, cleaned and sliced
> 2 tablespoons fresh lemon juice

In a large pot over high heat, bring the water and salt to a full rolling boil. Add the penne, stir once or twice until the water returns to a boil, and cook, undisturbed, for 10 minutes, or until al dente.

Meanwhile, warm the oil and garlic in a sauté pan over medium-high heat until the garlic begins to sizzle. Add the mushrooms and cook for 5 to 7 minutes, or until the edges just begin to brown. Add ½ cup of the pasta-cooking water and the lemon juice and cook until the liquid has evaporated to a glaze around the mushrooms. Drain the pasta, transfer it to a serving dish, and toss with the mushrooms. Serve at once.

Serves 2

Soba with Shiitake and Kale

Made with buckwheat flour, Japanese soba noodles have a distinctive taste that is easily appreciated with just a few drops of soy and some wasabi, or Japanese horseradish. Less ethe-real but more substantial additions give rise to satisfying entrées like this one.

> 1 pound fresh shiitake mushrooms
> 4 quarts water
> 2 tablespoons salt
> 1 pound soba noodles
> 3 tablespoons olive oil

1 tablespoon crushed red pepper flakes
1 tablespoon chopped garlic
1 pound curly green kale, cut into ribbons
2 tablespoons soy sauce

Remove the stems from the shiitake and cut the caps into ¼-inch slices. Set aside. In a large pot over high heat, bring the water and salt to a full rolling boil. Add the soba noodles, stir once or twice until the water returns to a boil then cook, undisturbed, for 10 minutes, or until noodles are cooked al dente. Meanwhile, warm the oil with the red pepper flakes and garlic in a sauté pan over medium-high heat until the garlic begins to sizzle. Add the mushrooms and the kale and cook for 5 minutes, or until the edges just begin to brown. Add ½ cup of the pasta-cooking water and the soy sauce and cook until the liquid has evaporated to a glaze around the mushrooms. Drain the pasta, transfer it to a serving dish, and toss with the mushrooms. Serve at once.

Serves 4

Mushroom and Tomato Lasagne

Mushrooms' affinity for pasta is nowhere more apparent than it is in this layered dish. The mellow smokiness of forest mushrooms is a perfect foil for the sharp tang of tomatoes.

2 pounds fresh porcini or 2 ounces dried porcini (about 1½ cups)
1 cup boiling water, if using dried mushrooms
1 small onion, thinly sliced
¼ cup olive oil
2 tablespoons chopped garlic
¼ teaspoon freshly ground black pepper
1 small sprig of fresh rosemary or ½ teaspoon dried rosemary
½ cup red wine
1 bay leaf
1 (18-ounce) can chopped peeled tomatoes
2 cups grated Parmesan cheese
¾ cup heavy whipping cream
1 pound lasagna noodles, cooked and rinsed in cold water

If using dried mushrooms, soak in boiling water for 30 minutes. Drain, reserving the soaking liquid. If using fresh mushrooms, brush clean and slice.

Preheat the oven to 350°F.

In a saucepan over high heat, sauté the onion in olive oil for 1 to 2 minutes, or until it just begins to brown. Add the garlic, pepper, mushrooms, and rosemary and sauté, stirring, for 5 minutes. Add the wine and bay leaf and let the mixture boil about 5 minutes, until the wine has evaporated. Stir in the tomatoes. Reduce the heat to medium and continue to stir for about 5 minutes, or until the tomatoes are heated through and the sauce is slightly thickened. Combine one quarter of the grated cheese with the cream and set aside. Coat a 13 x 9-inch baking dish with the tomato sauce, then layer noodles, sauce, and Parmesan until all are used. Top with the reserved cream mixture and cover with parchment paper and aluminum foil. Bake for 30 minutes, uncover, and bake 10 minutes more. Let stand for at least 10 minutes before serving.

Serves 6

Forest Mushroom Bread Pudding

Savory bread puddings, which may be thought of as stuffing baked in a pan, always surprise and satisfy. Since mushrooms enhance the flavor of any food with which they are served, this bread pudding makes a great companion to a roast. It also makes a satisfying main course for lunch or a casual supper.

> 8 ounces shiitake mushrooms
> 8 ounces chanterelles
> 8 ounces oyster mushrooms
> ¼ cup olive oil
> 2 teaspoons chopped garlic
> 1 teaspoon freshly ground black pepper
> ½ teaspoon freshly grated nutmeg
> 1 teaspoon dried thyme
> 6 eggs
> 2 teaspoons salt
> 2 cups chicken broth
> ½ cup heavy whipping cream
> 6 cups (1-inch cubes) bread

Preheat the oven to 350°F. Butter a 13 x 9 x 2-inch baking dish or an oval baker that holds 2 quarts.

Trim the stems from the shiitake caps. If they are bigger than 2 inches across, slice the caps; small caps may be left whole. Brush any forest debris from the chanterelles and slice them. Cut the oyster mushroom clusters into individual mushrooms and trim the stems to remove the tough fibers at their base. Warm the olive oil in a large skillet over medium-high heat, and stir in the garlic, pepper, nutmeg, and thyme. Sauté the mushrooms in the seasoned oil for 10 minutes, or until they are softened. Beat the eggs with salt in a mixing bowl, then stir in the broth and cream. Add the sautéed mushrooms and the bread and stir until the bread has soaked up most of the liquid. Transfer the mixture to the baking dish. Bake for 25 minutes, or until puffed and golden brown. Serve hot.

Serves 6 as a side dish

Matsutakes in Broth

Matsutakes have a powerful and distinctive scent. In the fall, when these mushrooms appear in markets, it is almost possible to follow their aroma to the produce stalls where they are displayed. The intoxicating aroma is matched by a superb flavor and an agreeable texture. If you like, use dashi no moto, *an instant Japanese broth made with dried bonito flakes and kombu or kelp. It is widely available in specialty stores and some supermarkets.*

> 2 cups chicken broth
> 1 teaspoon chopped garlic
> 1 teaspoon peeled and grated ginger
> 8 ounces fresh matsutake mushrooms
> 2 teaspoons vegetable oil
> Soy sauce

In a saucepan over high heat, combine the broth, garlic, and ginger. Bring the liquid to a boil, then turn off heat. Let the broth stand to absorb the flavor of the garlic and ginger while sautéing the matsutakes. Brush any forest debris or soil away from the mushrooms and slice them into ¼-inch-thick slices. Sauté the mushrooms in oil in another saucepan over medium-high heat for 3 to 5 minutes, or until softened. Strain the broth over the mushrooms and bring the liquid to a boil. Season to taste with soy sauce and serve at once.

Serves 4

Mushroom Bisque

Sherry is the predominant flavor in this soul-satisfying soup, which is equally at home on the lunch table or as the first course of a Christmas dinner. Sherry, which seems especially congenial to mushrooms, comes in a confusing array of types. For cooking I prefer amontillado, which is darker than fino and lighter than cream sherry. The bisque can be made very successfully with regular button mushrooms, but it takes on wonderful complexity when some or all of the button mushrooms are replaced with shiitake, chanterelle, or oyster mushrooms.

½ cup (1 stick) butter
1 large onion, thinly sliced
2 teaspoons chopped garlic
2½ pounds mushrooms, cleaned and coarsely chopped
6 cups milk
1 cup heavy whipping cream
1 cup sherry
2 teaspoons salt
½ teaspoon freshly ground black pepper
¼ teaspoon freshly grated nutmeg

In a large saucepan over medium heat, melt the butter. Add the onion and sauté for 10 to 12 minutes, or until soft and translucent. Add the garlic and the mushrooms and cook, stirring, for 5 minutes. Add the milk and cover the pan. As soon as the contents come to a boil, remove the pan from the heat and transfer the mixture in small batches to a blender. (Drape a dishtowel over the lid to prevent the contents from splashing out.) Blend each batch until smooth, then transfer to another container. Bring the cream and sherry to a full rolling boil in the pan in which the soup was first cooked, and cook for 3 to 5 minutes to evaporate the alcohol and reduce the mixture slightly. Stir in the salt, pepper, and nutmeg, then stir in the puréed mushroom mixture. Serve the soup at once or keep it hot by immersing the soup pot in a larger pot of simmering water.

Serves 8

Berries

I like strawberries and I like preserves, so I guess it was inevitable that sooner or later I would try preserving strawberries. I was living in Bellingham and traveling around town by bus when I saw the first flat of strawberries I couldn't resist. They were Skagit Valley berries, bright, beautiful berries that smelled of warmth and sunshine. I had been cooped up indoors at school and at work and on the bus for months on end, and I wanted nothing more than to make those red berries part of my life.   On the bus, the berries turned a few heads, and when I got off downtown

Berries

to change buses, I sat down across from two women who looked like they knew something about strawberries. One of them asked me if I was going to freeze them.   "No," I said. "I'm going to make strawberry preserves."

They exchanged knowing looks, then one of them said, "Berries like that won't make good preserves. You should freeze them." The other one nodded.

"I don't have a freezer," I said, still fairly cheerful. "And I love to make preserves."

"Strawberry preserves don't work," said the one who hadn't spoken before.

"It would be a shame to ruin those berries," said the first one.

I wasn't sure what to say to that. I suddenly felt very foolish for having a flat of strawberries at a bus terminal downtown. I felt ashamed of not having a freezer. The two women stared at me, waiting for my response. They seemed protective of the berries, and doubtful about my ability to take care of them properly. I mustered a smile and tried to look confident. But they had planted a seed of doubt.

At home, the seed of doubt sprouted. I proceeded with the jam-making plan as if I were making blackberry or raspberry jam. I had experienced some success with those berries, but I wondered if this would be different. The little sprout of doubt grew and grew. The berries became a syrupy mess that refused to set. I sealed it in jars anyway and tried to make the best of a bad situation.

One jar of the ruined jam was baked into a batch of overly sweet and alarmingly pink muffins. Then I tried stirring some of the syrup with some lemon juice into carbonated water to make a kind of strawberry soda. It was good, but I'm not really very big on strawberry soda. And so for several years the jars lingered on my pantry shelf while strawberry seasons came and went. If there's ever an Armageddon, I thought, someone will be glad I preserved these berries. Then at last, when I needed the jars to put up some applesauce, I cast the jam down the drain and determined that I would probably never make strawberry jam again.

As years went by, I had successes with other berries. I read a lot about jam making and looked at winning entries at county fairs. Once I made a good jam with strawberries and currants. The red currants had enough pectin to compensate for the complete lack of that stuff in the strawberries, and I gained confidence. Eventually, I tried again to make strawberry preserves. I followed the sage advice of Helen Witty in her book *Fancy Pantry*. The process was painfully long. It took two days and involved lots of soaking, boiling, and straining. The results were okay, but not substantially different from my first attempt. It seemed that the somber old sages at the bus terminal had been right. Once again, I determined that I didn't really like cooked strawberries and would probably forgo any further attempts at preserving them.

Then, at a farmstand in Eastern Washington one year, I came across a brochure of honey recipes distributed by the American Bee Keeping Federation. The cover featured a four-color photo of Naomi Gunther, the 1989 American Honey Queen. Inside, along with a formula for a honey facial cream and several other recipes and pearls of advice from Queen Naomi, there was a recipe for strawberry jam made with lots of packaged pectin and a modicum of honey. I still make that jam from time to time, but more often, I confine my jam-making activity to other berries.

While all berries share certain general qualities, each particular type of berry has its own distinctive character that makes it particularly valuable. Strawberries, for instance, are better in shortcake than they are in jam.

Sorting Berries

ODDLY ENOUGH, MANY OF THE BERRIES WE PILE ON CAKES, SLICE OVER BREAKFAST cereal, and purée into sauces are, according to the botanists, not really berries at all. Technically speaking, a strawberry is a "false fruit." Its voluptuous flesh is, botanically, part of the plant's flower that bears tiny fruits on its surface. The spots we call seeds are the real fruits, and each one, within its minuscule hull, contains the real seed. True berries (blueberries, cranberries, gooseberries, and currants) are real fruits containing seeds.

Since experts disagree on separation between varieties of cane fruits, no one is sure exactly how many there are. I find this somehow invigorating. It's as if Nature has triumphed over our obsessive need to catalogue everything she produces, and in the blurred margins between varieties of berries, I find new berries from time to time that defy my own attempts to categorize them. What, for instance, are the fine wild yellow raspberries that grow in the woods near Kalaloch on the Olympic Peninsula? Perhaps they are the same as the Arctic berries that grow in Scandinavia. Whatever they are, they are best enjoyed out of hand as soon as they are picked. Once, when I tried to gather enough to garnish plates at the restaurant, they disintegrated before I made it home with them.

Blackberries Clusters of numerous segments or drupelets, individual blackberries are actually made up of many smaller fruits. The same is true for the dozens of other cane fruits to which they are related. Several types of blackberries grow wild in the Northwest, but only one is native, and it is the best of the bunch. The low-growing vines that bear small strong blackberries are the native variety. Towering Himalaya berries were imported and escaped cultivation to devour the landscape. Their fruit is fragrant and good, but the drupelets are larger and so are the seeds. These larger berries contain a little more water and a little less flavor than the native berry so they make runnier pie fillings and slightly less flavorful jams. The widely cultivated Marion berry is a good choice for cobblers and pies. It also freezes well.

Raspberries The raspberry originated in Asia and probably migrated via birds and people to Europe, and from Europe to America. European colonists preferred the familiar raspberries of Eurasia to the wild raspberry of North America.

The berry's habitat now circumscribes the temperate regions of the globe. But if their range is wide, their season is relatively narrow. One day raspberries are everywhere, spraying their wild perfume into the air, silently coiled in their baskets, ready to unfurl like silken banners in our mouths, dripping from their canes like ruby honey. Then they are gone.

Of course they continue to trickle in from other places, but only local raspberries possess the qualities that make them irresistible. Only raspberries still warm from the sunshine have that peculiar custardlike consistency.

Fully ripened raspberries may be red, black, or yellow, but whatever their color, they may be quickly distinguished from blackberries by how they come away from the plant. When a raspberry is plucked from the vine, the pith stays behind. Pith is that bit of white fuzziness that constitutes the berry's core. A blackberry brings its core with it away from the plant, and stays solid, but a raspberry abandons its core as it's pulled off the vine, and becomes a little hollow cup.

The distinction is important when gathering certain wild berries. Black caps, for instance, are a variety of wild raspberry that should not be confused with blackberries. The peak season for black caps extends from late June to early August, and the berries are most likely to be found in distressed areas where bulldozers or forest fires have recently opened up patches of ground to sunlight.

Thimble berries, the soft and velvety wild berries that spring up around trailheads all over the Northwest, also leave their cores on the bush and are therefore, at least in my book, a kind of raspberry. These berries are particularly soft and sweet and capture I think the very essence of raspberry-ness. Thimble berries seldom survive a trip from the vine to a basket, and really must be enjoyed at the moment of being picked. Because of their delicacy, they cannot be expected to perform in recipes.

Raspberries, generally speaking, do not perform well in pies or cobblers. They are too soft and watery. And yet, raspberries do have a place in the kitchen. Tossed at the last minute on top of salads, they add considerable piquancy, and left uncooked, they are splendid on top of already-baked pastries.

Strawberries Tiny wild strawberries, always sweet and scarce, are best gobbled as quickly as they are picked. Most larger varieties of strawberries are the result of generations of cross-breeding. South American native varieties were delivered to Europe in the eighteenth century and hybridized with European native berries. Some are June bearing, others are ever bearing, but all seem to thrive in the Northwest. Like raspberries, strawberries are best enjoyed still warm from the field. Desserts made with strawberries usually feature the uncooked berries paired with pastry and/or creamy concoctions.

Blueberries and Huckleberries Cultivated more recently than other berries, blueberries were not seriously farmed until about 1910. Before that, they were gathered from the wild, and in the Northwest, many wild blueberries still thrive. We call them huckleberries, and while some may be red, they are still basically the same berry.

Between two of my neighbors' houses, a large evergreen bush produces what we call huckleberries. Its fruit looks and tastes like tiny blueberries, just like the huckleberries we gather in summer along mountain trails in the Olympic and Cascade mountain ranges, but other features of the bush bear little resemblance to the airy and sparsely leaved huckleberry bushes that grow in the mountains. These lowland huckleberry bushes are densely foliated with thick and shiny leaves, and the fruit hangs not like the tiny Christmas ornaments that hang on mountain bushes, but in packed clusters. When I pressed my neighbor for details and speculated that they must have been planted there, she insisted that the bushes were wild and indeed, I have since found them growing wild all over Bainbridge Island.

Cranberries These berries are closely related to blueberries. For the most part, when cooking with cranberries, I follow the recipes on the back of the bag, simply boiling them with sugar and water to make an annual batch of cranberry sauce, or cranberry orange relish. They also make a tasty garnish for winter desserts. First, pile them into a bowl with a lightly beaten egg white, or if you are nervous about eating raw eggs, use the sterilized egg whites or dehydrated egg whites available in most supermarkets. Shake off as much of the excess egg white as possible, then roll them in superfine sugar, spread them in a single layer on a baking sheet and freeze them. Once they are hard frozen, they can be transferred to a freezer bag and kept on hand for several weeks.

Currants and Gooseberries These bright little orbs seem especially exciting because they were forbidden for a time. The plants that bear them can be hosts to a certain fungus that spends part of its life on these canes and then finishes its cycle of growth on white pines. The fungus does not harm the berry bushes but it kills the white pines, and since the white pine is an important part of the economy in many regions of our country, the cultivation of these berries was discouraged, and in some states flatly outlawed. Fortunately, recent years have seen the proliferation of fungus-resistant varieties, and these once hard to find berries are coming back. Currants, red and black, have been grown for centuries in France. Gooseberries have been popular in England. The berries are rich in pectin and both make great additions to homemade jams and jellies.

Other Berries The variety of wild berries in the Northwest is staggering. Salmon berries, usually the first wild berries to ripen, range in colors from positively yellow to ephemerally red, and the oranges and pinks in between portend a range in flavors from earthy and acidic to perfumey and sweet. A few wild salmon berries pressed into oysters on the half shell make a kind of impromptu mignonette, like a squeeze of lemon juice. And boiled in wine then mounted with butter, they make a captivating sauce to accompany the fish for which they are named.

Salal, a common groundcover in Northwest landscaping projects and a basic component of the undergrowth in vast tracts of Northwest woodlands, bears a slightly fuzzy dark indigo berry that tastes something like a blueberry. Its pigment temporarily stains the teeth and tongue dark blue, but its flavor is well worth seeking out. Oregon grape, another basic element of the Northwest landscape, both wild and tame, bears clusters of tart berries that look like blueberries but taste more like sour grapes.

Freezing Berries

BLUEBERRIES AND HUCKLEBERRIES CAN BE PACKED DIRECTLY INTO STORAGE containers or plastic bags and simply frozen. Other berries need to be individually frozen before they are packed. Line a baking sheet with parchment paper and spread berries over the surface in a single layer. Try not to let the berries touch. Trim strawberries of their crowns before freezing. Place each strawberry, cut side down, on the parchment paper before freezing. Freeze the berries on the baking sheet for several hours, or until they are frozen through. Transfer the frozen berries to self-sealing food storage bags or small airtight containers and seal before returning to the freezer. Use frozen berries in baking projects as they come out of the freezer. Do not thaw before using unless the berries are to be puréed. Frozen berries make excellent jams and preserves.

Breasts of Chicken with Raspberries

After sautéing chicken or pork, deglaze the pan with a little berry vinegar; then, if they're in season, toss in a few of the berries themselves, just until they're warmed through. Serve this simple pan sauce with the sautéed meat. The formula that follows may be thought of as a basic plan on which variations can be improvised. Substitute turkey cutlets or pork chops for the chicken or exchange the raspberries for blackberries, and you have a whole new dish.

> **4 boneless half breasts of chicken**
> **1 teaspoon salt**
> **½ teaspoon freshly ground black pepper**
> **⅓ cup flour**
> **2 tablespoons olive oil**
> **½ cup chicken broth**
> **2 tablespoons Raspberry Vinegar** *(page 177)*
> **Steamed greens or green beans**
> **1 cup raspberries**

Sprinkle the chicken breasts with salt and pepper and roll in flour, shaking off any excess. Discard the remaining flour. In a sauté pan over medium heat, sauté the floured chicken in the olive oil for 5 minutes, or until well browned on one side. Turn and cook for 5 minutes on the other side. Add the chicken broth and Raspberry Vinegar and cook, uncovered, for 10 minutes more, or until the liquid is reduced to ¼ cup. Transfer the chicken to plates, resting each piece on a bed of steamed beans or green greens. Pile raspberries into the pan. As soon as berries are warmed through and just beginning to fall apart, spoon the berries and the sauce over the chicken. Serve at once.

Serves 4

Raspberry Tart with Alpine Cream

Unlike a pie, which may have two crusts or one, a tart has only one crust, never two. And unlike a pie, which is always baked with its filling, the best tarts boast uncooked fruit balanced on top of crisp baked pastry and some kind of creamy smooth filling. For this tart, the creamy smooth filling is a cream-and-yogurt–based concoction made firm with the addition of gelatin.

1 cup graham cracker crumbs
¼ cup (½ stick) butter, melted
Alpine Cream *(recipe follows)*
3 half-pint baskets fresh raspberries
½ cup Raspberry Jam *(page 176)* or red currant jelly
Raspberry leaves or fresh mint sprigs, for garnish (optional)

Line a 9-inch springform pan with wax paper or parchment paper, to prevent the metal pan from discoloring the Alpine Cream. Combine the crumbs and melted butter and press firmly into the bottom of the pan. Don't try to press the crumb mixture onto the sides of the pan, just on the bottom. Prepare the Alpine Cream and pour over crust. Refrigerate for at least 1 hour or for as long as overnight.

Spread the raspberries on top. In a small saucepan over medium heat, warm the Raspberry Jam or red currant jelly until it is thin enough to pour, then drizzle it over the berries. Decorate the tart with a few raspberry leaves or sprigs of fresh mint, if desired.

Makes one 9-inch tart

Alpine Cream

Because it consists largely of yogurt, this cream dessert is lighter than Italian panna cotta, which it resembles. It makes an admirable filling for a tart, but it also stands up well as a dessert in its own right. For those who would abandon the cookie crust altogether, Alpine Cream may be poured into little molds and refrigerated. Dip the molds in hot water and the cream will slide right out, keeping the shape of the mold. Serve the molded cream upright on a plate with a jumble of raspberries lying on the plate, paying homage to the cream. Or pour the cream into wine glasses, refrigerate them, and top with berries just before serving.

1 tablespoon unflavored gelatin
2 tablespoons cold water
1 cup heavy whipping cream
½ cup sugar
1½ cups plain yogurt
1 teaspoon vanilla extract
2 tablespoons fruit- or nut-flavored liqueur

In a cold saucepan, sprinkle gelatin over the water and let stand for 5 minutes. Add the cream and sugar and place the pan over medium heat. Stir until the sugar and gelatin are dissolved. Remove from the heat and add the yogurt, vanilla, and liqueur. Pour the mixture into a tart shell or wine glasses and refrigerate for 1 hour or until set. Serve topped with fresh fruit.

Serve 6

A Chocolate Raspberry Tart

I like to bake the chocolate crust for this tart in a rectangular shape and present it on a board. I saved the wooden end of a fruit crate and sanded it smooth for this very purpose. A cutting board, as long as it didn't smell of chopped onions, would serve equally well. The tart can also be made into a dozen individual tarts. Cut the cookie dough before it's baked, then finish each cookie as if it were a miniature tart.

> **Chocolate Shortbread, baked and cooled** (*recipe follows*)
> **12 ounces semisweet chocolate**
> **1½ cups heavy whipping cream**
> **3 pints raspberries**
> **Whipped cream, as an accompaniment (optional)**

Bake the chocolate shortbread and place it on a serving plate. Chop the chocolate into pieces no larger than ½ inch, put them in a mixing bowl, and set aside. In a saucepan over medium heat, heat the cream until it is barely simmering, then pour it over the chopped chocolate. With a wire whisk, stir the cream and chocolate until the chocolate is completely melted and the mixture is very smooth. Continue to stir until the mixture is cooled and beginning to thicken. Spread this chocolate ganache over the cooled chocolate shortbread, then top with the berries, pressing them gently into the chocolate so they won't tumble off. Let cool until the chocolate is set. Serve with or without whipped cream passed separately.

Serves 8 to 12

Chocolate Shortbread

Without the layer of ganache and the pile of berries that transforms it into a tart, this crumbly, not-too-sweet cookie crust serves very well as a plain chocolate cookie. Instead of baking it as a flat crust, shape the dough into a log, chill it, then slice the log into thin slices for cookies.

> ½ cup (1 stick) butter, softened
> ¼ cup sugar
> 1 cup semisweet chocolate chips, melted
> 1¼ cups flour

Preheat the oven to 325°F. Grease and flour a baking sheet and set aside.

In a mixing bowl, beat the butter and sugar until light and fluffy. Stir in the melted chocolate chips, then stir in the flour. As soon as the flour is moistened, stop stirring. Do not overmix. On a floured surface, bring the dough together to form a ball. Transfer it to the baking sheet and press it with your fingers into an 8 x 6-inch rectangle. Or roll it with a rolling pin. Use your fingers to make sharp edges on the rectangle. Bake for 12 minutes, or just until the surface is baked through. It will be soft, but will harden as it cools.

Makes 1 tart crust or 24 cookies

Blueberry and Lemon Tart

Since a blueberry is perfect the way it presents itself on the bush, cooking is quite unnecessary. But, perfection never stopped anyone from tampering with Nature's gifts and blueberries have cheerfully surrendered themselves to pies and muffins, crisps and pancakes for about as long as people have had ovens. While I enjoy these good baked things as much as the next guy, I usually make them with frozen berries, and save fresh blueberries for dishes in which they can be eaten raw.

Like the Raspberry Tart with Alpine Cream (see page 166), this blueberry tart is a composition of three separate elements: a crust, a filling, and fresh berries on top. To make the blueberries sparkle and stay on top of the tart, they are briefly tossed with a hot syrup that intensifies their flavor without really cooking them. If you wish to forgo that step, you may simply pile the berries on the lemon filling, but be prepared for most of them to roll off when you cut the tart.

2 lemons
¼ cup (½ stick) butter
2 eggs
⅔ cup sugar
1 Shortbread Pastry Crust, baked and cooled *(recipe follows)*
1 pint fresh blueberries or Glazed Blueberries *(recipe follows)*

Grate the zest of the lemons, then juice them. In the top of a double-boiler over medium heat, combine the zest, juice, and butter and cook until the butter is melted. In a mixing bowl, beat the eggs and sugar until the mixture is light and fluffy, then stir it into the lemon mixture. Cook, stirring constantly, until steaming hot and slightly thickened. Let cool, then refrigerate the lemon custard. Fill the cooled tart shell with the chilled lemon filling and top with blueberries.

Makes one 9-inch tart

Shortbread Pastry Crust

To give this tart a primal look and to free it from the confines of a pie plate, I like to bake the shortbread crust in a springform pan with removable sides, then remove it from the pan and fill it on a serving plate.

1 cup flour
2 tablespoons powdered sugar
½ teaspoon salt
½ cup (1 stick) butter, cold

Preheat the oven to 350°F.

In a food processor, combine the flour, sugar, and salt. Work in the butter until the mixture becomes crumbly, then pulsing on and off, continue to process until the mixture begins to come together to form dough. Remove it from the food processor and press the mixture into a ball. On a well-floured surface, roll the dough out to a 10-inch circle and tuck it into a 9-inch springform pan. Press the edges halfway up the sides of the pan to make a border about ½ inch high. Poke the pastry with a fork at 1-inch intervals to prevent it from puffing up while baking. Bake for 15 minutes or until lightly browned. Cool completely on a rack before removing the sides of the pan.

Makes one 9-inch pastry crust

Glazed Blueberries

A quick hot bath of boiling lemon juice and sugar gives blueberries a cooked consistency without robbing them of all their texture or flavor. Spooned on top of a filling in a tart shell or over the top of ice cream or a sponge cake, glazed berries have more flavor than plain berries.

> 1 pint blueberries
> ¼ cup fresh lemon juice
> ½ cup sugar

Pick through the blueberries, discarding any that are crushed or undeveloped. Rinse them in cold water, drain in a colander, and transfer to a bowl. In a small saucepan over medium-high heat, stir together the lemon juice and sugar and bring the mixture to a boil. Boil hard for 1 minute, then pour the hot syrup over the blueberries. With a rubber spatula, gently toss the berries in the syrup to coat them. The berries will keep refrigerated for up to 5 days.

Makes about 2 cups

Peak of the Season Strawberry Tart

The secret of this simple dessert lies in the perfection of the ingredients. Wait until the best local strawberries are available and rush them in from the garden, or home from the farmers' market, and pile them directly onto the tart just before serving. Don't refrigerate the berries or the finished tart unless you have to. The crust can be baked ahead and the filling can be pre-pared in advance and kept chilled, but assembly should take place as close to serving time as possible. If you have to make this tart with white-shouldered, out-of-season berries, you may engage in a little trompe l'oeil by brushing the finished tart with some melted red currant jelly. In winter, make this tart with Honey-Poached Pears (page 28) instead of strawberries.

> Vanilla Pastry Cream *(page 172)*
> 1 Shortbread Pastry Crust *(see preceding page)*
> 2 pints strawberries
> ½ cup red currant jelly *(optional)*

Make the pastry cream and chill it. Close to serving time, spread the cream filling over the crust, trim the crowns from the berries, and place them, trimmed side down, on the cream. If the berries are not perfectly red and ripe, melt the jelly in a small saucepan over medium heat and brush it over the top of the tart. Serve at once.

Makes one 10-inch tart

Vanilla Pastry Cream

The best use of this old-fashioned, thick, and creamy tart filling may be in this quintessential strawberry tart. But do not hesitate to use the filling with other berries or with sliced ripe peaches.

> ½ cup flour
> ¾ cup sugar
> ½ teaspoon salt
> 2 eggs
> 2 cups half-and-half
> 1 vanilla bean, split and scraped
> 2 tablespoons butter

In a small, heavy saucepan, whisk together the flour, sugar, and salt. Whisk in the eggs and stir until the mixture is perfectly smooth. Stir in the half-and-half and the split and scraped vanilla bean. Cook the mixture over medium-high heat, whisking constantly, until the mixture boils. Remove from the heat and stir in the butter. Let cool completely before filling the tart shell.

Makes about 2½ cups

Patty's Cake

One of my most reliable recipes for summer celebrations is a cake piled with as many different kinds of berries as I can find. About a half a dozen times, I've made it for my mother-in-law's birthday party. And because she appreciates it so much, I've come to think of it as Patty's Cake.

While the cake may be baked several hours or even a day in advance, and the filling may be made several hours ahead and stored in the refrigerator, actual assembly of the cake should wait until just before serving time. The cake will stand admirably for an hour or two, but then the juices from the berries start to run and it loses its first blush of exquisite beauty.

> **Sponge Cake** *(recipe follows)*
> **Lemon and Cream Cheese Filling** *(page 174)*
> 2 pints strawberries
> 2 pints blueberries
> 4 half-pints raspberries
> ½ cup red currant jelly
> Fresh mint sprigs

Prepare the sponge cake and cool it completely. Prepare the filling and refrigerate it in the pastry bag or food storage bag. Trim and split the strawberries. Pick through the blueberries and raspberries and discard any foreign matter and any underripe, overripe, or otherwise unpleasant berries. Put all of the berries in a large mixing bowl. In a small saucepan over medium heat, melt the currant jelly. Pour it over the berries and stir very gently to coat the berries without smashing them. Set aside. Split the cake in half lengthwise and place half the cake on a serving tray. Spread one quarter of the filling evenly over the surface of the cake on the tray. Spread half the berries on top of the filling and top with the other half of the cake. Spread the second cake layer with another quarter of the filling and top with the remaining berries. Pipe the remaining filling in even stripes up the sides of the cake to cover, leaving the top layer of berries completely exposed. Decorate the cake with mint sprigs and serve at once, or refrigerate for up to 2 hours before serving.

Serves 12

Sponge Cake

This recipe is the foundation of many of my favorite cakes. I have rolled it into jelly rolls, cut it into small rounds to be filled in various ways, and stacked it with everything from coffee-flavored buttercream to orange marmalade. If you need only half as much as this recipe makes, bake the full batch, and freeze the other half. It will come in very handy. Wrap it first in plastic wrap, then in foil. It keeps for 3 months in the freezer.

> 9 eggs
> 1½ cups sugar
> ¾ cup (1½ sticks) butter, melted
> 2 teaspoons vanilla extract
> ½ teaspoon salt
> 1½ cups flour

Preheat the oven to 350°F. Grease and flour the sides of a 16 x 12-inch half sheet pan and line the bottom with parchment paper.

Separate the eggs. Place the yolks in a large mixing bowl and place the whites in the bowl of an electric mixer or a deep mixing bowl for beating. Set aside. Beat the egg yolks with ¾ cup of the sugar until they are pale and run from the whisk in a wide ribbon. Stir in the melted butter, vanilla, and salt. Beat the egg whites until they hold soft peaks, then, still beating, stream in the remaining ¾ cup sugar until the egg whites hold firm peaks. With a rubber spatula, fold one third of the egg whites into the yolk mixture with ¾ cup of the flour. Add another third of the egg whites with the remaining flour and fold again. Fold the remainder of the egg whites into the batter and transfer immediately to the sheet pan. Bake the cake on the center rack of the oven for 15 minutes, or until it is lightly browned and springs back when pressed lightly in the center. Cool on a cooling rack, then turn the cake over, lift off the pan, and peel away the parchment paper.

Makes one 16 x 12-inch sheet cake

Lemon and Cream Cheese Filling

    1 cup heavy whipping cream, well chilled
    2 (8-ounce) packages cream cheese
    Zest and juice of 1 lemon
    ½ cup powdered sugar
    2 teaspoons vanilla extract

In the mixing bowl of an electric mixer, whip the cream until it holds firm peaks. Set aside. In a separate bowl, beat the cream cheese until smooth. Stir in the lemon zest and juice, powdered sugar, and vanilla. Fold one third of the whipped cream into the cream cheese mixture and when it is well incorporated, fold in the rest. Transfer filling to a pastry bag or a large self-sealing food storage bag and refrigerate.

Makes about 4 cups

Strawberries Brûlée

A berry lover's answer to crème brûlée involves berries tucked beneath a layer of whipped cream, sealed in turn by a layer of crisp burnt sugar. The best way to make it is to use a tool called a brûlée iron, designed for making crème brûlée. A metal knob is attached to a long handle and rests on a hot burner until it's red hot. The iron glides over the sugar and burns it without heating the food below. Unfortunately, brûlée irons are almost impossible to find. The second best option is to use a small propane torch, which can be purchased at the hardware store. If neither of these options seem feasible, simply place the dishes under a preheated broiler element and watch them closely. Keep the oven door open so the berries won't heat up underneath the cream.

  The Northwest Essentials Cookbook

If you cannot deal with the complexities of berries brûlée, consider a reasonable facsimile that involves no irons, no torches, and no broilers. Toss the berries with lemon and sugar as for berries brûlée, then top with sour cream and a sprinkling of brown sugar, and serve at once, or serve the plain berries with small individual bowls of sour cream and little saucers of brown sugar for dipping and rolling.

> 2 pints strawberries, hulled and split
> 1 tablespoon fresh lemon juice
> 1 tablespoon granulated sugar
> 1 cup heavy whipping cream
> 2 tablespoons powdered sugar
> 1 teaspoon vanilla extract
> ¼ cup granulated sugar, for sprinkling on top

In a small mixing bowl, combine the strawberries, lemon juice, and granulated sugar. Divide the mixture evenly among four 1-cup soufflé dishes and set aside. In a separate bowl, whip the cream, then stir in the powdered sugar and vanilla. Pile the whipped cream over the berries and with the straight side of a rubber spatula or a butter knife, flatten the cream on top of the berries. Preheat a broiler or light a small butane torch. Sprinkle about 1 tablespoon of sugar over the top of the whipped cream and place the dishes directly under the preheated broiler or run the flame of the lit torch over the sugar until it bubbles up and turns brown. The sugar will form a paper-thin layer of caramel over the surface of the cream. Serve at once.

Serves 4

Blackberry Sorbet

A sorbet can be made from any kind of berry. My favorite is dark as night and made with the giant Himalaya blackberries that consume the patches of ground wherever they are allowed to gain a foothold.

> 2 pints (packed) blackberries
> 1 cup sugar
> 1 cup water
> 2 tablespoons lemon juice or berry vinegar

In a blender, purée the blackberries with the sugar, water, and lemon juice. Pass the purée through a strainer to remove the seeds. Refrigerate for several hours or overnight. Freeze the sorbet in an ice-cream freezer according to the manufacturer's suggestions. Transfer it to airtight containers for storage in the freezer until ready to serve.

Makes 1 quart

Blackberry or Raspberry Jam

In jam- and jelly-making, timing is of the essence. Balanced amounts of sugar, water, pectin, and acid are brought rapidly to a jelling temperature. Small amounts work best; so never try to double a recipe for jam or jelly. If you want to make more, make several small batches.

> **4 cups (packed) blackberries or raspberries**
> **½ cup fresh lemon juice**
> **4 cups sugar**

Sterilize 5 or 6 half-pint canning jars in a kettle of boiling water and keep them simmering over low heat while the jam is prepared. In a large heavy-bottomed pot over high heat, mash the berries with lemon juice. Be sure to use a deep pot because the mixture will triple in volume as it boils. Bring the mixture to a boil and add exactly 4 cups of sugar. Stir gently until the mixture returns to a boil, then stop stirring and insert a candy thermometer. When the thermometer registers 220°F, remove jam from the heat. Transfer jam to sterilized jars, cover with new lids according to manufacturer's instructions, and process for 5 minutes in a boiling water bath.

Turn the jars upside down for 5 minutes, then turn right side up and allow them to stand, undisturbed, for at least 1 hour to seal. Any jars that do not seal can be stored in the refrigerator for several weeks. Sealed jars can be kept in a cool, dark pantry for at least 1 year.

Makes about 5 or 6 half-pint jars

Beekeepers' Strawberry Jam

Although strawberry jam isn't exactly like strawberry preserves—the strawberries are crushed instead of whole—this particular strawberry jam is extremely good, and I like to make it because it's quick and easy and the house smells wonderful when the strawberries are boiling in honey.

> 4 cups crushed strawberries
> 2 boxes powdered pectin
> 1¾ cups mild honey
> 2 tablespoons lemon juice

Sterilize 6 half-pint jars in a kettle of boiling water and keep them simmering while preparing the jam. In a 5-quart saucepan over medium-high heat, combine the strawberries and pectin. Bring the mixture to a boil. Boil hard for 1 minute, stirring constantly. Add the honey and lemon juice and bring the mixture back to a full, rolling boil. Boil hard for 5 minutes, stirring constantly. Remove from the heat, skim off the foam, and transfer jam to sterilized jars. Seal with new lids according to manufacturers' instructions.

Makes about 6 half pint jars

Raspberry Vinegar

Ordinary white wine vinegar or rice wine vinegar flavored with summer berries is one of the great joys of pantry-keeping. Without flavored vinegars, your cupboard may not be bare, but it is certainly less exciting than it could be. Vinegar can be flavored with any berries , but the ultimate berry vinegar and the one that commands a place of respect in the world of gastronomy is raspberry. So true is the exotic aroma of raspberry when it is suspended in vinegar that many chefs use raspberry vinegar to enhance the flavor of fresh berries, especially when the berries are to be served cold.

> 4 cups raspberries
> 4 cups white wine vinegar

In a large glass jar, combine the raspberries and wine vinegar and cover. Let the berries macerate in the vinegar for 2 weeks. Give the jar a shake or a turn every day to redistribute the contents. At this point, you may begin using the vinegar as is.

Makes about 4 cups

NOTE: Homemade berry vinegar will eventually form a cloud or even a raft of bacteria. This is harmless but unappealing. To lengthen the vinegar's shelf life, it can be pasteurized. Strain the berry vinegar into a saucepan. After pressing lightly on the pulp to remove most of the liquid, discard the solids and heat the liquid to a simmer. Keep the vinegar simmering, without boiling, for 3 minutes. Transfer it to a sterilized jar and seal it. The vinegar will keep perfectly for a year.

Raspberry Vinaigrette

Once you have raspberry vinegar, you have the means to make the quintessential Northwest salad dressing. Use a generous tablespoonful of the vinaigrette for each serving to dress salad greens. The vinaigrette keeps refrigerated for several weeks. If you prefer, make smaller amounts directly in the bowl in which salad greens are to be tossed. Just keep the proportions the same: one part vinegar to three parts oil.

⅓ cup Raspberry Vinegar *(page 177)*
1 tablespoon finely chopped garlic
1 teaspoon salt
1 teaspoon freshly ground black pepper
1 cup olive oil

In a clean, dry jar, combine all the ingredients and shake vigorously.

Makes 1 ⅓ cups

Mussels, Clams & Scallops

When my sister-in-law, Karen, was studying for a license to be a boat's captain, she came from Alaska to spend a winter with us on Bainbridge Island. She rose early every morning and took the ferry into town to sit in a makeshift classroom and study the details of marine navigation, an art she had already practiced in countless hours on fishing boats. We saw less of her than we would have liked but shared a few evening meals

Mussels, Clams & Scallops

with her around our little kitchen table and relished her stories of the daily commute. There were working mothers who left their babies on one side early in the morning and could not have them back until late in the evening. Some men in suits called the jam-packed passenger cabins "cattle cars," and avoided eye contact with one another.

Over the weeks, she established, as people will, certain routines. One of her daily rituals was a sort of aperitif or cocktail of hot clam nectar from Ivar's clam bar on the Seattle waterfront. This she sipped on the return trip each evening, as she chatted with one or another of the strangers who rode the boat with her, and, she said, the hot clam nectar revitalized her from the long day of study.

"Oh it's like the water of life," she insisted, and I knew that for her it was. "It's what my body needs." Personally, I would never go out of my way for the stuff, but a few good sips of the water in which some clams were steamed at home gives me a glimmer of the soul-satisfaction she seemed to draw from Ivar's clam nectar. Better still for my taste is the garlicky residue of wine that's been spent steaming shellfish, sopped up with bread when the clams or mussels or scallops are all gone. On certain occasions when I ate steamed shellfish and then drank the broth or ate chunks of bread soaked in it, I have felt the way Karen felt about that nectar from Ivar's.

There were days when we lived on San Juan Island, that my wife and I would gather clams at the shore and never bring them home. Instead, we would steam them right there on the beach, with our old Coleman campstove hissing its propane fuel in the sea breeze, and the kids all muddy and wet in their boots, and both of us feeling strengthened by the digging and the fresh air.

We were truly in the world then, digging for clams in the cool grey sand. And our campstove made it seem that we were far, not only from home but far from the bounds of time and civilization. In truth, home was less than ten miles away. But British Camp at the north end of San Juan Island, always seemed like another world. And the inhabitants of that world were soft-shelled clams, hiding in the sand.

If a clam, or the gathering of clams seems exotic or foreign to me, that is proof of how far removed I am from my own human roots, for clams are one of the oldest of all foods. Middens all over the world are a testament to early man's appreciation for bivalves. Heaps of charred clam and mussel shells, preserved over thousands of years, are plain evidence of mankind's long history of eating these creatures on beaches.

Hebrews were one exception. Dietary laws in the Old Testament forbid consumption of shellfish. Perhaps this prohibition protected the people from some diseases contracted by filter-feeding bivalves and carried to their human consumers. Certainly other people have seen the effects of shellfish-borne illness.

The Northwest Essentials Cookbook

Northwest Indians recognized paralytic shellfish poisoning; they called it the lip-numbing disease, for the first symptom is a numbing of the mouth.

The bacteria that cause it thrive in warm, nutrient rich, or polluted water, so, in the summertime, especially in waters that lie close to civilization, shellfish gathering is closed. Indians knew from experience that the disease could only be contracted in warmer months and so they avoided clams and mussels in summer and feasted on them in winter. These days waters from which shellfish are drawn for the commercial market are tested regularly, and every wholesaler must attach a state approved label to every container of live shellfish affirming that the water tested free of pathogens. In popular clamming areas, like English Camp, notices are posted if any danger of red tide is present, and in areas where pollution has rendered the shellfish unfit to eat, notices are also posted. Anyone who wants to gather clams in an area where there is any doubt should check the red tide hotline (800-562-5632) before gathering shellfish.

In most recipes, clams, mussels, and scallops in the shell are interchangeable. Any or all of them can be heaped together in a pot, splashed with water, wine, or beer, and seasoned or not with garlic or herbs to be steamed for a casual feast. With their colorful shells, and fresh-from-the-sea flavors, pink scallops, black mussels, and gray clams account for much of the character of Northwest seafood. In some of the recipes that follow, one type of shellfish may be substituted for another, but each has its particular virtues in specific dishes.

Clam Varieties

Native Littleneck Clam This is the clam that I think of when I think of clams at all. With its rounded shell, marked with both concentric and radiating lines, the native littleneck *(Protothaca staminea)* constitutes the ideal form for a steamer clam. They grow up to a very manageable 2½ inches in diameter, and the minimum size limit for legal harvest is 1½ inches across, at which size the clams are perfect for steaming or baking, or broiling on the half-shell. They are found at depths between 6 and 10 feet.

Manila Littleneck Clam An import from the Philippine Islands, the manila *(Tapes philippinarum)* has established itself very well in the Northwest and has won a place in the heart of avid clam lovers. Most clam growers prefer the manila over the native littleneck because it grows at a shallower depth (4 feet below the surface) and its meat is more tender. Recreational clam diggers seldom make a distinction between this import and the native clam.

Butter Clam Somewhat larger than littleneck clams, the butter clam *(Saxidomus giganteus)* grows up to 6 inches, but is best harvested at 3 or 4 inches across. Its chalky-white shells are marked by smooth concentric arcs and bear none of the radiating lines that mark littleneck clams. Butter clams are found between 12 and 18 inches below the surface of the sand. Small ones are good steamed and broiled, but larger specimens should be chopped and used in chowder or clam fritters.

Razor Clam The thin, oblong shell of the razor clam *(Siliqua patula)* does indeed resemble an old-fashioned single-edge razor. Covered with a smooth, light brown skin, this clam is shiny instead of chalky white. Unique to Pacific coastal beaches, the razor clam grows up to 6 inches and can be used like butter clams.

Horse Clam Something like a large butter clam, the horse clam *(Tresus capax* and *Tresus nuttalli)* is distinguished by its inability to retract its siphon. Its chalky shell is marked with yellowish-brown patches of flaky "skin." Found 1 or 2 feet below the surface, horse clams are often ignored by clam diggers seeking steamers; properly handled, however, the meat of these clams is very edible. The secret is to remove the tough outer membrane of the neck or siphon and chop the meat for use in recipes.

Geoduck Clam The Goliath of the clam family, the geoduck *(Panopea abrupta)* is found 2 or 3 feet below the surface and can weigh up to 10 pounds. It is the only clam that is large enough to make "clam steaks." Cut from the long siphon after it has been skinned, the cross sections of this clam can be sautéed in butter. Geoduck also can be chopped and used in chowder or fritters. Extra clam meat can be covered with clam nectar and frozen for later use.

Preparing Clams for Cooking

CLAMS RANGE IN SIZE FROM TINY 1-INCH SPECIMENS TO GARGANTUAN 10-pounders. Generally, the clams I call for in recipes lie at the small end of the continuum. The meat of larger clams is every bit as delectable in clam fritters or clam chowder, but preparing it is somewhat more rigorous. Instead of simply opening the clams by shucking, baking, or steaming, a cook who wishes to enjoy the meat of a large horse clam or geoduck must first clean and shuck, then fillet and skin the critter.

CLEANING CLAMS: Most clams sold at seafood counters are already free from grit, but those of us who gather our own must find ways to let the clams purge themselves of sand before we cook them. Boaters sometimes put the clams in a nylon mesh bag, and then suspend the bag from the stern of the boat for a day before enjoying the clams. Those who live near a saltwater dock can hang the clams from the end and allow them to purge themselves there. (One caveat: Be sure the line on which the bag is suspended is long enough to stay submerged during low tide.)

If neither of these options is available, allow freshly gathered clams to purge themselves in several changes of salt water over a period of hours. When the bucket or cooler in which the clams are held no longer has sand on the bottom, the clams should be grit-free. As a last resort, clams that still contain grit after steaming can be lifted from their nectar and rinsed under cold running water. The nectar should be strained and reintroduced to the grit-free clams.

SHUCKING CLAMS: In *The Fireside Cookbook*, James Beard states, "If you wish to serve raw clams, have the fish dealer open the clams for you." I'm not sure any of my fish dealers would oblige me in this way, but with an oyster knife and a steady hand, anyone can shuck a few clams for themselves. Clams can be shucked several hours ahead and kept refrigerated until serving time. Hold the clam in a cloth in one hand. With an oyster knife in your other hand, use the side of the blade to pry open the clam. Scrape the contents of the upper shell into the lower shell and cut the abductor muscle in the lower shell to free the clam. If you wish to serve the shucked clams on the half shell, arrange them open side up on a tray or a bed of ice and serve with lemon juice, mignonette sauce, or any cocktail sauce. If you plan to use the shucked clams in other recipes, scoop them, as they are shucked from their shells, into a bowl. Eight cups of small clams in the shell will yield about 1 cup of shucked clams.

Mussels

MY MOTHER-IN-LAW REMEMBERS WHEN PRACTICALLY NO ONE IN THE NORTHWEST ate mussels. "My brother and I ran away from home for a few hours when we were children," she says, "And he built a fire on the beach and cooked mussels in a coffee can. They were awful." Everyone knew they were edible, but no one thought they were worth the bother.

Even in the mid-1980s when I was cooking in a restaurant on San Juan Island, my local fishmonger thought I was crazy to pay for farm-raised mussels when "For one thing, you could just go down to the beach and pull them off the rocks, and for another thing, who wants to eat mussels anyway?"

The maturing of the American palate is clearly evidenced in the popularity of mussels on Northwest menus. They are universally accepted now not only as edible but as thoroughly desirable, and several Northwest sea farms produce fat succulent mussels of incomparable quality. Flavoring techniques borrowed from Mediterranean and Asian cultures have taught us to appreciate this lowly creature.

Part of this may be due to the preeminence of a particular variety of mussel grown in Totten Inlet off the coast of Washington. In an attempt to find a Pacific mussel *(Mytilus trossulus)* that would thrive in the slightly warmer water of the inlet, mussel farmers ordered seed from California, expecting to receive a variety of the blue mussels that grow all along the coast. Instead, the mussels grew into prized Mediterranean mussels *(Mytilus galloprovincialis)*. The seed must have inadvertently come from mussels attached to the hull of a ship coming from Europe, where the mussels have been enjoyed for thousands of years. No one ever thought to consciously transplant them to this part of the world. Once here, however, they thrived and the sweet-plump mussels from Totten Inlet are considered the best in the Northwest.

Buying and Bearding Mussels

EVEN MORE THAN OYSTERS, SCALLOPS, AND CLAMS, MUSSELS DETERIORATE RAPIDLY once they are removed from the water and it's critical to get them as fresh as possible. They must be alive right up until they are cooked. Do not buy mussels that are open and won't close, and do not buy mussels that are tightly wrapped in plastic wrap on Styrofoam trays. Store mussels, after they are purchased, for no more than a few hours, and keep them in the coldest part of the refrigerator closely wrapped in a wet towel. Just before cooking, beard the mussels one at a time. Hold a mussel firmly in one hand and with the other hand, snatch off the stringy tendrils that protrude from the shell.

Singing Scallops

IF EVER THERE WERE A SINGLE DISH THAT CAPTURED NORTHWEST STYLE, THAT dish would have to contain singing scallops (pink or spiny scallops—*Chlamys rubida* and *C. hastata*). Shells the color of clouds at sunset contain tender morsels of delicately flavored white meat, a rainbow arc of orange coral and a striped band of firmer muscle tissue with the texture of steamed clams. While larger scallops are generally "cleaned," or stripped of all but their cylindrical white abductor muscles, small, tender singing scallops are usually served in their entirety. They contain no waste meat.

Denizens of the deep, singing scallops are harvested by divers who collect them by hand and carry them up a few at a time in small net "goody bags." The first time I ever saw singing scallops, my co-worker told me that the name came from a whistling sound the scallops make when they are steamed. At first I believed her and listened intently for the scallop song every time I steamed them. I was frustrated when I couldn't hear it.

I only realized I had been hoodwinked when I learned that the scallops swim by opening and closing their shells. The pink shells opening and closing look like mouths singing in the silence below the waves. Divers say the motion of the scallops is reminiscent of butterflies in flight.

Scallops in the shell should be alive when they are purchased, but they live only a few hours out of the water. Kept well chilled, they will be good for a day or two. Ideally, their shells will be closed or will shut when you touch them. If they are no longer alive, but still look and smell fresh, they are still good.

Fresh singing scallops are amenable to just about any recipe calling for live mussels or clams, and if live singing scallops aren't available, you can substitute live mussels or clams for them in the recipes that follow.

Steamed Clams

Unlike mussels and scallops, clams are almost always steamed in water, almost never in wine. The water left behind, a rich liquor known as clam nectar, has tonic effects and should not be discarded.

> **2 pounds live clams**
> **1 cup water**
> **¼ cup (½ stick) butter, melted**

In a large kettle over high heat, cook the clams in the water for 12 to 15 minutes, or until they open. Serve at once with melted butter.

Serves 2 to 4

Baked Clams

At the risk of losing a little nectar and therefore a little flavor, you can bake clams open. The risk is that they will dry out and toughen, the advantage is that baking the clams makes shucking them infinitely easier. To prevent the clams from drying out, keep the baking time to a minimum.

> **Rock salt**
> **2 pounds live clams**
> **¼ cup (½ stick) butter, melted**
> **Lemon wedges**

Preheat the oven to 450°F and line a baking sheet with a ½-inch layer of rock salt. (As a contingency, crumpled aluminum foil can be used instead of rock salt.) Rest the clams on the bed of salt and bake 3 to 5 minutes for small clams or up to 15 minutes for large clams. In either case, bake just until clams pop open. Baked clams may be served at once with melted butter and lemon wedges passed separately, or they can be used in place of shucked clams in recipes.

Serves 2 to 4

Broiled Clams

Sizzling in their shells, each one like a miniature crust-covered casserole, clams broiled on the half shell are a little-known delicacy. I learned to make them when I was assistant to the chef at a small restaurant on San Juan Island. One of my daily chores was to open the clams with an oyster knife and set them up in gratin dishes before service. When I became chef, I stopped serving the clams for several years because I was so tired of shucking them. Shucking clams is tedious, but now I think it was worth the effort.

> 2 pounds (40 to 48) live clams, shucked
> 1 cup fresh bread crumbs
> ¼ cup fresh oregano, chopped, or 1 tablespoon dried
> 1 tablespoon chopped garlic
> 6 tablespoons melted butter
> 1 cup white wine
> Freshly ground black pepper, to taste
> Hot French bread as an accompaniment

Preheat the oven to 450°F. Divide the shucked clams among six 6-inch, shallow, oven-proof dishes (6 or 7 clams per dish) or place in one larger baking dish. Combine bread crumbs, oregano, garlic, and melted butter in a small bowl and put about 1 teaspoon of the bread-crumb mixture on top of each clam. Pour the wine over and around the clams, allowing most of it to land in the baking dish or dishes. Broil the clams for 5 to 6 minutes, or until well-browned and piping hot. Top with a grind of black pepper and serve at once with hot French bread.

Serves 6 as a first course

Fried Clams

Less common in my house than fried oysters, but no less delectable, fried clams demand a little more preparation. Instead of simply tossing them with seasoned flour, I like to apply layers of flour, egg, and bread crumbs. The crisp coating seems more appropriate to the firm texture of clams. Once fried, the clams should be heaped into a basket and passed with drinks before a meal. Of course, under the right circumstances, fried clams may be a meal in themselves. If the frying pan is overcrowded, the breading will not adhere properly, nor will it crisp as it should, so fry only 10 or 12 clams at a time.

> 2 pounds (40 to 48) live clams, shucked
> 1 teaspoon freshly ground black pepper
> ¾ cup flour
> 2 large eggs
> 2 tablespoons water
> 1½ cups panko *(see Note on page 208)* **or bread crumbs**
> Oil to form a 1-inch layer in skillet
> Cocktail sauce, Tartar Sauce *(page 209)*, **or Ginger Dipping Sauce** *(page 194)*, **optional**

Preheat the oven to 250°F. Line a baking sheet with paper towels or a brown paper bag and set aside.

Rinse the clams, pat them dry, and sprinkle with pepper; set aside. Put the flour on a plate. In a shallow bowl or a pie plate, beat the eggs with the water. Put the panko on another plate. In a large skillet, heat the oil until a candy thermometer registers 375°F or until a cube of bread dropped into the oil floats immediately to the surface and browns in 1 minute. Working with 10 or 12 clams at a time, toss the clams in the flour and shake off the excess. Dip the clams in the egg mixture and allow the excess egg to flow back into the bowl. Roll the clams in the panko and fry them for 4 minutes or until golden brown. Drain on paper towels and keep in the warm oven while frying the remaining clams. Serve hot with tartar sauce or dressed salad greens.

Serves 4 to 6 as an appetizer

Clam Chowder

While its roots may reach back to New England, chowder's branches are well-established over the Pacific Northwest. Here, in the creative hotbed of North American cuisine, variations abound. Smoked salmon is sometimes substituted for the traditional bacon, and firm apples may be used instead of potatoes. But the original is still more popular than any of the new-fangled twists on this American standard.

> 2 pounds Steamed Clams, *(see page 189)*
> 2 cups milk
> 2 large thin-skinned potatoes, preferably Yukon Gold, cut into 1-inch dice
> 8 ounces bacon, cut into ¼-inch dice
> 1 large onion, diced
> 4 stalks of celery, diced
> 1 tablespoon chopped garlic
> ¼ cup flour
> Salt and freshly ground black pepper

Set aside the clams to cool, reserving the clam nectar. Bring the milk to a slow boil in a large saucepan over medium heat, watching closely to prevent boiling over. Add the potatoes to the milk and cook for 12 to 15 minutes, or just until tender. Cook the bacon until well-browned in a soup kettle over medium-high heat. With a slotted spoon, lift the bacon bits out of the rendered bacon fat and set aside. Sauté the onion, celery, and garlic in the bacon fat for 5 minutes, or until soft and just beginning to brown. Stir in the flour, then stir in 1 cup of the milk in which potatoes have been cooked. Stir vigorously to prevent lumping. Stir in the remaining milk, the cooked potatoes, and the reserved clam nectar. Reduce the heat to medium-low. Chop the clams, add them to the soup, and simmer for 10 to 15 minutes. Season to taste with salt and pepper. Serve the chowder hot with bacon sprinkled on top.

Serves 6

Clam Fritters with Ginger Dipping Sauce

While Fried Clams (page 191) are made with whole clams in a crust, clam fritters are made with chopped clams stirred into a batter. The fritters can be made with any clams, but they are an especially appropriate way to use large clams. Cut away any tough parts of large butter clams; if you're using geoducks, razor clams, or horse clams, skin the necks or siphons and retain only the tender meat.

> ⅔ cup flour
> 1 teaspoon baking powder
> ¾ teaspoon salt
> ¼ teaspoon freshly ground black pepper
> 1 egg, plus 1 egg yolk
> ½ cup clam nectar or milk
> 1 cup clam meat, chopped
> ⅓ cup onion, chopped fine
> Oil to form a 1-inch layer in a skillet
> Ginger Dipping Sauce *(page 194)*

In a small mixing bowl, stir together the flour, baking powder, salt, and pepper; set aside. In a separate bowl, whisk together the egg, the egg yolk, and the clam nectar. Stir in the clam meat and onion, then add the flour mixture all at once and stir just until dry ingredients are moistened; do not overmix. In a large skillet, heat the oil until a candy thermometer registers 375°F, or until a drop of the batter or a cube of bread dropped into the oil floats immediately to the surface and browns in 1 minute. Drop the mixture by rounded tablespoonsful into the hot oil and fry, turning once, for about 8 minutes, or until fritters are golden brown and cooked through. If more than one batch is fried, the first batch may be held on a paper-lined baking sheet in a 200°F oven. Serve hot with Ginger Dipping Sauce.

Makes 12 fritters

Ginger Dipping Sauce

This light, almost clear sauce is as tangy and sweet as ketchup but it's infinitely more interesting. If there is extra sauce, consider using it as you would cocktail sauce for chilled crab or other shellfish. It keeps, refrigerated, almost indefinitely.

½ cup white vinegar
½ cup light corn syrup
1 tablespoon freshly ground ginger
2 teaspoons cornstarch
1 teaspoon salt

In a small saucepan, whisk together vinegar, corn syrup, ginger, cornstarch, and salt. Cook over high heat until mixture boils. Serve hot or cold.

Makes 1 cup

Steamed Mussels

The basic method of cooking mussels hasn't really changed much since my mother-in-law's crude introduction to mussels cooked in a coffee can; they are almost always simply steamed open. One would do well, though, to forgo the coffee can and use a proper kettle. Also replace the seawater with white wine and garlic. Serve the mussels with green salad, hot bread, and cold white wine for a simple dinner.

1 pound live mussels
1 cup dry white wine
1 tablespoon chopped fresh garlic
Freshly ground black pepper

Beard the mussels and rinse under cold running water. Set aside. Combine the wine, garlic, and pepper in a kettle, place over high heat, and bring the mixture to a boil. Add the mussels and cover the pan. Cook for 7 to 10 minutes, or until the mussels are opened. Season with freshly ground black pepper and serve at once.

Serves 2

  The Northwest Essentials Cookbook

Mussel Soup with Saffron and Cream

It's only a small step from simple steamed mussels to an elegant mussel soup. In this classic preparation, the pure fresh flavor of the sea rings out loud and clear. Base notes of saffron and garlic evoke the Mediterranean without infringing on the clear briny voice of the mussels themselves.

> **3 pounds live mussels**
> **2 cups white wine**
> **1 tablespoon chopped fresh garlic**
> **2 tablespoons butter**
> **2 tablespoons flour**
> **2 cups whipping cream**
> **About 1 teaspoon Spanish saffron threads**
> **6 leaves spinach or sorrel, cut into fine ribbons**

Beard the mussels and rinse under cold running water. Set aside. Combine the wine and garlic in a kettle, place over high heat, and bring to a boil. Add the mussels and cover the pan. Steam for 7 to 10 minutes, or until the mussels have popped open. Reserve the steaming liquor. As soon as the mussels are cool enough to handle, remove them from their shells and hold them in the reserved liquor.

Melt the butter in a clean pan and stir in the flour. Whisk in the cream and bring the liquid to a boil, whisking all the while. Add the saffron and mussels in their liquor. Allow the soup to come to a gentle boil and serve hot with fine ribbons of spinach or sorrel on each bowl for garnish.

Serves 6

Mussels Steamed with Coconut Milk

As with most preparations involving mussels, this Southeast Asian–flavored dish is accompanied by an abundance of flavorful broth. Serve the mussels in very large bowls, with the shellfish forming rings around mounds of fragrant basmati rice. Cook the rice before you begin and leave it covered in the pan in which it was cooked.

> 1 pound live mussels
> 1 (1-inch) length of fresh ginger, peeled and sliced ⅛ inch thick
> 1 stalk of fresh lemongrass, trimmed and cut into 6 or 7 pieces
> 1 teaspoon vegetable oil
> 1 tablespoon crushed red pepper flakes
> 1 (15-ounce) can coconut milk
> ½ cup fresh basil, cut into ribbons
> 1 cup basmati rice, cooked according to package instructions

Beard the mussels and rinse under cold running water. Transfer to a colander and set aside to drain. Sauté the ginger and lemongrass in the oil in a large kettle over high heat for 1 minute, then add the red pepper flakes and cook for a few seconds more. Add the coconut milk and bring the mixture to a full rolling boil. Add the mussels, cover, and cook for 7 to 10 minutes, or until mussels are fully opened. Stir in basil and serve at once with hot basmati rice.

Serves 2

Singing Scallops Steamed with Garlic and Herbs

Like other shellfish, singing scallops are quickly and easily steamed. Here, an impromptu bath of white wine, garlic, and herbs makes a flavorful broth around scallops that are ready to eat at once or easily adapted to a chilled presentation.

> 1 pound live singing scallops
> ½ cup white wine
> 1 tablespoon *herbes de Provence* or Italian seasoning
> 1 teaspoon chopped garlic
> A grind of black pepper
> Fresh herb sprigs for garnish (optional)

In a covered saucepan over high heat, cook the scallops with the wine, herbs, garlic, and pepper for 5 to 6 minutes, or until the shells are opened. Transfer to a large bowl or divide between 2 bowls and pour on the steaming liquid. Decorate, if desired, with sprigs of fresh herbs. Serve at once with bread for soaking up the juice.

Serves 2 generously as a starter

Chilled Singing Scallops on the Half Shell

Well chilled and dressed with a bright green mayonnaiselike sauce, singing scallops make an elegant passed hors d'oeuvre. Line the tray on which they are served with ribbons of spinach to set off the pretty pink shells. This recipe works beautifully with steamed mussels as well.

> 1 pound Singing Scallops Steamed with Garlic and Herbs *(see preceding page)*
> 1 egg yolk
> 1 teaspoon lemon juice
> ½ cup fresh chopped sorrel, dill, basil, mint, or parsley, or a combination
> ¾ cup olive oil

Save the liquid that comes off the scallops and strain it into a saucepan. Remove one of the shells from each opened scallop, then free the scallop from the other half shell so it slips off easily. Arrange the scallops on their half shells on a baking sheet or tray and put in the refrigerator.

Boil the liquid in which the scallops were cooked until it has reduced to ¼ cup. Place 2 tablespoons of this liquid in a blender and discard the rest. Add the egg yolk, lemon juice, and chopped herb or herbs, and blend until thoroughly combined. With the motor running, add a few drops of oil and then carefully stream in more oil, a teaspoon at a time, to create a smooth emulsion. Transfer the sauce to a self-sealing food storage bag and refrigerate. Just before serving the scallops, snip off one corner of the bag and pipe the sauce in a little whirl on top of each scallop. Serve cold.

Makes 24 to 30 pieces to serve 6 as an hors d'oeuvre

A Mixed Shellfish Steam

Since all the bivalves respond so well to steaming, it's only natural that they should be piled in a great big pot and steamed all together. This preparation, perfumed with garlic and thyme, is infinitely variable. Choose another herb, or for an Asian flavor replace the garlic and thyme with ginger and cilantro. If not all the shellfish are available, use only one or two varieties. Do give the clams and oysters a little head start or the scallops and mussels will be falling out of their shells before the slower-cooking shellfish are opened. The dish may be served communally with finger bowls and extra napkins or divided among individual serving bowls.

>1 cup white wine
>1 tablespoon chopped garlic
>1 teaspoon dried thyme
>Freshly ground black pepper
>1 pound live clams
>6 live Pacific oysters, such as Kumamotos
>1 pound live singing scallops
>1 pound live mussels
>Sprigs of thyme, for garnish
>Lemon wedges

Bring the wine, garlic, thyme, and pepper to taste to a full rolling boil in a covered saucepan over high heat. Add the clams and oysters, cover, and steam for 8 minutes, then add the scallops and mussels and steam for 5 minutes more, or until the shells are open. Serve at once with sprigs of thyme and wedges of lemon.

Serves 6

Other Fish in the Sea

I've never been much of a fisherman. There is no excuse for this. I've had every opportunity to learn, and perhaps someday I will. But so far, my efforts at survival have been focused on other tasks, and fishing has never been a real priority. Once or twice though, with the aid of my wife, Betsy, who can tie fishing line with the same easy dexterity that allows her to braid her hair behind her back, I have dangled a hook in the water and pulled up something with scales. ✐ Once, before we had children, we piled our tent and cooler and ourselves along with a couple of friends into an

Other Fish in the Sea

aluminum boat with an outboard motor and set out to camp on one of the small islands in the San Juan archipelago that has been set aside as a state park. Along the way we were fishing for our supper and I was the only member of the expedition who had any luck. I caught a rockfish, and we kept the fish in a bucket in the bottom of the boat and called him Frisky.

Frisky was probably an olive rockfish; certainly he was one of the various Pacific rockfish that inhabit the deep rocky, underwater hillsides that run along the Pacific coast from southern California to Alaska. If he were here today I could probably identify him, but memory serves poorly at taxonomy.

When we arrived and set up our tent and camp stove, I cleaned and filleted my scaly prize. I sprinkled the fillets with salt and pepper, rolled them in cornmeal and fried them in a shallow puddle of olive oil. It was a fairly large specimen and we each had a nice piece of fish. But that large head was wasted. When I cook rockfish at home, I use the head and skeleton to make a stock. Then I poach the fish in the stock so that nothing is wasted. The same procedure can be employed with other fish.

Fish Varieties

Rockfish This is a loose and not entirely specific name for any number of fish. In the Chesapeake Bay area, rockfish means striped bass. In the Northwest, Pacific rockfish is used to describe all members of the genus *Sebastes*. With names like Bank, Widow, Yellowtail, and Canary, the various species are recognized mostly by their skin color, which ranges from bright vermilion to black with myriad hues in between. In fillet form, one species is virtually indistinguishable from another. The fillets are also easily confused with fillets of snapper and cod, and these more consumer-friendly names are sometimes erroneously applied to the fish. Unless you can get the fish whole and fillet it yourself, you probably cannot identify it, but whatever it is, rockfish fries well, broils well, and generally makes people happy.

Snapper More than two hundred varieties of saltwater snapper exist, the most familiar being the red snapper of the Gulf and Atlantic coasts. Gray snapper, yellowtail snapper, and others are gastronomically equal to popular red snapper, but their unfamiliarity presents a challenge to marketers who simply label all of them red snapper—even fish that are not snapper at all. In short, snapper is an unofficial shorthand for any fish that meets consumer demand for a versatile firm white fillet. Such is the case with many rockfish. Orange roughy, a popular Pacific fish, used to be routinely labeled red snapper, but a growing public familiarity with it has prompted fishmongers to sell it under its own name.

Lingcod Another versatile denizen of Northwest waters, lingcod (*Ophiodon elongatus*) is seldom mistaken for anything else, but its name does generate some confusion. It is neither a ling nor a cod, rather it's a member of the greenling family. When it was more abundant, lingcod was the first choice for fish and chips. Now it's more likely to be served in white-tablecloth restaurants in swank dishes where it can command the higher prices that it rightfully demands. Lingcod performs very well under the broiler, and pan-seared, it rivals the most coveted fishes of the Mediterranean. But it is perhaps best served inside a tempura batter, where it softens into an incomparable delicacy and harkens the days of its fish-and-chips glory.

Petrale Sole Like sand dab and starry flounder, petrale sole (*Eopsetta jordani*) is one of several flatfish found in Pacific waters from Mexico to Alaska. No one seems to know why it's called petrale. It's larger than Dover sole and smaller than the smallest halibut, and tastes something like a cross between the two. When I call for sole in a recipe, I'm thinking of this one. The delicate fillets respond equally well to poaching or frying, but not so well to oven-broiling.

Halibut Of all the flounders, halibut (*Hippoglossus stenolepsis*) is distinguished primarily by its enormous size. It is never mistaken for anything else nor is any other fish taken for halibut, but it is the West Coast's answer to turbot, the noble flatfish of the Atlantic. Properly cooked, it breaks into large silken flakes that have good flavor. Oven-broiling is usually my first choice for halibut, but it also responds well to poaching, especially in a stock made from its own bones. (Fish stock made from halibut is the best fish stock you can make.) Most fishmongers will be happy to sell you or even give you part of a halibut frame to make your own fish stock.

Preparing Fish for Cooking

FILLETING FISH: For some, the prospect of filleting a fish can be intimidating, but with a sharp knife and a sense of adventure, even a novice can take satisfaction from this task. A fish is, after all, considerably less anatomically complicated than, say, a chicken, and boning it is not that difficult.

For round fish, follow the advice on filleting salmon on page 39. For flatfish, cut down the center of each side of the fish until you hit bone, then work the knife between the flesh and bones until the flesh comes free. A flatfish like halibut or sole yields four fillets, two from each side.

If you don't feel comfortable or competent filleting your own fish, perhaps you can find a fishmonger who will show you how or, at least, save you the skeleton from the fish he fillets. Rejoice over the skeletal frame left behind, for in it, you have the means to make a great poaching liquid for the fillets you have removed from the fish.

SKINNING FISH FILLETS: With a sharp knife and a fairly steady hand, anyone can skin a fish fillet. The secret is to move the fish and hold the knife steady. Place the fish on a cutting board, skin side down, with the tail end toward you. If you are right-handed, hold the knife in your right hand and the fish in your left. Starting about half an inch from the tip closest to you, cut into the fish just until you reach the skin; do not cut through the skin. Grasp the bit of fish and skin at the tail end in your left hand, and with your right hand, hold the knife steady. Pull the skin toward you, wriggling it back and forth, from left to right. Ideally, the knife will be wedged between the fish and the skin. This operation is more easily demonstrated than described, and it's easier still to perform. After one or two tries, anyone can be a pro.

Poaching Fish

COOKING FISH IN LIQUID SHOULD NOT BE THOUGHT OF AS BOILING, WHICH implies a certain rough handling that could destroy delicate fillets of fresh fish. Slipped gently into a simmering bath of barely bubbling liquid, fish should fare very well indeed. The liquid could be a stock, referred to in some circles as fumet, made from the carcass that yielded the fillets, or it could be a classic court bouillon, a light broth made from aromatic vegetables. In a pinch, plain white wine and water make a fine poaching liquid, especially if a few fennel seeds or a sprig of fresh fennel is added. Fish may also be considered poached when baked under cover with ample liquid around it. One great advantage of poaching is that the poaching liquid can be reduced and enriched to form a sauce.

Fillet of Sole with White Grapes

Sole Véronique, or sole with grapes, is an old dish that was chronicled by Escoffier and was once part of every serious chef's repertoire. A hundred years ago, when it appeared on menus all over Europe and America and in first-class dining rooms on passenger ships making their way between the two continents, it was prepared quite differently from the way I offer it here. The fillets of sole were poached in fish stock and a little pyramid of peeled Muscat grapes accompanied every serving. I don't always have fish stock on hand, and I shudder at the thought of peeling grapes and piling them into a pyramid, but I do like the combination of sweet grapes and savory fish fillets. For added piquancy, I follow the lead of my late friend Gerald Knight who added capers to his Sole Véronique. Serve the fish with sautéed spinach and a gratin of potatoes.

> 6 large or 12 small sole fillets (about 1½ pounds)
> Kosher salt
> 1 cup white wine
> ¼ cup heavy whipping cream
> ½ pound green grapes, sliced in half lengthwise
> 1 tablespoon capers (optional)
> ¼ cup (½ stick) butter, cold, cut into 1-inch pieces

If the fillets are large, cut them in half lengthwise. Sprinkle the fillets lightly with salt, then roll each one into a little individual scroll. In a large sauté pan arrange the rolled fillets in a single layer and pour on the wine. Cover the pan and cook over medium heat for 10 minutes. With a slotted spoon, transfer the fish rolls from the cooking liquid to a warm platter or individual serving dishes. Increase the heat to high and boil the cooking liquid until it is reduced to about ¼ cup. Add the cream and continue to boil on high heat until the mixture is slightly thickened. Add the grapes and capers, if using, then swirl in the butter. As soon as the butter has melted into the sauce, spoon the grapes onto the plates, pour the sauce over the poached fillets and serve at once.

Serves 4

Fillet of Sole with Dungeness Crabmeat

Along the same lines as Sole Véronique is this capricious dish that should have been a part of the classical tradition but wasn't. I like to tuck spoonfuls of crabmeat inside scrolls of sole and poach them in the oven with white wine and cream. Fragrant crabmeat permeates the sole and makes a little crab go a long way. This dish would be nicely complemented by a gratin of potatoes and forest mushrooms and a sémillon from Eastern Washington.

> 6 large or 12 small sole fillets (about 1½ pounds)
> Kosher salt
> Freshly ground black pepper
> 4 ounces Dungeness crabmeat
> 1 tablespoon chopped fresh dill
> ½ cup white wine
> ½ cup heavy whipping cream

Preheat the oven to 400°F.

If the fillets are large, cut them in half lengthwise to form 12 narrow fillets. Lay the fillets out on wax paper or a clean countertop with the darker sides up and the lighter sides down. Sprinkle the fillets with salt and pepper. In a small bowl, combine the crabmeat and dill. Place a spoonful of the crabmeat mixture in the center of each fillet and roll it up. Arrange the crab-filled rolls in a glass or ceramic baking dish and pour on the wine and cream.

Bake for 15 minutes, or until the surface is slightly browned and the fish is cooked through. With a fish spatula or a slotted spoon, lift the fillets from the cooking liquid in the pan and arrange them on plates. Transfer the cooking liquid to a saucepan and cook over high heat for 3 minutes, or until sauce is thickened. Spoon the sauce over the fillets and serve at once.

Serves 4

Panfried Fish with Tartar Sauce

A potato may be fried au naturel, for its starchy nature responds beautifully to hot oil, but foods that are mostly protein would be made hard and chewy by direct exposure to the hot oil. So fish, before it's fried, should be enrobed in a starchy case: a thin layer of cornmeal, a tempura batter, or a three-layered fantasy of flour, egg, and bread crumbs like the one described below. The same technique may be applied to shucked clams or oysters. Use the Japanese crumbs known as panko (see Note, below), or dried bread crumbs.

> 4 rockfish, lingcod, or sole fillets (6 to 8 ounces each)
> Salt and freshly ground black pepper
> ¾ cup flour
> 2 large eggs
> 2 tablespoons water
> 1½ cups panko *(see Note, below)* or bread crumbs
> Oil, for frying
> Lemon wedges, for serving
> Tartar Sauce *(recipe follows)*

Sprinkle the fillets with salt and pepper. Put the flour on a dinner plate. Beat the eggs with water in a shallow bowl or pie plate. Put the bread crumbs on another plate. In a large skillet, heat a 1-inch layer of oil over medium-high heat until a candy thermometer registers 375°F or until a cube of bread dropped into the oil rises immediately to the surface and becomes golden brown in 1 minute. Coat each fish fillet in flour, shaking off any excess. Next, dip it into the beaten egg mixture, allowing the excess to run off. Finally, coat with bread crumbs. Test the oil temperature, then gently add breaded fillets. After 3 to 5 minutes, or when each fillet is delicately browned, turn and cook 2 to 4 minutes more. Drain on paper towels or clean brown paper and serve hot with wedges of lemon and tartar sauce.

Serves 4

NOTE: An import from Japan, panko is a manufactured bread crumb sold under many different brand names. Traditionally used for making Japanese dishes like the crispy-fried pork cutlet known as *tonkatsu,* panko is unsurpassed for coating foods that are to be fried, and it is a kitchen staple in many Northwest homes. Light and dry, it looks like shredded coconut. It can be purchased in the imported foods section of almost any grocery store. Day-old French bread grated on the coarse side of an ordinary cheese grater will yield a similar result, but for those who like their fried foods extra crispy, nothing works like panko.

  The Northwest Essentials Cookbook

Tartar Sauce

Very much like a homemade mayonnaise, homemade tartar sauce, which is based on mayonnaise, is a revelation to anyone who has only had the bottled kind.

1 soft-boiled egg yolk
1 teaspoon dry mustard powder
1 tablespoon fresh lemon juice
¾ cup light olive oil or vegetable oil
1 small kosher dill pickle, grated
1 tablespoon chopped parsley
Salt and freshly ground black pepper

In a food processor, combine the egg yolk, mustard, and lemon juice. With the motor running, add a few drops of oil, and when they are incorporated, add a few more. Stream in the remaining oil very slowly to make a thick emulsion. Stir in pickle and parsley. Add salt and pepper to taste. Serve at once or transfer to a clean glass jar and store, refrigerated, for up to 1 week.

Makes 1 cup

Beer-Battered Lingcod with Red Chilies and Lime

Traditional tempura batter, made with egg, water, and flour, forms a delicate crust around anything suitable for frying. Tempura batter can also be made with beer instead of egg and water. Try using extra batter to coat herbs from the garden or slices of sweet onion to accompany your fried fish. Keenly aware that fried food is best eaten as soon as it is cooked, Japanese tempura chefs fry only a few bite-size pieces at a time and diners wait for their next bite while it fries. When I fry enough for the whole family, I keep the first batches hot in a warm oven on a baking sheet lined with brown paper.

1 cup flour
1 cup lager beer
1 pound lingcod fillets
Corn oil or other vegetable oil, for deep-frying
Red Pepper and Lime Sauce *(recipe follows)*

Preheat the oven to 250°F, and line a baking sheet with a brown paper bag or paper towels.

Whisk together the flour and beer in a small bowl, cover, and set aside. Remove any bones from the fillets and cut the fish into ½-inch-wide strips. Heat 3 inches of oil in a large frying pan (I use cast-iron) over medium-high heat, until a candy thermometer registers 375°F, or until a cube of bread dropped into the oil floats immediately to the surface and browns in 1 minute. Working with 3 or 4 strips of the fish at a time, dip the fish in the batter and allow excess batter to drip back into the bowl. Fry the fish for about 2 minutes on each side, or until golden, then transfer to the paper-lined baking sheet and keep warm. Repeat the procedure with the remaining fish. Never overcrowd the pan. Serve immediately with sauce for dipping.

Serves 2 to 4

Red Pepper and Lime Sauce

Well-made soy sauce is such a complex and complete sauce in itself that it stands perfectly well alone. But the addition of lime and red pepper flakes transforms it into something livelier and more compelling.

> 1 tablespoon crushed red pepper flakes
> 1 tablespoon boiling water
> 1 lime
> 2 tablespoons soy sauce

Cover red pepper flakes with water and set aside. Working over a small bowl, grate the colorful outer zest from the lime, then squeeze the juice from the lime into the bowl. Stir in the soy sauce and crushed red pepper and serve with fried fish.

Serves 2 to 4

Oven-Broiled Fish Fillets with a Glaze

Almost any fish fillets can be brought to the table without a lot of fuss in a matter of minutes if you broil them in the oven, then finish them with a flavorful glaze of homemade mayonnaise or one of the other glazes that follow.

4 rockfish, halibut, or other white fish fillets (6 to 8 ounces each)
6 tablespoons Homemade Mayonnaise or one of the glazes on pages 212–213

Preheat the broiler or oven to 450°F, and lightly oil a baking sheet.

Arrange fillets in a single layer on the oiled sheet, and bake or broil for 10 to 12 minutes. Cover the baked fish with a thin layer of mayonnaise or another glaze of choice and pop the pan back into the hot oven or under the glowing broiler element. As soon as the glaze is bubbling, it's done. Serve at once.

Serves 4

Homemade Mayonnaise

Making your own mayonnaise is easier than you think. When I was a boy, homemade mayonnaise for potato salad was a part of the preparation of every important holiday meal. I was always captivated by the process of bringing oil and liquid together into an emulsion and frequently volunteered to help. We sometimes used the ancient Sunbeam Mixmaster upright mixer; sometimes we would use the Waring blender, but the mixture always became too thick for the blender before all the oil was added. By the time I was in my early teens, I was whisking the mayonnaise together in a mixing bowl with a wire whisk. I still find this to be the most satisfactory method, especially if a kitchen partner is willing to slowly stream in the oil while I do the whisking. Since not everyone takes the same delight I do in wielding a whisk and since food processors have become so common, I've given food processor directions.

2 egg yolks
1 tablespoon vinegar
½ teaspoon white pepper
½ teaspoon sugar
½ teaspoon dry mustard
½ teaspoon salt
1 cup light olive oil or vegetable oil

In a food processor, combine the egg yolks, vinegar, pepper, sugar, mustard, and salt. With the motor running, add a few drops of olive oil and when it is well incorporated, add a teaspoon of oil at a time until one quarter of the oil has been slowly and thoroughly incorporated. Stream in the remaining oil very slowly, processing all the while to make a thick emulsion. For glaze, spread about 1 tablespoon of the mayonnaise over each fish fillet. Return the glazed fish to the oven and broil for 30 seconds, or until the glaze is bubbling hot. Serve at once. Store the remaining mayonnaise, covered, in the refrigerator for up to 1 week.

Makes about 1½ cups

Parsley Glaze

Taken off the side of the plate and placed center stage in this brilliant green glaze, ordinary curly parsley shines as a flavorful accompaniment to broiled rockfish, snapper, halibut, or cod. Pernod, an aperitif with a strong suggestion of fennel or anise, makes a nice addition to the glaze. If you don't have any, don't fret. The sauce is still delicious without it.

> 2 egg yolks
> 1 tablespoon fresh lemon juice
> 1 teaspoon chopped garlic
> ½ teaspoon salt
> ¾ cup roughly chopped curly parsley
> 1 cup light olive oil or vegetable oil
> 1 tablespoon Pernod (optional)

In a food processor, combine the egg yolks, lemon juice, garlic, and salt. Toss the parsley in. With the motor running, add a few drops of olive oil and when it is well incorporated, add a teaspoon of oil at a time until one quarter of the oil has been slowly and thoroughly incorporated. Stream in the remaining oil very slowly, processing to make a thick emulsion. If desired, stir in the Pernod. For glaze, spread over each fish fillet. Return the glazed fish to the oven and broil for 30 seconds, or until the glaze is bubbling hot. Serve at once. Store any extra parsley glaze, covered, in the refrigerator for up to 1 week.

Makes about 1 cup

Stone-Ground Mustard Glaze for Seafood

Pommerey mustard from France is very good for this dish, but so are many of the American-made mustards. I have used Creole mustards from Louisiana and a popular brand produced in Beaverton, Oregon, with equally good results. They key is to choose a mustard with lots of visible brown mustard seeds and a satisfying, not too vinegary, flavor.

2 egg yolks
¼ cup stone-ground mustard
1 teaspoon salt
1 cup light oil

In a food processor, combine the egg yolks, mustard, and salt. With the motor running, add a few drops of oil, and when they are incorporated, add a few more. Stream in remaining oil very slowly to make a thick emulsion. For glaze, spread over each fish fillet. Return the glazed fish to the oven and broil for 30 seconds, or until the glaze is bubbling hot. Serve at once. Serve as a cold sauce with cracked crab. Store any extra mustard glaze, covered, in the refrigerator for up to 1 week.

Makes about 1½ cups

Red Bell Pepper Glaze for Seafood

Glazing broiled fillets of fish doesn't have to mean mayonnaise. A simple brush of soy sauce can be a very effective flavor enhancer, and the dark and shiny finish it leaves over the surface of the fish is just as appealing as some of the more complicated glazes. Another simple way to enhance broiled fish fillets is to brush them with a purée of roasted red bell pepper.

4 cloves garlic
2 large red bell peppers, roasted, peeled, and seeded, or 1 cup bottled
  roasted red bell peppers
1 tablespoon balsamic vinegar, or to taste
Salt and freshly ground black pepper

In a food processor or a blender, chop the garlic until fine by pulsing on and off, scraping the larger bits from the sides with a rubber spatula. Add the red bell pepper and purée until smooth. Whirl in the vinegar and add salt and pepper to taste. For glaze, spread over each fish fillet. Return the glazed fish to the oven and broil for 30 seconds, or until the glaze is bubbling hot. Serve at once. Or serve as a dipping sauce with fried fish. Store any extra sauce, covered, in the refrigerator for 2 weeks.

Makes about 1 cup

Baked Halibut with Three Citrus Fruits

In this preparation, halibut is served with long curls of zest and juicy segments from three different citrus fruits. Something like a squeeze of lemon taken to another level, this vibrant citrus fruit mixture can be served with other fish as well.

> 3 tablespoons extra virgin olive oil
> 6 halibut fillets (8 ounces each)
> Kosher salt and freshly ground black pepper
> 2 oranges
> 2 limes
> 2 pink grapefruits
> 1 tablespoon sugar

Preheat the oven to 425°F. On a baking sheet, drizzle olive oil over halibut fillets, turning to coat the fillets evenly. Arrange the fillets, skin side down, 2 inches apart and sprinkle with salt and pepper. Bake for 10 minutes.

With a zester, carefully remove the colorful outer zest from the oranges, limes, and grapefruits. Place the zest in a small bowl. With a very sharp paring knife, cut the tops and bottoms from the fruits, then cut away and discard the remaining peel and white pith. Holding the fruit over the bowl containing the zest, cut out the sections of pulp, allowing them to fall in with the zest. Squeeze any juice from the remaining pulp into the bowl. Add the sugar, 1 teaspoon salt, and ½ teaspoon pepper. Spoon the citrus fruit mixture over the baked halibut fillets and bake for 1 minute more. With a metal spatula, transfer fillets with citrus fruit to serving plates. Drizzle the remaining juices over each portion and serve hot.

Serves 6

Fish Baked in a Pastry Crust

Simple fillets of snapper or a large side of halibut can become an entrée worthy of note when baked under a layer of puff pastry. For an even grander dish, you might want to cover the surface of the fish with a layer of sautéed spinach or mushroom duxelles before you cover it with the pastry, but neither one is necessary. The dish is very easy to accomplish if you buy frozen puff pastry, and it's not really difficult even if you make your own Mock Puff Pastry. If you go the homemade route, make the pastry the day before or at least several hours ahead and chill it.

4 fish fillets (8 ounces each), or one 2-pound fish fillet
Salt and freshly ground black pepper
½ cup sautéed spinach, patted dry, or Mushroom Duxelles *(page 150)*, optional
1 (14 x 9-inch) sheet frozen puff pastry or Mock Puff Pastry *(recipe follows)*
1 egg
1 teaspoon sugar

Preheat the oven to 400°F. Lightly oil a baking sheet. Arrange the fish on top of the baking sheet. Sprinkle generously with salt and pepper. If desired, cover the surface of the fish with the sautéed spinach or Mushroom Duxelles. Cover with puff pastry and trim into the shape of a fish. Using the metal tip of a pastry bag or a knife, score the pastry with circular marks to represent scales and straight lines to imitate fin lines. In a small bowl, beat the egg with the sugar, then brush the pastry with the egg mixture. Bake for 15 minutes for individual fillets or 25 minutes for 1 large fillet. For a large fillet, transfer to a serving platter. Individual fillets should be transferred directly to dinner plates.

Serves 4

Mock Puff Pastry

2¼ cups flour
1 teaspoon salt
¾ cup (1½ sticks) butter, divided
¾ cup water

In a mixing bowl or a food processor, combine the flour with the salt. With a fork or with the steel blade of the processor, cut in half of the butter until the mixture is uniformly crumbly. Add the water all at once and stir or process until mixture comes together to form a soft dough. On a well-floured surface, roll the dough into a 16 x 9-inch rectangle. Spread the dough with half of the remaining butter. Fold the dough letter-style into thirds, then rub the surface with the remaining butter, and fold it into thirds once again, to form a smaller rectangle. Wrap the dough in plastic and refrigerate it for several hours or overnight before rolling it out again into a 16 x 9-inch rectangle.

Makes one 16 x 9-inch sheet

Fish Stock

When I purchase fillets of fish, I don't really miss fish stock. I simply broil or fry or steam the fish fillets and enjoy them. But when I get my hands on a whole fish, I celebrate by making stock for a stew or for a rich sauce around poached fillets. Often, there's enough stock to make a second meal from a single fish, and unlike chicken or beef stocks, fish stock doesn't need to simmer for hours. All the flavor and nourishment is extracted from a fish frame in a matter of minutes.

> 2 pounds fish head, tails, fins, and bones
> 1 onion, unpeeled and sliced
> 2 stalks celery, roughly chopped
> ½ teaspoon fennel seed
> ½ cup white wine or 2 tablespoons lemon juice
> 6 cups water, or just enough to barely cover the fish

In a large saucepan or stockpot over high heat, combine the fish pieces, onion, celery, fennel seed, and wine, and pour in enough water to barely cover. Bring the liquid to a boil, reduce the heat to low, and simmer for 20 to 30 minutes. Strain to remove solids. The stock may be used immediately or frozen for future use.

Makes about 6 cups

Simple Rockfish Stew

Simplicity is a dubious virtue. Too often it means bland or boring, but in its proper sense it can mean pure and uncomplicated. This stew is so completely innocent of the garish flavor additives encountered so often in modern food, that reading the recipe you might think it would yield an uninteresting dish. In fact, it is a dish of subtle charm that honors its main ingredient in a very flavorful way.

If you are fortunate enough to encounter live, or very, very fresh, rockfish or snapper, fillet the fish and skin the fillets, make a stock, assemble this stew, and serve it with a bottle of Washington chardonnay or Oregon pinot gris and a loaf of artisan bread. You will experience simplicity at its best. Use a heavy saucepan. I use an enameled iron pot like Le Creuset or Cousance. Leave the fish fillets whole while they cook, and let them fall apart when you ladle the stew into bowls.

> ¼ cup (½ stick) butter, olive oil, or a combination
> ¼ cup flour

½ teaspoon freshly ground black pepper

6 cups Fish Stock *(see preceding page)*

1 cup white wine

Kosher salt

3 pounds firm rockfish fillets

3 to 4 tablespoons chopped parsley, dill, or sorrel

In a soup kettle over medium-high heat, melt the butter and stir in the flour. Add the pepper. Whisk in the stock and wine and bring the mixture to a boil. Add salt to taste. The sauce should taste good even without the fish. Ease the fish fillets into the simmering sauce and when the mixture returns to a gentle boil, reduce the heat to low. Poach the fish for 10 minutes, or until the fillets are curled and beginning to flake. With a ladle, transfer the stew to large shallow bowls and sprinkle on the freshly chopped herb of choice.

Serves 6

Seafood Stew with Saffron and Tomatoes

This genial blend of intensely flavored foods casts some notions of simplicity out the window, but in its own way, a vibrant Mediterranean-style seafood stew built upon a base of onions in olive oil is every bit as basic as a stew made with a roux. Reminiscent of cioppino with echoes of bouillabaisse, this dish derives its robust character from onions, tomatoes, garlic, and kale. With crusty bread and an honest red wine, it lifts spirits dampened by fall and winter chills. Against the advice of several experts, I have successfully used Salmon Stock (page 48) and salmon fillets in this stew, but a white fish like halibut or snapper is more conventional. If you wish, add variety with shrimp and scallops.

1 medium onion, thinly sliced

3 tablespoons olive oil

2 teaspoons dried oregano

¼ teaspoon freshly ground black pepper

⅛ teaspoon cayenne (optional)

½ cup red wine

3 cups Fish Stock *(see preceding page)*

Generous pinch of saffron threads

1 tablespoon crushed garlic

1 (22-ounce) can crushed Italian-style tomatoes

3 pounds fish fillets or a combination of fish, shrimp, and scallops

1 bunch kale, cut crosswise into fine ribbons (about 4 cups, packed)

In a large, heavy saucepan over medium-high heat, sauté the onion in the olive oil until it just begins to brown. Stir in the oregano, pepper, and cayenne. Add the wine and let the mixture boil until the wine has evaporated and you can hear the onions beginning to fry again. Stir in the stock, saffron, and garlic and bring the mixture to a boil. Add the tomatoes. (The stew may be made ahead of time and kept refrigerated until 20 minutes before serving time.) Bring the stew to a boil, add the fish fillets and kale. Reduce the heat to low and simmer for 15 minutes. Serve at once.

Serves 6

Snapper à la Vera Cruz

An initial searing in a small amount of butter or oil, followed by gentle simmering in a flavorful liquid or sauce constitutes braising. A cooking method that is more typically applied to meat and poultry dishes, braising can also be applied successfully to fish. The initial blast of higher heat in the first step of braising gives some seafood dishes a deeper flavor than would ever be achieved by mere poaching or baking. Even greater flavor can be developed during the subsequent simmering time if the simmering liquid is a mixture of wine and lemon and the juices of a ripe tomato.

> 4 snapper or rockfish fillets (about 8 ounces each)
> Salt and freshly ground black pepper
> 1 large onion, thinly sliced
> 4 tablespoons olive oil
> 4 cloves garlic, chopped
> 1 large tomato, sliced vertically ¼ inch thick
> 2 tablespoons capers, drained
> ¼ cup green olives, pitted and sliced
> ½ cup white wine

Remove any bones from the fish fillets and sprinkle them with salt and pepper. Set aside. In a large sauté pan or skillet over medium-high heat, sauté the onion in 2 tablespoons of the olive oil until soft and translucent. Add the garlic and tomato and sauté for 1 or 2 minutes. Push the tomato mixture to the side of the pan and drizzle the remaining olive oil over the exposed surface of the pan. Cook the fish fillets, best-looking surface down, for 3 to 5 minutes. Turn the fillets and toss in the capers, olives, and wine. Shake or gently stir to blend tomato mixture into wine. Reduce the heat to medium-low and cook for 5 minutes. Transfer fish fillets to warm plates and spoon sauce over each serving.

Serves 4

Lentils, Split Peas & Chickpeas

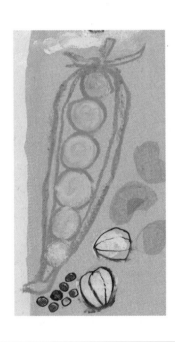

*T*he pioneers who came to Western Washington thought of Eastern Washington as the last leg of an inland desert, a wasteland that had to be crossed. Newcomers to the Northwest often feel the same way—at least I did. There is a tendency to think of Eastern Washington simply as a place to be passed through on the way to the greener Washington west of the mountains, just as our predecessors did a hundred years ago. ✑ My own

Lentils, Split Peas & Chickpeas

crossing of the Inland Empire came in 1980. Mount Saint Helens had recently blanketed the region in a layer of pale gray ash. From the windows of a car bound for Bellingham, where I would attend Western Washington

University, I stared out at a bleak landscape and wondered why I had ever chosen to come to Washington. But as soon as I crossed the mountains and rose out of the ashes, I was satisfied that this was indeed a decent place.

Now, I have come to see the eastern block of the Northwest not as a wasteland but more as an agricultural Eden. Trips east of the mountains to gather tomatoes, peaches, apples, and pears in their seasons have helped me see the region for the fertile land it really is. The ash that rendered the landscape depressingly monochromatic when I first saw it is just the latest in a series of fertilizing volcanic rains that have fallen on that region for millennia, building on a foundation of mineral riches deposited when melting glaciers left a wealth of crushed rock in their wake at the end of the Ice Age.

At the heart of the Northwest breadbasket, a region known as the Palouse occupies parts of Idaho, Oregon, and Washington. With Moscow, Idaho, roughly at its center, the region is generally considered to be the best in the world for growing lentils, peas, and chickpeas.

Even before farmers began irrigating the Columbia River Valley in the early years of this century, rain-watered winter wheat was successfully grown in Eastern Washington. And few Washingtonians realize it, but Washington produces more soft white winter wheat than any other state in the union. Many of the acres devoted to wheat are covered between harvests with lentils, peas, and chickpeas. These crops help fertilize the soil for growing wheat, and they yield a second harvest that constitutes one of the most significant crops in the region. More lentils and peas are harvested in the Northwest than anywhere else, and they are exported all over the globe, mostly to India and to the Middle East.

Lentils and peas have been cultivated in the river valleys of the Middle East for more than eight thousand years. Along with wheat and barley, they were among the first plants ever domesticated; and they were often grown together with those ancient grains, just as they are now, because they helped to replenish the soil. Much of the bread that was the staff of life in ancient times was baked with lentil and chickpea flour incorporated into the dough.

Consider, too, the biblical tale of Isaac's sons. Esau, the older son, was a hunter who traveled far and wide in search of game. Jacob, the younger son, tended the fields close to home. One day when Esau returned from the hunt

Lentils, Split Peas & Chickpeas

empty-handed and hungry, he was forced to rely on his brother's soup for sustenance; and the hunter traded his birthright for a bowl of Jacob's soup.

The story can be read metaphorically: The days of a hunter-gatherer society were coming to a close, and the great social transition to farming had begun. It is significant that the writer, so often sparing us any details, points out that the soup was made from lentils. Specific crops like lentils had an enormous impact on those societies. A reliable crop of lentils made it possible to abandon a nomadic lifestyle and settle the land. Likewise, the harvest of lentils and peas from the once barren soil of the Inland Desert helped make it possible for settlers to establish homes and farms east of the mountains.

Brown lentils and green split peas are always on hand in Northwest kitchens. In a clean dry jar, they are virtually immortal, and their attractive forms make them popular choices for ornamental space fillers on many kitchen shelves. But they are more than decorative, they are a practical and wonderful addition to the pantry.

Because these legumes cook in about thirty minutes without any presoaking, they are often preferred over other beans. They are an excellent source of fiber and a great alternative to meat. Ounce per ounce, lentils and split peas have more protein than beef and they contain a more generous supply of vitamins and minerals, especially iron.

Lentils, Split Peas & Chickpeas

Lentils From the tiny red lentils that turn terra cotta when they're cooked to the delicate French green ones to the somewhat larger brown ones, there is considerable variety among lentils (*Lens* species). All the different types are more or less interchangeable, but subtle differences make some varieties more suited to certain preparations than others. For soups, any type will do. For simple buttered lentils to be served as a side dish, my first choice would be the small green variety, available at specialty food stores and co-ops. For salads, choose the big brown ones; they keep their shape better.

Split Peas The pea (*Pisum sativum*) probably originated in India, but it has thrived in the Northwest, just as it has in practically every other part of the world. Varieties grown in the Palouse include whole green peas and green and yellow peas for splitting, which are shipped around the world. Throughout history, these legumes have been dried and stored as insurance against famine. Their simple goodness is reassuring and satisfying even in times of plenty.

Chickpeas or Garbanzos Since the chickpea (*Cicer arietinum*) requires soaking before cooking, it is for all practical purposes more like beans than it is like lentils and peas. But unlike most beans, which originated in the New World, the garbanzo's pedigree can be traced to the Old World where it grew in fields within sight of the pyramids of Giza and even in Stone Age Switzerland. In Pompeii, when the volcano buried that city two thousand years ago, chickpeas already cooked with bacon were for sale at the market in amphorae. Now eaten mostly in countries where they are appreciated for their low cost and high nutritional value, chickpeas are less a staple than a novelty. But the Northwest is one of the world's leading suppliers of this historic food.

Lentil Cakes

In the Middle East, legumes are sometimes soaked, puréed, and seasoned, then pressed into little cakes—falafel—that are fried and served as an hors d'oeuvre or as street food. A few years ago, I was determined to make something more substantial than soup out of lentils. My experiment led to these Lentil Cakes. Serve them with a green vegetable and tahini sauce or plain yogurt for garnish.

> 5 cups water
> 1 tablespoon salt
> 1 bay leaf, preferably fresh
> 2 cups red lentils
> 2 stalks celery, thinly sliced
> 1 large carrot, thinly sliced
> 1 large onion, thinly sliced
> ¼ cup olive oil
> 1 cup bread crumbs
> Olive oil, for brushing the pan and patties

In a saucepan over high heat, bring the water, salt, and bay leaf to a boil. Stir in the lentils, reduce the heat to low and cook, stirring occasionally, for 25 minutes, or until the lentils have begun to burst. Meanwhile, sauté the celery, carrot, and onion in olive oil for 5 minutes or until the vegetables are golden brown and just becoming tender. Remove the bay leaf from the lentils and process the lentils and sautéed vegetables in a food processor to make a smooth paste. Stir in the bread crumbs and spread the mixture out over a large platter to cool. Refrigerate for 30 minutes, or until completely cooled.

Preheat the oven to 375°F. Coat a baking sheet with olive oil.

With lightly oiled hands, shape the paste into twelve 4-inch cakes, patting smooth. Brush the cakes with olive oil and place on the pan. Bake for 10 minutes, or until lightly browned and heated through. Serve immediately.

Makes 12 cakes to serve 6

Lentil Cassoulet

In Paris, just before Christmas one year, my wife and I ate at a restaurant specializing in the foods of southwest France. We ate lavishly, and the highlight of our meal was a cassoulet made not with the traditional white beans but with lentils. Here in the Northwest, this seems like a very appropriate way to interpret one of the great dishes of France and to celebrate one of our own agricultural gems. I like to use bulk sausage, pressed into patties, but I have also had success with large Italian-style sausages and even with ordinary breakfast links.

For a really singular cassoulet, make a Confit of Duckling; for a simpler dish, substitute bacon for the confit. Either version should be served with your favorite mustard and plenty of good bread. At the Paris restaurant the cassoulet came after a salad of wilted savoy cabbage and bacon, which would have been a meal in itself. I like to serve the cassoulet with steamed mustard greens dressed with a splash of vinegar.

6 cups water
1 tablespoon salt
1 bay leaf, preferably fresh
1 pound small green lentils
Confit of Duckling *(recipe follows)* or 1 pound sliced bacon
1 medium onion, thinly sliced
3 to 4 cloves garlic
1 pound pork sausage links or 1 pound bulk sausage pressed into 8 patties
2 tablespoons brandy
1 cup fresh bread crumbs

In a flameproof casserole bring the water, salt, and bay leaf to a boil over high heat. Add the lentils, reduce the heat to medium and cook for 20 to 25 minutes, or until they are tender but not falling apart. Meanwhile, in a frying pan over medium-high heat, melt ½ cup of the fat from the confit or fry the bacon and set it aside, leaving ½ cup of the fat in the pan. Save an additional 2 tablespoons of fat to moisten the bread crumbs. Cook the onion in the fat, stirring for 5 minutes, or until it is tender and beginning to brown. Stir in the garlic and cook for 1 minute more. Stir the onion mixture into the lentils and tuck the pieces of duck or the strips of bacon into the lentils. Brown the sausages in the saucepan and tuck them into the lentils.

Preheat the oven to 300°F. Pour the brandy into the pan and swirl it around to pick up any flavorful bits. Fold gently into the lentils. Moisten the bread crumbs with either duck fat or the reserved bacon fat and cover the lentils with bread crumbs. Bake for 45 minutes to 1 hour, or until the juices are bubbling up around a layer of browned crumbs. Serve hot.

Serves 6 to 8

Confit of Duckling

In the classic lexicon of French cookery, a confit is a preserve, and in the days before refrigeration, meats were sometimes preserved with salt and fat. First, a coating of salt was applied to draw out any moisture, then the meat was slowly cooked in its own fat. Finally, the meat was packed into crocks and covered with the rendered cooking fat to seal it. Meats preserved in this way were used to add flavor and interest to pulses and grains.

In my simplified version, the duckling is not really preserved; rather, it is transformed into a flavorful condiment that enhances dishes like cassoulet. Incidentally, the same technique may be applied to goose with very savory results.

> **1 duckling (3 to 4 pounds)**
> **About ⅓ cup kosher salt**
> **1 tablespoon freshly cracked black pepper**

Cut the duckling in half lengthwise, then cut each half into 3 pieces. Rinse under cold running water, then sprinkle fairly heavily with kosher salt and cracked pepper. Arrange the pieces on a rack over a pan and let drain for 1 hour.

Preheat the oven to 325°F.

Rinse off as much of the salt as possible. Place the duck pieces in a baking dish and bake for 90 minutes. Use the duckling immediately, or pack the cooked duckling pieces into a crockery container just large enough to hold them, or a Pyrex loaf pan, then pour the cooking fat over the meat and store it in the refrigerator for up to 1 week.

Makes about 6 cups of confit

Red Lentil Dal

Dal, sometimes spelled dahl, is a generic name for small bean-based dishes that constitute the foundation of the Indian diet. Dal can be prepared in many ways. I like this version, which may not be particularly authentic but is a formula I have devised out of convenience. The lentils are cooked in water until tender, then a mixture of fried spices and onion, known as a tadka or tarka, is stirred in at the end.

6 cups water, plus more if needed
2 teaspoons salt
2 bay leaves
2 cups red lentils
1 teaspoon mustard seeds
3 tablespoons clarified butter or oil
1 medium onion, thinly sliced
1 tablespoon finely chopped garlic
1 teaspoon crushed red pepper flakes, or to taste

In a soup kettle over high heat, bring the water, salt, and bay leaves to a boil. Stir in the lentils. Reduce the heat to medium-low, cover, and cook for 30 minutes, or until lentils are tender and beginning to disintegrate. While cooking, keep the lid of the pan slightly ajar to prevent the soup from boiling over.

Meanwhile, prepare the *tarka*. Cook mustard seeds in clarified butter in a sauté pan over medium-high heat for a few seconds, or just until they pop. Add the onion, garlic, and red pepper flakes to taste. Sauté for 5 minutes, or until the onion is soft and beginning to brown. Add the mixture to the lentils. Cover and simmer for 10 to 15 minutes, or until the mixture has the consistency of a thick purée. Serve hot with Chapati and Fresh Mango Chutney (recipes follow).

Serves 6

Chapati or Poori

Whenever I make dal, I also make Indian flatbread to go with it. Sometimes I make light and soft-baked Chapati; other times, I make crisp, deep-fried Poori. Both breads are based on the same simple formula and come together in less than half an hour. Use all white flour or up to half whole wheat flour.

2 cups flour
1 teaspoon salt
¾ to 1 cup water
Hot oil, for frying poori

In a mixing bowl, or a food processor, stir together the flour and salt. Add just enough water to make a fairly stiff dough. Mix and knead until smooth and elastic. Cover the dough with a damp paper towel and let rest for 10 minutes.

To make chapati, divide the dough into 6 equal portions and on a well-floured surface roll each portion out into an 8-inch circle. Cook the chapati in a dry cast-iron skillet over medium-high heat for 3 minutes on each side, or until slightly puffed and beginning to brown. Serve hot.

To make poori, divide the dough into 12 equal portions and on a well-floured surface, roll each portion into a 6-inch circle. Drop the breads, one at a time, into hot oil and fry, swishing hot oil over the top of the poori, for 2 minutes, or until puffed and golden. Turn and fry 1 minute more. Drain on brown paper and serve hot.

Makes 6 chapati or 12 poori

Fresh Peach or Mango Chutney

The hearty goodness of dal is made more interesting with condiments like chutney. I usually keep a few jars of homemade chutney in the pantry, but it's also nice to toss together the essential ingredients of chutney and serve it fresh as a kind of relish. If fresh peaches are out of season, I use mangoes instead. They do not grow in the Northwest, but the influence of Pacific cultures has had such a tremendous impact on Northwest cooking that this tropical fruit is almost ubiquitous here. Palm sugar, available in specialty food stores and Asian markets, has a subtle, caramel flavor that evokes the tropics, but brown sugar is a reasonable alternative.

¼ cup rice vinegar
¼ cup palm sugar or brown sugar
2 tablespoons finely chopped crystallized ginger
3 ripe peaches or 2 mangoes

In a small bowl, combine the vinegar, palm sugar, and crystallized ginger and set aside. If using peaches, dip whole peaches in boiling water for 1 minute, pass under cold running water, and slip off the skins. Cut the peeled peaches in half, remove the pits, and slice the peaches. If using mangoes, cut the sides of the mangoes away from the pit, then with a spoon work the half mangoes out of the skin. Place the peeled mango pieces on a cutting board and slice. Toss the sliced peaches or mangoes with the vinegar mixture. Serve at room temperature or refrigerate and serve cold.

Makes 2 cups

Lentil, Tomato, and Basil Salad

Perhaps anything would taste good with red ripe plum tomatoes, fresh basil, and extra virgin olive oil. Certainly lentils do. The combination of tomatoes and basil brings these hearty Northwest legumes back to their sunny Mediterranean roots. The dish is substantial enough to serve as a light entrée; it also makes a good side dish at a backyard barbecue.

> 3 cups water
> 1 teaspoon salt
> 1 cup lentils, preferably large brown lentils
> 3 tablespoons apple cider vinegar
> 3 tablespoons extra virgin olive oil
> 4 plum tomatoes, chopped
> 2 cups basil leaves, cut into ⅛-inch ribbons

In a deep saucepan over high heat, bring the water and salt to a boil. Stir in the lentils, cover, and reduce the heat to low. Cook, undisturbed, for 20 minutes, or until just tender but still intact. Strain the lentils, discarding the cooking liquid. Combine the vinegar, oil, tomatoes, and basil in a salad bowl. Add the lentils and toss to combine. Serve at room temperature within 1 hour or refrigerate and serve cold.

Serves 6

Duck Soup with Yellow Split Peas and Sage

Use Confit of Duckling (page 227) or leftover roast duckling to flavor this satisfying winter soup. Wait to add salt until after the soup is cooked because the confit may be salty enough to season the split peas. I like to garnish this soup with fried sage leaves, and what better medium to fry them in than duck fat?

8 cups water
2 bay leaves
2 cups dried yellow split peas
¼ cup duck fat
2 medium onions, sliced
1 tablespoon fresh sage leaves, minced, or 1 teaspoon dried sage
1 cup Confit of Duckling *(page 227)*, cut from the bone
Salt and freshly ground black pepper
Fresh sage leaves fried in a little duck fat, for garnish (optional)

In a soup kettle over high heat, bring the water and bay leaves to a boil. Stir in the split peas. Reduce the heat to medium, cover, and cook for 30 minutes, or until the peas are just tender. Keep the lid of the pan slightly ajar to prevent the soup from boiling over.

Meanwhile heat the duck fat in a skillet over medium-high heat, and add the onion. Sauté for 8 to 10 minutes, or until very soft and golden brown. Stir in the sage. Transfer the mixture to the soup kettle with the peas. Cut the duck meat into ½-inch pieces and stir into the soup. Simmer for 15 minutes more, or until the peas have dissolved into the broth around them. Season to taste with salt and pepper. If desired, place a few fried sage leaves on top of each serving.

Serves 6

Green Split Pea Soup with a Mirepoix

Very often, pea soup is a vehicle for leftover ham. In this version, the peas themselves are the stars, and twinkling between them are little points of aromatic vegetables. In French this combination of tiny diced aromatic vegetables is known as a mirepoix; it is at the foundation of many classic dishes. Be sure to allow the vegetables ample time in the olive oil so that they begin to brown and caramelize.

    2 quarts water
    2 teaspoons salt
    2 bay leaves
    1 pound green split peas
    1 medium onion, peeled
    4 stalks celery
    2 medium carrots, scrubbed
    ¼ cup olive oil
    ½ teaspoon freshly ground black pepper
    1 cup chopped parsley
    1 tablespoon chopped garlic

In a soup kettle over high heat, bring the water, salt, and bay leaves to a boil. Stir in the split peas. Reduce the heat to medium, cover, and cook for 30 minutes, or until the peas are just tender. Keep the lid of the pan slightly ajar to prevent the soup from boiling over.

Meanwhile cut the onion, celery, and carrots into fine dice, as small as the peas. Heat the olive oil in a skillet over medium-high heat and add the diced vegetables. Sauté for 8 to 10 minutes, or until the vegetables are soft and beginning to color. Add the pepper, parsley, and garlic. Continue to sauté for 1 to 2 minutes more. Add the mixture to the peas. Simmer for 10 to 15 minutes longer, or until the peas begin to disintegrate. Serve hot.

Serves 6

Green Purée

Fernand Point, who achieved fame at his restaurant La Pyramide, once worked closely with Salvador Dali to produce a cookbook called Gala. Long out of print, the book is legendary. Years ago, I was afforded a cursory look at the book and was taken with a bizarre green purée. Attempts to reproduce it resulted in this recipe for a most unusual side dish that adds a brilliant

green to plates and provides a very satisfying accompaniment to roast meats when more pedestrian vegetables just won't do.

> 3 cups water
> 1 teaspoon salt
> 1 bay leaf
> 1 cup green split peas
> 3 tablespoons olive oil
> 1 medium onion, thinly sliced
> 1 teaspoon chopped garlic
> 8 ounces spinach leaves, washed and stemmed
> Salt and pepper

In a saucepan over high heat, bring the water, salt, and bay leaf to a rolling boil. Stir in the split peas and reduce the heat to low. Cover and cook for 30 minutes, or until the peas have begun to disintegrate. Remove from the heat.

In a sauté pan over medium-high heat, heat the oil and sauté the onion for 3 minutes, or until it is soft and translucent. Add the garlic and cook 1 minute more. Add the spinach and cook until tender. Transfer the mixture to a food processor and pulse on and off to purée. Remove the bay leaf from the peas, strain, reserving any liquid, and put the peas into the food processor. Purée until smooth, adding reserved cooking liquid if necessary to create a smooth, thick paste.

Serves 6

Boiled Chickpeas

Chickpeas, or garbanzo beans, are sold pre-cooked in cans, but the canned beans never seem to taste as good as the ones I cook myself. I almost never eat them plain, but use them instead to make hummus or soup.

> 2 cups dried chickpeas
> 6 cups water
> 2 teaspoons salt

Sort the chickpeas and remove and discard any bits of gravel or other unwanted matter. In a stockpot or a soup kettle over high heat, bring the water to a boil. Add the chickpeas and as soon as the water returns to a boil, turn off the heat. Let stand for 1 hour. Drain off the water, replace it with fresh water, and add the salt. Bring back to a boil over high heat.

Reduce the heat to low and cook for 1 hour, or until the chickpeas are tender. Chickpeas may be drained, buttered, and served at once as a side dish, or they may be used in soup or a dip.

Makes about 5 cups

Garbanzo Pepper Pot.

Philadelphia pepper pot is a traditional American soup in which tripe figures prominently. When I was a teenage vegetarian, I loved the sound of pepper pot but shuddered at the thought of eating tripe. I made a variation on the theme using garbanzo beans (chickpeas). I've never forgotten that soup. When I don't have time to cook the beans, I substitute canned chickpeas with their juice.

> ¼ cup olive oil
> 2 small onions, thinly sliced
> 1 tablespoon chopped garlic
> 1 green bell pepper, seeded and thinly sliced
> 1 red bell pepper, seeded and thinly sliced
> 1 small can (4 ounces) whole green chilies, sliced lengthwise
> 2 cups cooked chickpeas in their cooking liquid *(see page 233)*
> 2 cups chicken broth
> Crushed red pepper flakes

In a heavy-bottomed soup kettle over medium high heat, heat the olive oil. Add the onion and cook, stirring, for 5 minutes, or until soft. Add the garlic and green and red bell peppers. Cook for 1 minute, or until peppers are soft. Add the green chilies, chickpeas, and broth. Bring to a boil and add red pepper flakes to taste. Serve hot.

Serves 4

Hummus

Traditionally served with pita bread and accompanied by olives, cucumbers, and tomatoes, the spread goes equally well with Chapati or Poori (page 228). Spread some hummus on a fresh warm chapati, then season it to taste with salt, pepper, and olive oil. Add shredded spinach and chopped tomato and you have something like a taco. Some people like to slip off the papery skins of cooked chickpeas to make the finished paste silky smooth. I rather like the texture of the skins.

1 cup cooked chickpeas with ¼ cup cooking liquid *(see page 233)*
⅓ cup tahini
3 tablespoons fresh lemon juice
1 teaspoon chopped garlic
Salt
⅛ teaspoon cayenne, or more to taste
¼ cup olive oil

In a food processor, chop the chickpeas by pulsing on and off. Add the cooking liquid and purée. Add the tahini, lemon juice, and garlic. Purée until the mixture forms a thick paste. Taste the mixture and if it needs salt, add it. Add the cayenne and 2 tablespoons of the olive oil and process until smooth. Transfer the mixture to a serving dish, then drizzle the remaining olive oil over the surface of the hummus. Serve at once with flatbread or crackers.

Makes 2 cups

Hazelnuts

There was a time when pecans rained down in slow motion around me, and on the bare ground beneath the trees, where grass could barely stake a claim in the sandy soil, I would gather the nuts and put them into a brown paper bag. The trees were in my grandmother's yard and I was only five years old, but occasionally, when dappled light comes through the leaves of other trees, I am a child again and pecans are falling around me again.

I have lived in the Northwest longer now than I lived in the South, but like any expatriate who remembers a childhood far away, I am nostalgic

Hazelnuts

about the foods of that other time and place. As children, my brothers and sisters and I gathered bags full of nuts and in the deep shade of my grandmother's porch, we struggled with little metal pliers to crack them and keep them whole. Almost always we broke them into smaller bits. Some of the nuts must have landed in a bowl where they were eventually drafted into pies, but most of them found their way into our mouths.

My ancestors who settled in the south in centuries past were probably as nostalgic about hazelnuts as I am about pecans. Their *noisettes* or *noccioli*, as they called them in France and Italy from whence they came, were the most common and most versatile nut in the Old World kitchen. But hazelnuts were not native to the Gulf Coast, nor would imported trees thrive in that climate. So European settlers like my ancestors had to make do with an American nut, a nut the Algonquian people called *paccan*. But making do with pecans is easy, and the pecan filled the niche of the hazelnut admirably. In most of the United States, it still does, for it became the nut of choice in dishes that eventually became American classics.

Panforte, a holiday classic of dried fruits and nuts from Italy, evolved into the dense, dark fruit cakes chock full of pecans that appeared on our holiday tables. Nourishing porridges that had been made since ancient times by stirring hazelnuts and other nuts into simmering grains inspired southern cooks to stir pecans into long-grain rice to become an elegant side dish for the plantation table. Buttery tart shells filled with caramelized sugar and hazelnuts, once a staple of French pastry kitchens, evolved into pecan pie.

As Americans moved into the Pacific Northwest, all that changed. Here, at least in many parts of "here," hazelnuts grew in abundance, just as they once did in Italy, France, and Turkey, the world's leading hazelnut-growing countries. Domestic varieties from the Old World were introduced to the Northwest in the mid-nineteenth century, and they immediately took root.

According to Lucy Gerspacher, the Oregonian author of *Hazelnuts & More*, the first domestic hazelnut tree was planted in Oregon by an English sailor, Sam Strickland, in 1858. Offshoots of that tree continue to produce nuts to this day. A Frenchman, David Gernot, planted a row of the trees to supply his family's needs in the 1870s. It may have been Gernot's success that inspired Felix Gillet, another Frenchman, who was growing them commercially by 1885.

Others followed Gillet's example and today, Oregon's Willamette Valley produces over 90 percent of the country's hazelnuts. Home gardeners also appreciate this diminutive member of the birch or Betulaceae family, and several species are grown for ornamental purposes. With rounded leaves, ruffled at the edges in summer, and showy male catkins hanging on the bare branches throughout the winter, the twenty-foot trees are very attractive. The nuts are harvested in September and October.

So settlers coming west from the eastern states at the turn of the century began substituting local hazelnuts for pecans in their favorite recipes. Today in the Northwest, hazelnuts stand in for pecans just as pecans once stood in for hazelnuts. You might say we have come full circle. In any case, the hazelnut is *the* Northwest nut. It is as closely associated with the region's table as apples or salmon.

Trying out familiar southern standards with the Northwest nut, I have discovered that hazelnuts make a fine version of New Orleans–style pralines. The pecans that used to seem mandatory in my mother's Waldorf Salad can be replaced with hazelnuts with happy results. And hazelnuts lend any favorite recipe for southern pecan pie a decidedly Pacific Northwest flavor.

One challenge of using hazelnuts is that most recipes call for toasting the nuts and rubbing between clean dry cloths to remove the clinging, paper-thin dark brown skins. With some varieties of hazelnuts, this is not possible. If you have large, round Oregon-grown hazelnuts, peel them (see page 242). But be aware that many Washington growers produce a smaller, elongated nut that needs no peeling, and in fact will not be peeled effectively at all.

Peeling Hazelnuts

PREHEAT THE OVEN TO 300°F. SPREAD SHELLED HAZELNUTS IN A SINGLE LAYER ON A baking sheet and roast for 15 to 20 minutes, or until the nuts have just begun to turn golden. The best indicator that the nuts are ready is the delicious aroma they emit when they begin to turn brown. With a clean lint-free kitchen towel, rub the hot nuts to remove the skins. Some of the nuts will not give up their skins, and even the peeled nuts will retain tiny patches of skin. Not to worry. Once the skins are rubbed off the nuts, the papery brown skins need to be discarded. Use a stiff index card or a playing card to push the nuts and skins to one end of the baking sheet. Tilt the pan and the nuts will roll down, leaving the skins at the top of the pan.

Northwest Waldorf Salad

My mother often made Waldorf salad, and I admire her now for persevering in this effort, because she was surrounded in those days by people—my siblings and me—who didn't appreciate her efforts at all. "Gross!" we would say, as if we knew something about what was good. My father liked Waldorf salad, but not enough to request it. Most of the things she made were made to please him. But it was her own good taste, and her determination to gratify it, that drove my mother to make that salad. She liked to make it with a particular apple, Winesap, her favorite—red-veined, tart, and heady scented. A craving for the salad led more than once, as I recall, to a special trip to the store just to buy those apples, the freshest possible celery, and the pecans required to make it.

These days, I do appreciate Waldorf Salad, but I make mine a little differently. I prefer a spicy, homemade dressing to the bottled stuff we used when I was a kid, and I prefer the dense, starchy celery root, also known as celeriac, to green celery. I also like to put my Waldorf mixture on an unconventional bed of watercress because I like the challenging bite of the cress and I like the way the dark green leaves look behind the pale apples and celery root.

1 large celery root, peeled and cut into julienne strips

Waldorf Salad Dressing *(recipe follows)*

6 large Winesap, Gala, or Criterion apples

1 tablespoon fresh lemon juice

1 tablespoon sugar

1 bunch (6 ounces) watercress, rinsed and spun dry

1 cup toasted and skinned hazelnuts

Freshly ground black pepper

In a small bowl, combine the julienned celery root and salad dressing and set aside. Slice the apples into ⅛-inch-thick crescents, leaving the cores behind. In a clean bowl, toss apple slices with the lemon juice and sugar. Divide watercress among 6 chilled salad plates. Arrange dressed apple slices on top of watercress, then place a mound of celery root on top of each salad. Top with hazelnuts and a generous sprinkling of pepper.

Serves 6

Waldorf Salad Dressing

2 soft-boiled egg yolks

1 tablespoon coarse mustard

1 tablespoon fresh lemon juice

1 tablespoon sugar

½ teaspoon salt

½ teaspoon freshly ground black pepper

½ cup light olive oil or corn oil

In a small mixing bowl, smash the soft-boiled egg yolks. Stir in the mustard, lemon juice, sugar, salt, and pepper, and continue to stir until the mixture is very well combined. Gradually stir in the oil, a few drops at first, then a tablespoonful at a time, until a smooth and creamy dressing is made.

Makes about 1¼ cups

Mixed Greens with a Hazelnut-Goat Cheese Fritter and Raspberry Vinaigrette

Toasted nuts add such depth of flavor and texture to a salad that they have almost become a standard component. With hazelnut oil in the dressing, whole toasted hazelnuts tucked between the leafy greens, and a round of goat cheese crusted in more hazelnuts, this salad reverberates with the nut. It's also studded with whole raspberries whose flavor is reflected in the raspberry vinaigrette. This is not a salad to appear on the side of the plate at a buffet. Rather, it should be contemplated as a course unto itself or even a meal in itself.

    1 pound mixed salad greens, rinsed and spun dry
    1 cup Raspberry Vinaigrette *(page 178)*
    1 pint fresh raspberries
    1 cup toasted hazelnuts
    8 Hazelnut–Goat Cheese Fritters *(recipe follows)*
    Freshly ground black pepper

In a mixing bowl, toss mixed greens with the vinaigrette. Transfer to 8 chilled salad plates. Sprinkle on raspberries and hazelnuts and place a warm fritter on top of each salad. Offer freshly ground black pepper with each serving.

Serves 8 as a first course at dinner, or 4 for a main course at lunch

Hazelnut-Goat Cheese Fritters

    1 log (11 ounces) soft, white goat cheese
    ½ cup flour
    2 eggs
    ½ teaspoon salt
    2 tablespoons water
    ½ cup bread crumbs
    ½ cup toasted and skinned hazelnuts, finely chopped
    Light olive oil or corn oil, for frying

With a sharp knife dipped in hot water, cut the cheese into 8 rounds, each about ¾ inch thick. Place 3 soup plates side by side. In one, put the flour; in the next, beat the eggs with salt and water. In the third, combine the bread crumbs and chopped nuts. Roll each piece of cheese in flour, shaking off the excess, dip into the egg mixture, and roll in the hazelnut mixture to coat. Set aside. Fritters may be prepared ahead up to this point and refrigerated for several hours or overnight.

Just before serving, heat the oil to 375°F, or until a cube of bread floats immediately to the top and sizzles. Fry the breaded cheese, 3 or 4 pieces at a time, without crowding, for 2 minutes on each side, or until golden. Drain on paper towels. Serve hot.

Makes 8 fritters

Breasts of Chicken in a Hazelnut Crust with Pears and Riesling

In the South, breasts of chicken are occasionally rolled in pecans before they are fried. The delicious entrée is typically served with pan gravy or simply sour cream warmed in the frying pan in which the chicken was fried. My Northwest take on the dish calls for aromatic hazelnuts in place of the pecans and sweet refreshing pears and riesling in place of the gravy or sour cream.

> 4 chicken breast halves, skinned and boned
> 1 teaspoon kosher salt
> ½ teaspoon freshly ground black pepper
> 1 cup flour
> 2 eggs
> ½ cup milk
> 1½ cups chopped toasted hazelnuts
> ¼ cup (½ stick) butter
> 4 ripe pear halves, peeled and cored
> ½ cup riesling wine

With a tenderizer or the side of a knife, pound the chicken breasts on a cutting board to flatten. Sprinkle with salt and pepper and set aside. Place the flour on a soup plate. On a second soup plate, beat the eggs with milk. Place the hazelnuts in a third plate. Roll a breast of chicken in the flour, shaking off the excess, and dip it in the egg mixture, allowing the excess to drip back into the bowl. Roll the chicken breast in hazelnuts to coat and set aside. Repeat with the remaining chicken breasts. Chicken breasts may be made ahead up to this point and refrigerated for several hours.

In a large sauté pan over medium-high heat, melt the butter and add the hazelnut-coated breasts of chicken. Cook for 4 to 5 minutes, or until the breasts are evenly browned, then turn and cook 5 minutes more. When cooked, the meat will be resilient when pressed with a fingertip, and the juices run clear when the meat is poked with the tip of a sharp knife. Transfer the chicken breasts to a warm platter and keep warm. Sauté the pear halves in the pan until lightly colored, pour in the riesling, and let the wine boil around the pears until it has reduced by about half and the pears are heated through. Serve hot.

Serves 4

Hazelnut Rice Pilaf

The combination of grains and nuts is very satisfying. Here, the sweetness of a slightly caramelized onion and a splash of nutty Madeira or Marsala enhance the fragrant appeal of this age-old combination. Serve the rice with roast chicken or with grilled salmon.

> 2 tablespoons butter
> 1 medium onion, chopped
> 2 teaspoons chopped fresh garlic
> 1 cup long-grain rice
> 1¾ cups chicken broth
> ¼ cup Madeira or Marsala wine
> 1 cup skinned and toasted hazelnuts, chopped
> ¼ cup chopped parsley

In a saucepan over medium-high heat, melt the butter, stir in the onion, and sauté for 5 minutes, or until translucent and just beginning to brown. Add the garlic and rice and stir for 1 minute to coat the rice with the butter mixture. Stir in the broth and wine. As soon as the mixture boils, reduce the heat to low. Cover and cook for 20 minutes over low heat, then stir in the chopped hazelnuts and parsley, re-cover the pan, and let the rice stand for 5 minutes. Serve hot.

Serves 4

Hazelnut Tart

It may be that the best and highest use of the hazelnut is this extraordinary variation on the pecan pie, which itself probably was a variation on a caramel and hazelnut tart from the Dauphinoise region in the French Alps where hazelnuts are extensively cultivated.

Brown Sugar Pastry *(page 248)*
1½ cups toasted and skinned hazelnuts
3 eggs
1 egg yolk
1 cup (packed) brown sugar
1 cup corn syrup
¼ cup (½ stick) butter, melted
1 teaspoon vanilla extract
½ teaspoon salt
Whipping cream, for serving

Preheat the oven to 350°F.

Prepare the pastry and roll it into a 12-inch circle. Sprinkle the rolled dough with flour and fold it so that it can be moved without stretching or tearing. Unfold the pastry into a 9-inch springform pan. Fold the rough edges down to create a smooth finish at the edge of the crust. Spread the hazelnuts into the pastry shell and set aside. Whisk together eggs, egg yolk, and brown sugar in a mixing bowl. Stir in the corn syrup, melted butter, vanilla, and salt. Pour the mixture over the hazelnuts. Bake for 45 to 50 minutes, or until a sharp knife inserted in the center comes out clean. Cool on a rack for at least 1 hour. Remove the sides of the springform pan. With a metal spatula, free the bottom crust from the pan. Carefully transfer the tart to a serving plate. Serve at room temperature with dollops of whipped cream.

Makes one 9-inch tart

Brown Sugar Pastry

1 cup flour
⅓ cup (packed) brown sugar
1 teaspoon salt
½ cup (1 stick) cold butter, cut into 1-inch pieces
1 egg white

In a food processor fitted with a metal blade, combine the flour, brown sugar, and salt. Add the butter and process, pulsing on and off, until the mixture resembles coarse bread crumbs. Add the egg white and process, pulsing on and off, until the dough comes together to form a ball. Transfer the dough to a well floured surface, sprinkle more flour on top, and roll out to a 12-inch circle.

Warm Chocolate Hazelnut Cakes

This is a fancy restaurant dessert that is fairly easy to reproduce at home. The cakes are made ahead and refrigerated before baking. The cold batter bakes quickly on the outside of each dish but remains slightly underbaked in the center. Serve these cakes hot from the oven while the center is still gooey.

1 pound bittersweet chocolate
1 cup (2 sticks) butter
1 cup toasted and skinned hazelnuts
⅔ cup sugar
1 tablespoon cornstarch
6 eggs, separated
1 teaspoon salt
1 teaspoon vinegar
Whipped cream, toasted hazelnuts, and fancy chocolate shapes, for garnish

Brush the insides of eight 8-ounce ramekins with butter, sprinkle with sugar, shaking out excess sugar, and line the bottom of each dish with a round of parchment paper. Set aside. Melt the chocolate and butter in a double-boiler or a large, stainless steel mixing bowl set over barely simmering water, stirring occasionally. While the chocolate is melting, combine the hazelnuts, ⅓ cup of the sugar, and the cornstarch in the workbowl of a food processor. Process, pulsing on and off, until the mixture is uniformly crumbly, then process steadily until the hazelnuts are finely ground and the mixture is almost pastelike. Set aside. Stir the egg yolks into the chocolate mixture and continue stirring until the mixture is very smooth. Set aside. In the bowl of an electric mixer, beat the egg whites with the salt and vinegar until they hold soft peaks. With the motor running, stream in the remaining ⅓ cup of sugar and continue to beat until the whites are firm. Fold half the whites and the hazelnut mixture into the chocolate mixture, then fold in the remaining whites. Transfer the batter to prepared ramekins and refrigerate for at least 1 hour or for up to 24 hours.

Preheat the oven to 350°F. Bake for 15 minutes, or until the top of the cakes are crisp. At serving time, place a plate on top of the ramekin, then flip the plate and ramekin together to invert. Let stand on the plate in the ramekin for 1 or 2 minutes to set. Remove the ramekin, peel away the parchment liner, and garnish with a sprinkling of whipped cream, toasted hazelnuts, and a vertical chocolate garnish.

Makes 6 large servings

Hazelnut Cream Dessert

Astute readers will recognize this as a variation on Alpine Cream (page 167). It is reminiscent of the blancmange that was once a standard element of most recipe collections. A kind of custard made with almond milk, or simply a plain white pudding thickened with cornstarch, blancmange was once considered restorative. This creamy dessert is the same way.

> ½ cup toasted and skinned hazelnuts
> ½ cup sugar
> 1 tablespoon (1 envelope) unflavored gelatin
> 2 tablespoons cold water
> 1 cup heavy whipping cream
> 1 cup plain yogurt
> 2 tablespoons hazelnut-flavored liqueur
> Fresh fruit or berry purée, as an accompaniment
> Toasted hazelnuts, for garnish

Have six 4-ounce dishes or disposable cups ready to fill. In a food processor, grind the hazelnuts with the sugar for 90 seconds, or until mixture is very finely ground. In a saucepan, dissolve the gelatin in the water. Add the cream and cook over medium heat, stirring until gelatin is dissolved. Stir in the hazelnut mixture, yogurt, and hazelnut liqueur, then transfer to dishes or cups and chill for 2 hours or until set. The dessert may be served directly from the container in which it was chilled, but it makes a better showing if it is unmolded and presented on a plate with fresh fruit, or in a pool of berry purée with a few toasted hazelnuts on the plate for decoration. If disposable cups are used as molds, dip them in hot water deep enough to reach almost to the top of the cup, and the cream will slip right out.

Serves 6

Dried Cherry and Hazelnut Biscotti

One European tradition that has taken root as deeply as hazelnut trees is the twice-baked Tuscan cookies known as biscotti. Northwest variations are innumerable. In Italy, the cookies are fairly uniform. Flavored with anise and almonds, they are baked hard as rocks, so that they keep for a very long time. To soften them, the cookies are dipped in espresso or sweet dessert wine.

The biscotti I make are softer than the Italian originals. I follow a formula that comes indirectly from the sister of Angelo Pellegrini, the late Professor Emeritus of English at the University of Washington. Pellegrini was the author of The Unprejudiced Palate, *a culinary classic. His family made biscotti more or less in the traditional way, but slightly softer. When I came into possession of Aunt Clara's recipe, I couldn't help dabbling. This version, in which I abandoned anise and almonds for hazelnuts and cherries, has become my favorite biscotti recipe.*

> 3 cups flour
> ½ cup lightly toasted and skinned hazelnuts
> 2½ teaspoons baking powder
> 1 cup sugar
> ½ teaspoon salt
> 3 large eggs, beaten
> ½ cup (1 stick) butter, melted and cooled
> ½ cup dried tart cherries

Preheat the oven to 350°F.

Line 2 baking sheets with parchment paper. In a large mixing bowl, combine the flour, hazelnuts, baking powder, sugar, and salt; set aside. In a separate bowl, combine the eggs with the melted butter and dried cherries. Make a well in the center of the flour mixture and stir in the egg mixture. Turn out onto a lightly floured surface and knead briefly just until the dough is smooth. Shape the dough into 4 rolls, each about as wide as your thumb, and arrange the rolls several inches apart on the baking sheets. Bake for 25 minutes, or until the rolls are golden brown and slightly flattened. Transfer the rolls to a cooling rack and cool for 10 minutes. Slice each roll on a long diagonal into ½-inch slices and lay the slices on the baking sheets. Bake for 8 minutes, or until slightly brown, then turn each cookie over and bake for 5 minutes more. Cool the cookies on racks and store tightly covered.

Makes 2 dozen large cookies

Creole Pralines with Hazelnuts

Pralines are the direct descendant of a French confection developed centuries ago, shortly after the development of refined sugar. The French version is sugar browned over high heat, inundated with almonds and allowed to harden into a crackly mass that is broken and crumbled over fruit, custard, or cakes. Creole colonists imitated the sweet they remembered, substituting native pecans for the traditional hazelnuts. They surpassed the original by creating a smoother, less brittle candy that could be enjoyed alone. The candy comes full circle to the Northwest where hazelnuts are native and pecans are not.

    1 cup (packed) brown sugar
    1 cup granulated sugar
    ¾ cup half-and-half
    Pinch of salt
    2 tablespoons butter
    1 tablespoon vanilla extract
    1 cup chopped roasted and skinned hazelnuts

Line a baking sheet with buttered parchment paper and set aside. In a deep heavy saucepan over medium-high heat, combine the brown sugar, granulated sugar, half-and-half, and salt. Stir until smooth. When mixture comes to a full boil, stop stirring. Let boil until a candy thermometer registers 235°F, or until a spoonful dropped in cold water forms a soft ball. When candy tests done, remove from the heat, stir in the butter, vanilla, and hazelnuts, and stir until mixture just begins to lose its sheen. Drop spoonfuls onto buttered parchment paper and cool until hard.

Makes 48 pralines

Index

T–Z